Road to ASEAN-10

The Japan Center for International Exchange wishes to thank

The Nippon Foundation

Road to ASEAN-10

Japanese Perspectives on Economic Integration

edited by
Sekiguchi Sueo *and* Noda Makito

Tokyo • Japan Center for International Exchange • *New York*

The surnames of the authors and other persons mentioned in this book
are positioned according to country practice.

Copyediting by Michael D. Evans and Pamela J. Noda.
Cover and typographic design by Becky Davis, EDS Inc., Editorial &
Design Services, Tokyo. Typesetting and production by EDS Inc.
Cover photograph © 1997 The Studio Dog/PhotoDisc, Inc.

Printed in Japan.
ISBN 4-88907-033-8

Distributed outside Japan in North and South America, Europe, and Africa by
Brookings Institution Press, 1775 Massachusetts Avenue, N.W.,
Washington, D.C. 20036-2188 U.S.A.

Japan Center for International Exchange
9-17 Minami Azabu 4-chome, Minato-ku, Tokyo 106-0047 Japan

URL: http://www.jcie.or.jp

Japan Center for International Exchange, Inc. (JCIE/USA)
1251 Avenue of the Americas, New York, N.Y. 10020 U.S.A.

Contents

Tables and Figures

Foreword

THIS VOLUME presents the research of a study group of emerging intellectual leaders in Japan organized in early 1997, under the guidance of Sekiguchi Sueo, professor of economics at Seikei University in Tokyo, to examine the prospects of ASEAN-10. The study project is part of the Global ThinkNet Fellows Program, which is an integral part of the Global ThinkNet Program of the Japan Center for International Exchange (JCIE). The Global ThinkNet Program is a multipronged, policy-relevant research and dialogue program launched in 1996 with the generous support of the Nippon Foundation. The program is designed to stimulate joint policy research and dialogue domestically and between Japan and other countries by building a broad network of policy research institutions and researchers.

The Global ThinkNet Fellows Program was conceived as an effective way to develop the human resources in Japan that are essential to augment Japan's positive contributions to the international community. Seven study groups have been organized since the inception of the program in 1996. The study groups are organized around a critical international issue and with the participation of six or seven promising young researchers under the guidance of one or more senior scholars. These young scholars participate in a monthly study seminar, often with resource persons such as senior scholars, political leaders, and government officials, and also take part in field trips within Japan or abroad. The participants are expected to submit papers in Japanese and English; these papers are turned into publications such as this volume.

The ASEAN-10 study project, the fifth project of the Global ThinkNet Fellows Program, was launched before the advent of the Asian economic crisis in July 1997. The crisis has certainly dampened the earlier bullish prospect of the region and has also brought about major political upheaval, such as the resignation of President Suharto of Indonesia, who had been considered to be a cornerstone of ASEAN solidarity. Nevertheless, ASEAN has moved on to come closer to achieving its earlier aspiration of "one Southeast Asia" by acceding Cambodia into the organization on April 30, 1999. The focus of the ASEAN-10 study group seemed to be fully justified despite the recent setbacks, as ASEAN continues to function as a viable regional group in the political as well as the security arena, and the future of the association is bound to have a major impact on the future of Asian regional order as well as on the international community at large.

This belief in the continuing importance of closely watching the evolution of the regional organization was reinforced when the members of the study group made an eight-day field trip to ASEAN member countries in 1997. They met with intellectual leaders in workshops in Myanmar, Thailand, and Singapore to discuss their draft papers, and they also met with government leaders such as Myanmar Foreign Minister Ohn Gyaw and Brigadier General David Abel, minister of national planning and economic development. These extremely productive and stimulating meetings were made possible through the efforts of Aye Lwin, director-general of ASEAN affairs of the Myanmar Ministry of Foreign Affairs, and of close friends and regular collaborators of JCIE in the region, including Suchit Bunbonkarn of Chulanlongkorn University of Thailand and Chia Siow Yue, director of the Institute of Southeast Asian Studies in Singapore. I wish to take this opportunity to thank them for their generous support on behalf of Professor Sekiguchi and the entire group.

This project would not have been possible without the dedicated leadership of Professor Sekiguchi, who paid personal attention to each of the participants of the study group as they prepared their research papers. I also wish to express my gratitude to the participants of the project, who endured the rigorous activities of the study group and produced the papers which constitute this volume.

Last but not least, I wish to express my most sincere appreciation to the Nippon Foundation for its generous financial support not only for this particular study group but for the entire Global ThinkNet Program.

Yamamoto Tadashi
PRESIDENT
JAPAN CENTER FOR INTERNATIONAL EXCHANGE

Abbreviations

ADB   Asian Development Bank
AFTA   ASEAN Free Trade Area
AIA   ASEAN Investment Area
AIC   ASEAN Industrial Complementation (scheme)
AICO   ASEAN Industrial Cooperation (scheme)
AMM   ASEAN Ministerial Meeting
APEC   Asia-Pacific Economic Cooperation (forum)
ARF   ASEAN Regional Forum
ASC   ASEAN Standing Committee
ASEAN   Association of Southeast Asian Nations
ASEAN-5   Indonesia, Malaysia, the Philippines, Singapore, and Thailand
ASEAN-4   Indonesia, Malaysia, the Philippines, and Thailand
ASEAN-ISIS   ASEAN Institutes of Strategic and International Studies
ASEAN-PTA   ASEAN Preferential Trading Arrangement
ASEAN-7   Brunei, Indonesia, Malaysia, the Philippines, Singapore, Thailand, and Vietnam
ASEAN-6   Brunei, Indonesia, Malaysia, the Philippines, Singapore, and Thailand
ASEAN-10   Brunei, Cambodia, Indonesia, Laos, Malaysia, Myanmar, the Philippines, Singapore, Thailand, and Vietnam
ASEM   Asia-Europe Meeting
BBC   Brand-to-Brand Complementation (scheme)
CEPT   Common Effective Preferential Tariff (scheme)
CER   Closer Economic Relations (pact)
CMEA   Council for Mutual Economic Assistance
CSCAP   Council for Security Cooperation in the Asia Pacific
EAEC   East Asian Economic Caucus
FDI   foreign direct investment
FUNCINPEC   National United Front for an Independent, Neutral, Peaceful and Cooperative Cambodia

GATS   General Agreement on Trade in Services
GATT   General Agreement on Tariffs and Trade
GDP   gross domestic product
G-8   Canada, England, France, Germany, Italy, Japan, Russia, and the United States
GNP   gross national product
G-7   Canada, England, France, Germany, Italy, Japan, and the United States
HS   Harmonized Commodity Description and Coding System
IMF   International Monetary Fund
JETRO   Japan External Trade Organization
MAPA   Manila Programme of Action
MITI   Ministry of International Trade and Industry (Japan)
NAFTA   North American Free Trade Agreement
NATO   North Atlantic Treaty Organization
NGO   nongovernmental organization
NIEs   newly industrializing economies (generally Hong Kong, South Korea, and Taiwan)
OHQ   operational headquarters
PAFTAD   Pacific Trade and Development Conference
PECC   Pacific Economic Cooperation Council
PMC   (ASEAN) Post Ministerial Conference
RCA   revealed comparative advantage (index)
SEATO   Southeast Asia Treaty Organization
SITC   Standard International Trade Classification
SLORC   State Law and Order Restoration Council (of Myanmar)
SOE   state-owned enterprise
SOM   (ASEAN) Senior Officials Meeting
SPDC   State Peace and Development Council (of Myanmar)
TAC   Treaty of Amity and Cooperation (in Southeast Asia)
TFP   total factor productivity
UNCTAD   United Nations Conference on Trade and Development
UNDP   United Nations Development Program
WTO   World Trade Organization

Road to ASEAN-10

– 1 –

Introduction

Sekiguchi Sueo

T HE ASSOCIATION OF SOUTHEAST ASIAN NATIONS (ASEAN) was
formed in 1967 mainly to counter the political influence of communist countries such as China and North Vietnam but shifted its emphasis to economic cooperation as the threat of communism faded. The
original members—Indonesia, Malaysia, the Philippines, Singapore, and
Thailand (the ASEAN-5)—have been joined by Brunei, Vietnam, Laos,
and Myanmar. Cambodia, whose participation was delayed because of
domestic political unrest, was admitted to ASEAN in April 1999, making the ASEAN-10 a reality.

The ASEAN-10 have a market of 480 million people (see table 1) but
lack a common political system. Among the new entrants, for example,
Myanmar's military dictatorship targets economic stability and development, Vietnam's official aim is to construct a socialist market economy,
and Cambodia remains politically unstable despite the birth of a new
regime under the leadership of Hun Sen after the election in 1998.

The ASEAN-5 should continue to play a guiding role. The democratization of the ASEAN-5 has been subordinated to economic development.
In this regard, almost all ASEAN members have been "developmental-
istic." In most member countries, the top political leaders stayed in
power for many years and then handpicked their successors. The Philippines has been an exception since the mid-1980s when the Aquino administration replaced the Marcos regime. Thailand is another exception
in that power has shifted quickly among political leaders, even though
military factions remained prominent in these struggles.

Anticommunism was once the ASEAN-5's most important unifying
factor. The threat of China, North Vietnam (backed by China), and the

3

Table 1. Main Economic Indicators of ASEAN-10 in 1995

	Code	Population (000)	GDP: MP (1987 US$mn)	GNP (US$mn)	GDP per Capita (US$)	M-Exports (US$mn)	M-Imports (US$mn)	Trade Surplus (US$mn)
Brunei	BRN	285	3,109	7,170	10,908	NA	NA	NA
Cambodia	KHM	10,024	1,328	2,718	133	855	1,213	-358
Indonesia	IDN	193,277	139,065	190,105	720	45,417	40,918	4,499
Laos	LAO	4,882	1,772	1,694	363	348	587	-239
Malaysia	MYS	20,140	62,597	78,321	3,108	74,037	77,751	-3,714
Myanmar	MMR	45,106	NA	NA	NA	846	1,335	-489
Philippines	PHL	68,595	43,193	71,865	630	17,502	28,337	-10,835
Singapore	SGP	2,987	40,173	79,831	13,451	118,268	124,507	-6,239
Thailand	THA	58,242	107,365	159,630	1,843	56,459	70,776	-14,317
Vietnam	VNM	73,475	59,940	17,634	816	5,026	7,272	-2,246
ASEAN-10		477,012	458,541	608,967	1,062	318,758	352,696	-33,938
Japan	JPN	125,213	3,018,176	4,963,587	24,104	443,116	335,882	107,234
North Korea	PRK	23,867	NA	NA	NA	NA	NA	NA
South Korea	KOR	44,851	254,003	435,137	5,663	125,058	135,119	-10,061
Japan + Koreas		193,931	3,272,179	5,398,724	19,241	568,174	471,001	97,173
China	CHN	1,200,241	577,486	744,890	481	148,797	129,113	19,684
Hong Kong	HKG	6,190	73,726	142,332	11,911	173,754	192,774	-19,020
Macao	MAC	450	3,621	NA	NA	1,976	2,021	-45
PRC and related		1,206,881	654,834	887,222	543	324,527	323,908	619
Mongolia	MNG	2,461	3,183	767	1,294	NA	NA	NA
Grand Total		1,880,285	4,388,737	6,895,679	2,392	1,211,459	1,147,605	63,854

Source: World Bank (1997).

Note: GDP per capita is in constant US$ prices of 1987. Population of the countries for which GDP is unavailable is deducted in calculating per capita GDP of the region. MP: Market prices; "M" in M-Exports and M-Imports: Merchandise trade.

former Soviet Union strengthened ASEAN solidarity. The end of the cold war, however, raised a new flag for ASEAN unity, one of economic co-operation to accelerate development. Thus, since 1992 the ASEAN Free Trade Area (AFTA) has become one of the members' most important agendas. In connection with this agenda, ASEAN has tried to promote cooperation on foreign direct investment (FDI) and technology trans-fers.

The United States and many Western European nations have pro-tested Myanmar's participation in ASEAN because Myanmar's military regime prohibits the establishment of a parliamentary democracy and restricts the political freedom of the country's leading proponent of democratization. ASEAN argues that a shift to Western-style democracy throughout the region would endanger economic stability. Democracy, it asserts, should be pursued steadily with economic development in a manner suitable for each nation. Because most ASEAN economies place top priority on economic development and, in doing so, sacrifice some democratic processes, the political leaders of these nations justify their own regimes by defending Myanmar's.

ASEAN as a Unit of Regional Integration

Whether ASEAN as an institution has contributed significantly to the economic development of its members is debatable. The association has upgraded members' bargaining power in negotiating with the rest of the world, and the voice of the group has become more important than that of any member. ASEAN has also actively promoted the ASEAN agenda in Japan, the United States, and Western Europe. Other nations are certainly paying greater attention to ASEAN than before.[1]

This volume focuses on the economic aspects of the ASEAN-10. Al-though no consensus exists on ASEAN's specific contributions to the economic development of its members, many observers acknowledge that ASEAN has facilitated trade and investment in the region through frequent conferences hosted by member governments. Conferences and consultations have contributed directly and indirectly to common stand-ards for business practices and administrative procedures. These stand-ards, in turn, have promoted intraregional transactions. As integration progressed among the ASEAN members, their regional market became increasingly attractive to nonmembers as well. Not only local corpora-tions but also multinational enterprises have expanded their investments in the ASEAN market. One can argue, therefore, on the one hand that ASEAN has contributed to the creation of a favorable investment climate.

On the other hand, it is questionable whether ASEAN's institutional integration through discriminatory mechanisms has enhanced the economic development of its members. Preferential trade arrangements for certain members have obstructed intraregional trade, and most members try to protect similar industries. AFTA remains incomplete in that it allows 5 percent import tariffs even in its target year for implementation. The success of AFTA depends on the efforts of member governments that still protect their domestic industries against those of other members.

Member governments' efforts to gain preferential trade arrangements for themselves have borne little fruit. Industrial cooperation to create a division of labor among members failed because most countries planned to develop the same industries. AFTA is an attempt to break through individual protectionism, but the list of import tariffs offered for elimination reveals the hesitation of member governments. As a result, by the mid-1990s AFTA had made little progress. These facts suggest that institutional arrangements within ASEAN have contributed little to the development of members' economies.

What then caused the rapid growth of the ASEAN economies in the latter half of the 1980s? Except for Singapore, these economies depended heavily on foreign technology and investment. Member governments controlled resource allocation, including foreign exchange, through regulations and administrative guidance.

Although the industrialized economies adopted the floating exchange rate system after 1973, most ASEAN economies continued to peg their currencies to the U.S. dollar (see figs. 1–3). Through the 1970s and the 1980s, ASEAN governments claimed that they had actually pegged their currencies to a basket of major currencies. Exchange rate data, however, revealed ongoing pegging to the U.S. dollar. The significant depreciation of the U.S. dollar in the latter half of the 1980s led to the undervaluation of the ASEAN currencies, which, in turn, created booms in ASEAN's exports. As they improved their infrastructures, Thailand and Malaysia, in particular, attracted investment not only from the industrialized economies but also from the newly industrializing economies (NIEs). Consequently, the wages of engineers rose significantly

Figure 1. Won and Yen per US$

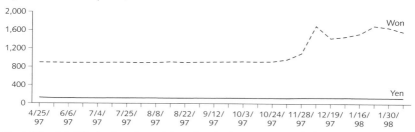

Source: Nihon Keizai Shimbun (Japan Economic Journal), various issues reporting interbank exchange rates of selected currencies.

Figure 2. Baht and NT$ per US$

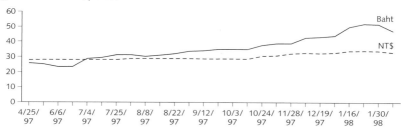

Source: Nihon Keizai Shimbun (Japan Economic Journal), various issues reporting interbank exchange rates of selected currencies.

Figure 3. Renminbi, HK$, and S$ per US$

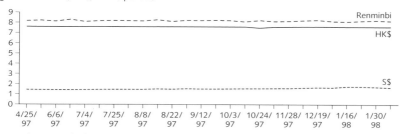

Source: Nihon Keizai Shimbun (Japan Economic Journal), various issues reporting interbank exchange rates of selected currencies.

and land prices soared (see Montes 1998). High interest rates and currencies pegged to the U.S. dollar promoted capital importation throughout ASEAN.

Some ASEAN economies declared that they were now NIEs, not the middle-income group. Meanwhile, *deregulation* became a byword in government strategies, especially among the industrialized economies. The overconfident governments of some ASEAN economies deregulated foreign exchange transactions as well as their financial sectors. Manufacturers and local financial institutions actively imported foreign capital during the investment boom. Deregulated foreign exchange transactions, under such circumstances, triggered huge capital outflows as investors and lenders doubted the sustainability of borrowing abroad. Many ASEAN currencies were already overvalued in the early 1990s in terms of purchasing power parity. These factors were the direct causes of the currency crises in Thailand and Indonesia (see figs. 4–7).

The U.S. dollar has appreciated since the mid-1990s, as have the currencies pegged to it. As domestic booms became bubbles in some ASEAN economies, their currencies were clearly overvalued. In contrast, the currencies of the ASEAN economies' major competitors, notably India's rupee and China's renminbi, remained stable. As a result, many ASEAN economies' exports became less competitive in world markets. Stagnant exports and massive capital outflows led to balance-of-payment shortages. Thus, most ASEAN currencies depreciated drastically from late 1996 through 1997.

The situation varied by country. Although Singapore experienced a foreign investment boom and domestic inflation, the depreciation of the Singapore dollar was slight, reflecting market concern about the negative effects of defaults in neighboring countries. Local investors and lenders expected losses in Singapore attributable to defaults by borrowers and other countries. Thailand has responded to its financial crisis by strengthening regulations and stabilizing its markets with stricter supply-demand management. Financial cooperation by industrialized countries through the International Monetary Fund (IMF) is supporting the Thai government's efforts. Some of Thailand's political leaders have resigned to take responsibility for the crisis. In Indonesia, which has received substantial financial assistance from the IMF and the industrialized countries, the situation remains unpredictable. The long-lasting Suharto administration showed no signs of restructuring relations between the government and President Suharto's family, and violent public protests in May 1998 resulted in Suharto's relinquishing power to H. B. Habibie. Business groups, however, are still controlled by Suharto's family, which suggests the need for drastic reform of governmental systems. The Habibie administration needs to urgently reconstruct the economy under the leadership of a "clean government."

Figure 4. Exchange Rate Index and Wholesale Price Index in Thailand (1990 = 100)

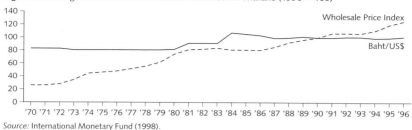

Source: International Monetary Fund (1998).

Figure 5. Balance of Goods, Services, and Income, and Overall Balance of Payments in Thailand (US$ billion)

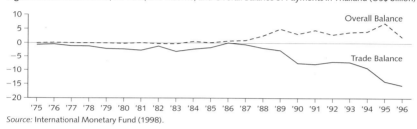

Source: International Monetary Fund (1998).

Figure 6. Exchange Rate Index and Wholesale Price Index in Indonesia (1990 = 100)

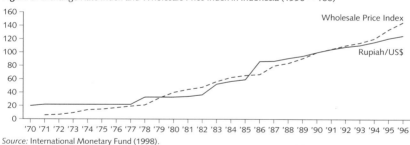

Source: International Monetary Fund (1998).

Figure 7. Balance of Goods, Services, and Income, and Overall Balance of Payments in Indonesia (US$ billion)

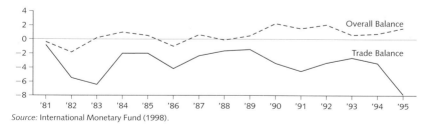

Source: International Monetary Fund (1998).

But it is too early to predict how successful Habibie will be because the quality of his political leadership is unknown. For the time being, international financial institutions supporting the new government seem to favor giving technocrats positions of responsibility.

The issue of succession of political power attracted attention in Malaysia as well. A political system that permits smooth changes in the leader of the governing party and the prime minister must be created. As of January 1999, expectations were that either Foreign Minister Abdullah Ahmad Badawi or Education Minister Najib Razak would eventually succeed Prime Minister Mahathir bin Mohamad. The long existence of the Mahathir regime means that the next prime minister will be handpicked by Mahathir. As a similar situation exists regarding the succession of the leader of the governing party and the prime minister in Japan, this is no surprise to the Japanese. The real issue is who is capable of strengthening the economy and reforming the political system. Whoever takes power, the new prime minister is sure to lack the leadership and charisma of Mahathir.

Whether the recent currency crises promote or deter regional integration in ASEAN is debatable. Conditions imposed by the IMF on borrowers prohibit governmental intervention and regulation of foreign exchange and instead emphasize the importance of stricter supply-demand management. If borrowers faithfully follow the IMF's guidance, foreign trade and investment should remain free as regulations are restrained. Because the costs of transport and communications within the region are low, natural integration will occur, though the economies might not fully complement each other. If the ASEAN members strengthen preferential trade to save hard currency, they could distort trade flows. The gains from preferential trade might be less significant because trade opportunities within the region are limited.

Mahathir emphasizes a strategy to promote intraregional trade and investment and has attacked some U.S. speculators in foreign exchange. He argues that the ASEAN economies should use local currencies to settle intraregional trade and save U.S. dollar reserves. Although his intentions are understandable, the feasibility of his ideas remains dubious. Intraregional trade growth depends more on the complementarity of member economies. Artificially forcing external trade could increase production costs in the ASEAN economies. Moreover, exporters would probably not accept payment in unstable local currencies.

AFTA is still in its start-up phase and its impact on trade between ASEAN and the rest of the world will be negligible for a decade or so. Its effect on attracting foreign investment will also be modest.[2]

Short-Term Difficulties and Long-Term Prospects

The long-term growth potential of the ASEAN economies cannot be denied because of the currency crises of 1996–1998. However, Paul Krugman (1994) questions this potential by pointing out that the economies' growth has depended more on increased factor inputs than on technological progress. He cites this same reason as the cause of the failures of the former Soviet Union and Eastern European countries. The NIEs differ significantly from centrally planned economies in that competition and market mechanisms work. Their past dependence on increases in factor inputs simply reflects the early stage of their economic development.

Financial crises are neither the subject of Krugman's analysis nor the determinants of long-term growth potential. He correctly argues that the NIEs' growth depended heavily on rising factor inputs, a fact confirmed by Alwyn Young (1994), who correctly applied growth accounting to these economies. Krugman is wrong to impose the characteristics of centrally planned economies onto the NIEs, despite the NIEs' recent dependence on foreign investment and technology transfer. This dependence is indicative of the "catching-up" phase. The NIEs and the middle-income countries in East Asia can sustain high economic growth rates relative to those of the fully industrialized economies.

As economic development progresses, local institutions must adapt. Governments played important roles during the earliest stage of development by providing administrative guidance, regulations, and tax breaks for industries. Changing economies necessitate institutional reform. In the late 1980s, *deregulation* was a key word in most NIEs and middle-income countries. Partial deregulation with residual protection and restrictions has caused a bubble phenomenon in recent years, as government strategies failed during the transitional growth phase. Nonetheless, there is no direct relationship between medium-term and long-term growth potential.[3]

Most ASEAN economies still depend on foreign capital; they finance domestic investment with imported capital. Not surprisingly, they have current account deficits in their balance of payments. The issue is whether these deficits are sustainable. They are as long as sovereign borrowers grow at a higher rate than interest rates rise. Because most ASEAN economies have surplus labor, they are wise to accelerate growth using foreign capital. Technology imports are indispensable during the present phase of development and will help the NIEs maintain high growth rates relative to the industrialized economies. Investment in research and development will gradually increase in the NIEs.

Economic development is not without turbulence. The ASEAN economies might occasionally fluctuate during times of political reform and institutional change, both of which are needed for economic development. Through these fluctuations, they will grow fast for a few decades. At the same time, intraregional trade and investment opportunities will emerge, as higher per capita income creates more bilateral trade. Such change, however, is not promoted by government intervention but by the progress of economic development.

The Structure of This Volume

This volume examines the medium- and long-term prospects of the ASEAN-10 and their relations with major trading partners. Although recent developments in politics and economics are addressed, the volume primarily explores a longer-term outlook. ASEAN as a regional institution is the focal point, and therefore international and domestic politics are important factors. Thus, this volume begins with a chapter on politics in the ASEAN-10.

Chapter 2 discusses the political problems facing the ASEAN-10 and possible solutions. Because the members are not isolated and most also belong to the Asia-Pacific Economic Cooperation (APEC) forum, it is important to examine the roles that the ASEAN-10 play in broader regional cooperation. Changes in ASEAN's relations with its neighbors and other countries in APEC are also examined. The chapter also includes a discussion of future relations between the ASEAN-10 and Japan. Special attention is given to new members Myanmar, Vietnam, and Cambodia. The functions and limits of the ASEAN Regional Forum (ARF) are reviewed, as well as external relations with the countries wielding the greatest influence on ASEAN—China, Japan, and the United States.

Chapter 3 turns to economic issues by examining ASEAN's position in APEC. ASEAN looks forward to economic assistance within the APEC framework, but it resists drastic deregulation and the liberalization of foreign trade, particularly in manufactured goods and financial services. A larger ASEAN might have difficulty reaching the consensus essential to its policy making. This would make it more difficult for ASEAN and APEC to adjust to each other. The chapter discusses not only ASEAN's views on APEC and its major subregions but also looks at how the other members of APEC interact with ASEAN.

Chapter 4 focuses on financial networks in the major ASEAN economies. Currency crises and financial instability are currently the dominant issues. This chapter deals with the long-term development of financial markets and freer movements of international capital. Because of biases in capital allocation in the international marketplace, interest rates do not converge. When a net debtor country (one with a current account deficit) borrows foreign capital, some of the funds are directly related to trade in goods and "real" or direct investment. There were massive capital inflows pursuing high interest rates in some ASEAN economies during the so-called bubble years, followed by drastic outflows when the sustainability of foreign borrowing looked doubtful. Obviously, regulation and deregulation of the banking sector and foreign exchange transactions are interrelated issues. Deregulation, however, often remains partial. Foreign entrants into the ASEAN economies' financial sectors have been strictly controlled. This chapter compares the performance of some ASEAN economies in allocating financial resources and stabilizing currency values.

Chapter 4 also presents the internal economic relations of the ASEAN-10. The intensity of trade as well as investment among ASEAN members has thus far not been significant compared with that among the major industrialized economies. Therefore, when examining trade and investment within ASEAN, the text refers to relations with non-members when appropriate. Although covering new members country by country is desirable, it is not feasible. Vietnam was chosen as representative of the economic issues that will emerge as new members adapt to ASEAN.[4]

Chapter 5 examines intra- and interregional trade among the ASEAN-10, though because of the limited available data the focus of the chapter is on the core ASEAN-5. Intraregional trade grew rapidly in the latter half of the 1980s owing to an expansion of intra-industry trade in such sectors as the electrical and electronic equipment industry. This new industry developed mostly through FDI. The ASEAN-10's new members increase trade opportunities among the grouping as Vietnam and Myanmar export mineral fuels and natural resources as well as labor-intensive manufactures. Although preferential trading arrangements have played a part in promoting intraregional trade, industrialization through FDI has contributed more to the expansion of trade among the ASEAN economies. More important for ASEAN over the long term than intraregional trade, however, is interregional trade with non-ASEAN members—mostly developed countries and the NIES—because they import a large portion of ASEAN's finished products.

Chapter 6 focuses on investment, another important link among the ASEAN-10. This introductory chapter suggested that, except for Singapore, ASEAN economies are recipients of FDI. This is an oversimplification. In fact, Thailand invested in Indochina when the latter opened its market. FDI is promoting an industrial shuffle within ASEAN. Nonetheless, investment from non-ASEAN members, including the NIEs, might be more important. The countries and sectors that receive this investment affect the division of labor among ASEAN members and determine future trade patterns.

Chapter 7 examines Vietnam's development since it opened up and began promoting foreign trade with, and receiving foreign investment from, market-driven economies. Vietnam is an experiment for ASEAN in that it maintains a significantly different political system. If ASEAN successfully integrates socialist countries and military dictatorships, it can teach an important lesson: Harmony between different political systems and mutual economic prosperity contribute to peace and development in Southeast Asia. New members might negatively affect this integration until they adjust to ASEAN's rules. ASEAN, for its part, might have to slow the pace of integration. Furthermore, new members might not support schemes that force members to switch to intraregional trade, as Malaysia's Mahathir has proposed.

Chapter 8 reviews the functions of nongovernmental organizations (NGOs) within the ASEAN-10. NGOs have increased their roles in the many fields in which market forces are not solving urgent problems, for example, environmental protection, education, training, and community development in underdeveloped countries. NGOs are also active in preliminary discussions of human rights and democratization, two areas in which official negotiations often damage bilateral relations. Before formal talks between governments, NGO discussions contribute to establishing common ground and avoiding conflicts.

Finally, chapter 9 offers a bird's-eye view of the preceding chapters' topics and issues. In short, chapters 2–8 look at the trees and chapter 9 looks at the forest.

Notes

1. As evidence of ASEAN's growing influence, Japan and Australia sought ASEAN's support for their creation of the Pacific Economic Cooperation Council by promoting only the activities that ASEAN approved.

2. For the theoretical aspects of the effects of free trade areas, customs, and unions on foreign trade and investment, see Sekiguchi (1998).

3. Socialist market economies, despite strict currency regulations, cannot prevent monetary turbulence during the reform of their institutions and systems. China and Vietnam might face more serious transition-related problems in the future. However, if they learn by watching other countries' struggles, they can reduce their own difficulties.

4. Although the present volume does not contain a chapter on Myanmar, some members of the study group for this volume have made their first visit to that country in preparation for future studies.

Bibliography

International Monetary Fund. 1998. *International Financial Statistics 1997*. CD-ROM. Washington, D.C.: International Monetary Fund.

Krugman, Paul. 1994. "The Myth of Asia's Miracle." *Foreign Affairs* 73(6): 62–78.

Montes, Manuel F. 1998. *The Currency Crisis in Southeast Asia*. Singapore: Institute of Southeast Asian Studies.

Sekiguchi Sueo. 1998. "Chiikitōgō to kokusaitōshi" (Regional integration and international investment). *Kaigaitōshi kenkyūshohō* (Journal of overseas investment) 24(3): 4–25. Published by the Export-Import Bank of Japan.

World Bank. 1997. *World Bank Development Indicators 1997*. CD-ROM. Washington, D.C.: World Bank.

Young, Alwyn. 1994. "The Tyranny of Numbers: Confirming the Statistical Realities of the East Asian Growth Experience." NBER Working Paper No. 4680. Cambridge, Mass.: National Bureau for Economic Research.

– 2 –

The ASEAN-10 and
Regional Political Relations

Takano Takeshi

A UNIFIED SOUTHEAST ASIA, at least in a political sense, is emerging. The prospect of the Association of Southeast Asian Nations en-
compassing all the states in the region as its members should bring new
hope to a region once about to lose confidence in its ability and aspiration to overcome its vulnerabilities. The economic crises that began in
mid-1997 hit all of East Asia hard and have had sweeping ramifications,
most obviously in Indonesia. These crises, coupled with the political
turmoil in Cambodia, have delayed and impeded ASEAN's agenda to
unite the region. However, as the 21st century approaches ASEAN is expected to embrace a new era in its long history since inception in 1967;
in this new era all the states of the region are to share the fruits of meaningful political, economic, and functional cooperation. The codes of
conduct originally envisaged but realized only much later—including
peaceful solutions to problems between states, "work ethics" for development, and, ultimately, "regional resilience"—will be shared by the
newly acceded members as well.

The original rhetoric notwithstanding, all is not rosy ahead for
ASEAN. Concerns surrounding the association and its member countries abound at the domestic, regional, and international levels. In this
chapter, those concerns are analyzed from two perspectives: over the
short to medium term, and over the medium to long term. This chapter
focuses on four points:

- Under what conditions has the enlargement of ASEAN occurred?
- How will the new member states affect the association?

16

- How will external relations with the association change (or not change)?
- What is Japan's role in the region with regard to ASEAN enlargement?

Here, the emphasis is on regional politics and security. This focus includes the nonmilitary aspects of regional security, especially on whether and how the so-called ASEAN way (Chalmers 1996, 13–39; Mutalib 1997; Narine 1997) works (or doesn't work) in relations between the old and new members and between members and ASEAN's dialogue partners in the Post Ministerial Conference (PMC) and the ASEAN Regional Forum (ARF).

The Process of Enlargement

In August 1967, in the thick of the "hot" cold war being fought in the region, ASEAN was created among the noncommunist countries; the then-neutral regional states of Burma (now called Myanmar), Cambodia, and Laos did not join for their respective reasons. The participation of either South Vietnam or North Vietnam was out of the question from the beginning. Admission of South Vietnam, a hard-line anticommunist state, would surely have induced severe criticism from the socialist camp. The enlargement process began in January 1984, when Brunei became the sixth member state. But even then there was little expectation among ASEAN leaders and bureaucrats that the rest of the regional states—Myanmar, Cambodia, Laos, and a unified Vietnam—would join ASEAN. Although ASEAN was not begun as an anticommunist alliance, the common political systems in the founding five countries and the strong sentiment against domestic communist movements led to the suspicion, criticism, and even denunciation of ASEAN as a second Southeast Asia Treaty Organization (SEATO) by socialist states both inside and outside the region (see, for example, Buszynski 1983).

Political Background

The road to the ASEAN-10—the expansion of the organization to all ten countries in the region—began not with the inclusion of Brunei but with Vietnam's formal accession to the association in July 1995. The end of the cold war necessitated Vietnam changing its attitude toward ASEAN, the political enemy it used to denounce as a puppet of the "imperialist" camp. ASEAN leaders, too, realized that the inclusion of a nonaggressive Vietnam brought certain benefits to regional security.

Vietnam, which historically has had a love-hate relationship with China, its adversary during Vietnam's military occupation of Cambodia, was considered by the ASEAN members as a possible counterforce— or at least a buffer—against China. In the late 1980s, when Vietnamese armed forces were expected to withdraw, sooner or later, from Cambodia (thanks in part to ASEAN's diplomatic efforts to solve the problem peacefully), China instead emerged as a potential threat to the regional security environment.

The threat perception vis-à-vis China that prevailed in the region at that time was mainly attributed to China's military, especially with regard to Chinese naval action in the East and South China seas. There, the Paracel and Spratly islands were the source of territorial disputes by several regional claimants, among which China and Vietnam were (and still are) two significant players. The naval clash off the Spratlys between these two countries in March 1988 aroused serious concern among the other claimants (Brunei, Malaysia, the Philippines, and Taiwan). Even among the nonclaimant regional states (Indonesia, Singapore, and Thailand), concerns were raised regarding damage to the relatively peaceful and benign regional security environment by the arbitrary actions of China.

In January 1988, Vietnamese Foreign Minister Nguyen Co Thach indirectly and unofficially spoke of Vietnam's aspiration to join ASEAN.[1] A month earlier, at the third summit meeting of ASEAN in Manila, Hanoi extended an unprecedentedly amicable message to the association suggesting that it would no longer regard ASEAN as an adversary. On the contrary, Vietnam claimed to appreciate the achievements of the association, saying that "[ASEAN] created a new opportunity to enable all the regional states to coexist peacefully."

Vietnam's armed forces completed their withdrawal from Cambodian territory in September 1989. With the abrupt termination of financial and military assistance from the Soviet Union, Vietnam had to turn its attention to new providers of resources for reconstruction and development, especially for the purpose of driving its *doi moi* (which literally means renovation) reform programs further forward. The rapidly developing economies in its neighborhood were expected to provide Vietnam, for the first time in the history of the socialist republic, with an attractive opportunity to cooperate. Security concerns also drove Vietnam toward ASEAN, which shared with Vietnam a chariness regarding China's military buildup and growing influence in the region. Even during Vietnam's occupation of Cambodia, countries such as Indonesia and Malaysia did not conceal their sympathies for Vietnam and cautious attitudes toward China. There existed, in effect, a de facto ASEAN entente supporting the association's stance in the international arena.

Although it would take five more years until Vietnam formally joined ASEAN, by around 1990 the possibility of Vietnam as a member had already emerged. By then, mutual understanding between the ASEAN-6 (the founding five countries plus Brunei) and Vietnam had increased, largely as a result of sitting at the same negotiating table. But it was far from easy: The historical antagonism and distrust that Thais, for example, felt toward Vietnamese still loomed. However, improved communication enabled the once mutually hostile parties to recognize their common interests (especially regarding national and regional security) beyond differences in ideologies and political systems.

Myanmar's approach to ASEAN differed from Vietnam's (as did ASEAN's approach to Myanmar differ from that to Vietnam), but some similarities existed. Ideological constraints became negligible, a quasi-market economy was adopted in the process of reform, and participation in world affairs became increasingly urgent. These factors spurred Myanmar to join ASEAN.

Institutional Aspects

Vietnam gained status as an ASEAN observer at the 25th ASEAN Ministerial Meeting (AMM) in Manila in July 1992. At the same time, Vietnam signed the Treaty of Amity and Cooperation in Southeast Asia (TAC), a prerequisite to full membership in ASEAN. Laos also acquired observer status at this meeting, but at the 28th AMM in Bandar Seri Begawan, Brunei, in July 1995, Lao Foreign Minister Somsavat Lengsavad expressed the country's desire to enter ASEAN in two years' time. Vietnam was formally admitted in 1995. Also at the Brunei meeting, Cambodia was accorded observer status, and Myanmar signed the TAC and applied for observer status, which was granted at the 29th AMM. At the 30th AMM, in Kuala Lumpur in July 1997, Laos and Myanmar were accorded full membership in ASEAN but Cambodia's entry was postponed.

Laos was unable to join ASEAN together with Vietnam in July 1995. Given the administrative and personnel difficulties in "acquiring

familiarity with the complex structures, processes, and modus ope-
randi of ASEAN functional cooperation"—problems Vietnam also experienced—Laos clearly needed more time to prepare for entry (Chin
1995, 427–428). It was only in 1995 that the Lao Ministry of Foreign
Affairs set up an ASEAN Division in its Department of Asia-Pacific and
Africa. That department was later upgraded, and a director-general was
appointed early the next year. In February 1996, a fact-finding team
from the ASEAN Standing Committee (ASC) was sent to Vientiane and
presented the "Road Map Toward Membership in ASEAN" in a meeting
with senior Lao officials. Meanwhile, the ASEAN Secretariat trained
seven Lao officials in attachment programs ranging from three to five
weeks with funds from the United Nations Development Program
(UNDP). In addition, the Secretariat staff conducted intensive briefings
on ASEAN affairs and the ASEAN Free Trade Area (AFTA), and held
technical discussions with Lao officials on establishing an e-mail link
to facilitate information exchange with the Secretariat.[2] Many of these
same procedures were also applied to Cambodia.

The procedures applied to Myanmar were essentially the same, but
the process was slightly different and quicker. In 1994, Myanmar Foreign Minister Ohn Gyaw was invited to the 27th AMM in Bangkok as an
official guest of the host government of Thailand. He also attended the
following year's AMM in Brunei (under the same guest status), when
Myanmar's application for observer status was received, a step that enabled the country to become an ASEAN observer at the 29th AMM in
Jakarta.[3] A year later, Myanmar joined ASEAN. Myanmar's entry was ex-
ceptionally swift relative to that of Vietnam and Laos.

Two factors supported Myanmar's entry into ASEAN: First, political
decisiveness was exerted in the ASEAN leaders' decision-making process. At an informal ASEAN summit meeting in Jakarta, in December
1996, some of the leaders were reportedly reluctant to admit Myanmar;
they thought its entry was premature. Indonesian President Suharto,
however, strongly supported Myanmar's bid. He insisted that Myanmar's
alleged human rights violations were not sufficient reason to continue
to isolate the country from the international community and that it
should be admitted to ASEAN as soon as possible.

Second, Myanmar possessed highly competent administration and
personnel. Of course, Myanmar underwent training programs to famil-
iarize its officials with ASEAN affairs, and the Secretariat also sent its staff
for briefings in Yangon (formerly Rangoon). However, compared with

other new member states, their English education background, for example, seemed to provide Myanmar officials with a definite advantage in handling a large (and growing) quantity of complex programs and works.

New Factors Following Enlargement

The enlargement process entails difficulties at various levels of ASEAN activities. Will the new members pull their own weight along with the ASEAN-6? Besides concerns about competence among government officials, what are the political and security implications of enlargement? How will it affect the nature and behavior of the association over the medium to long term? Especially important in this regard are Vietnam and Myanmar, which share some common features as new members of ASEAN. Both countries

- have experienced major economic reform from a socialist to a market economy since the late 1980s (Myanmar even abandoned the "Burmese way to socialism");
- enjoyed near-double-digit economic growth in the years following their economic transition;[4] and
- share a border and a distinctive relationship with China in terms of geography, history, and strategic interests.

Vietnam as a New Asian Tiger?

Vietnam's entry into ASEAN has been broadly considered to have embraced a latent Sino-Vietnamese conflict within the association. Territorial disputes in the South China Sea and over some land borders are still a source of concern between the two states. For Vietnam, China is still a potential adversary, despite the restoration of diplomatic relations between the two communist regimes in November 1991, followed by the normalization of ties at the party-to-party level. Beijing has implied that the countries could be comrades but no longer allies (Nishihara and Morley 1996, 120), rather like the characterization of China and North Vietnam as "lips and teeth" during the first and second Indochinese Wars in the 1950s and 1960s.

Yet it is misleading to view their relations only in an adversarial context. The two countries now share similar interests. Both badly need a benign and stable regional security environment for substantial economic reform and development to take place. Entry into ASEAN opened a path for Vietnam to really participate in global affairs and to become integrated into the world economy. Indeed, Hanoi normalized its relationship with Washington at almost the same time. The neighboring economies, especially Singapore and Hong Kong, as well as the Western nations such as France and Japan have so far made remarkable contributions to the economic reconstruction of Vietnam.

It is noteworthy that Taiwan, and not China, has played a significant role in assisting Vietnam's reform efforts. Although this development may still cause tensions in Sino-Vietnamese relations, it did prod China to enhance its economic relations with Vietnam in the early 1990s. These economic and political-security motives drove Beijing into an accelerating rapprochement with Hanoi. Beijing was still suffering from the economic sanctions imposed by the Western nations after the crackdown on the student demonstration in Tiananmen Square on June 4, 1989, and it desperately needed friends.

In recent years, Sino-Vietnamese economic relations have been quite active: Bilateral trade now amounts to US$1 billion annually, border trade resumed with the reopening of the land border, the border railroad is running again, and Chinese investment in Vietnam has been increasing steadily. Northern Vietnam has turned into a vast market for Chinese consumer goods, which are relatively cheap and of high quality. In fact, some economic domination by China has been observed in the border areas of its other neighboring countries, especially in the area the Chinese call the "golden quadrangle," including Laos, Myanmar, Thailand, and Northern Vietnam (Seekins 1997, 531).

Vietnam and China will be increasingly discussed in terms of rivalry or competition in Asia Pacific, or the East Asian economic structure, especially as a potential market for foreign direct investment (FDI). The regional economy is now in bad shape and will continue to struggle for the time being, but Vietnam will surely emerge as the next "tiger." It will be a strong competitor to China and to some of the ASEAN-5, notably Indonesia and the Philippines.

Myanmar as China's Pawn?

If Vietnam's entry into ASEAN implies a potential conflict or rivalry vis-à-vis China, Myanmar's membership might well draw the association into China's sphere of influence. Since the emergence of military rule after the coup in 1988, the Yangon regime, or the State Law and Order Restoration Council (SLORC), has fostered its relationship with Beijing from many aspects: overseas and border trade, investment, financial and military assistance, and internal as well as external security. Relations between the two countries could be compared to that of a guardian and protégé. These two internationally isolated states naturally became closer after Rangoon's abrupt invalidation of the 1990 general election, which followed Beijing's violent crackdown on students in Tiananmen Square almost a year earlier.

China used to be a cause of concern for Burma, especially from the late 1960s to the early 1970s (Seekins 1997, 527–528). The Chinese Communist Party supported its Burmese counterpart while radically propagating Maoism among the local Chinese during the Cultural Revolution. In 1967, this resulted in a ban on the domestic Maoist movement by Ne Win's military regime; riots even broke out against the local Chinese community in Rangoon. Diplomatic relations between the two countries were suspended until 1971, when Ne Win visited Beijing and restored the relationship. Burma also experienced the same kind of serious insurgency problems as did Malaysia, the Philippines, and Thailand. Only in recent years have Sino-Burmese ties significantly improved.

Relations between the two countries are now integrated in almost every aspect of life. Especially remarkable—and thus worrisome to neighboring countries—is the security dimension. Myanmar has purchased an estimated US$1.5 billion in arms from China, weaponry that appears to be relatively advanced. The two governments also signed a military cooperation agreement in late 1996. The agreement reportedly stipulates that China will provide Myanmar with military training (especially for its navy and air force) and financial assistance (which means selling arms to Myanmar at a "friendly" price). The two countries will also apparently exchange information regarding "mutual threats" (*Far Eastern Economic Review* 30 January 1997, 12). Moreover, China has assisted in the construction of military facilities in Myanmar, most notably the naval and radar facilities on the islands and coastal areas along the Andaman Sea and the Bay of Bengal.

Today, Myanmar is not hostile to any particular neighbor, and none of its neighbors are hostile to it, despite some lingering historical antagonism against the Burmese (especially among the Thais). The diffusion of China's influence into Myanmar may therefore not cause serious concern, much less the possibility of armed conflict in mainland Southeast Asia, at least in the foreseeable future. Nonetheless, one reason why the ASEAN-5 states were quick to accept Myanmar's entry was to lessen Myanmar's excessive dependence on China and to draw Myanmar into ASEAN's sphere of influence.

There is another aspect to this tug-of-war between ASEAN and China on Myanmar. Myanmar's entry into ASEAN has inevitably elicited harsh criticism on human rights and democracy by the Western governments. In this respect, China shares many of the same views as ASEAN, both of which advocate "Asian values." Defending Myanmar serves the interests of both ASEAN and China, but some of the ASEAN-5 states, notably Indonesia and Malaysia, insist that Myanmar should be engaged with the rest of the world through ASEAN and not through China. ASEAN has also adopted a constructive engagement policy toward China. Malaysian Prime Minister Mahathir bin Mohamad visited Yangon in March 1998, his second official visit since 1988, and reportedly met with General Than Shwe, chairman of the State Peace and Development Council (SPDC; the moniker SLORC was dropped in late 1997). Mahathir consulted with the general on matters concerning the general principle of unity and a future ASEAN common currency program. This visit was quite meaningful, given the continuing regionwide economic crisis, Suharto's struggles with the International Monetary Fund (IMF), and the imminent London gathering of the Asia-Europe Meeting (ASEM).

Cambodia as a Troublemaker?

Cambodia attained full membership in ASEAN on April 30, 1999. However, it is still difficult to predict if the country will even be governed peacefully under the new government. Ousted First Prime Minister Norodom Ranariddh, now the House speaker, and his co-premier, Hun Sen, who is now the only prime minister, were legitimate leaders elected in a U.N.-supervised general election in May 1993. However, in early July 1997, a few days after the Thai baht depreciated, Hun Sen ousted Ranariddh by force, and in the next month the position of first premier went to, as was expected, Foreign Minister Ung Huot, another member of the National United Front for an Independent, Neutral, Peaceful and Cooperative Cambodia (FUNCINPEC). The coalition in the Cambodian government was obviously a pretense (see Peang-Meth 1997 for recent political developments in Cambodia).

Premier Hun Sen is a shrewd political maneuverer both domestically and internationally. Right after what amounted to a coup d'état—though he denied that such was the case—Hun Sen rejected ASEAN's offer to mediate between the warring factions. Hun Sen took advantage of ASEAN's principle (and past practice) of noninterference in the domestic problems of any member state. But he later reversed his position and accepted ASEAN's diplomatic efforts while justifying his actions toward Ranariddh as necessary to maintain peace and order in Cambodia. ASEAN, for its part, had no choice but to avoid criticizing the second prime minister by name, and to express its hope to see a peaceful Cambodia as a member as soon as possible. Hun Sen won yet another political battle, this time with ASEAN.

More than eight months later, in late March 1998, Ranariddh returned, but his influence in domestic politics seems to have been reduced significantly, despite his popularity among the general public. In mid-April, Pol Pot, the notorious genocidal leader of the Khmer Rouge —and another long-standing political enemy of Hun Sen—died, resulting in the apparent dissolution of the Khmer Rouge (*Mainichi Shimbun* 15–18 April 1998). Hun Sen has now outstripped the power of almost all his political rivals. Cambodia under him and his grip on power after the general election may be relatively stable, and his power base will certainly be consolidated with the dominance of his Cambodian People's Party. But Cambodia will almost certainly remain a trouble spot, considering the self-righteous attitudes of Hun Sen, the tendency to solve political problems by force, and the fragility of its constitutional monarchy, given the declining physical condition of King Sihanouk, who remains based in Beijing, not in Phnom Penh. The prospect of the post-Sihanouk monarchy is quite uncertain; Cambodia may well remain a problem for its neighbors even after joining ASEAN.

Regional Security

The ASEAN members may still have to cope with political maneuvering during the process of enlargement. Enlargement will also affect relations with ASEAN's dialogue partners, which could lead to an overall restructuring of ASEAN's external relations. Nonetheless, China, Japan, and the United States remain the most important countries to ASEAN. The roles of China and the United States are central to overall regional security. Regional powers such as China and India might emerge as poles of regional international politics and security, whereas the only remaining superpower after the cold war, the United States, might play a balancing role, in contrast to its role of "world police officer" in the immediate post–cold war world. In this context, the core of ARF—essentially an enlarged ASEAN—will become one such pole that will exert more influence in the future affairs of the region.

Regional Security Environment

The regional security environment in Asia Pacific in the late 1990s is by and large benign and stable, with the exception of the unpredictable situation on the Korean peninsula (see, for example, Oberdorfer 1997). Even the turmoil in Cambodia, which clouds the political future of that country, does not affect regional security to the extent that it did in the late 1970s and 1980s. It was once presumed that regional powers such as China, India, or even Japan might try to fill the power vacuum in the region following the end of the cold war. This kind of argument aroused serious concern among the ASEAN members, especially in the early 1990s (see, for example, Chin 1995); at that time, it was unclear whether the United States would maintain its military bases in the Philippines —which had been long considered both implicitly and explicitly as a keystone in the security of post–Vietnam War Southeast Asia. As anticipated, by the end of 1992 all U.S. troops and facilities withdrew from the Subic and Clark bases, which left the ASEAN members to develop a new framework of security cooperation.

The years 1989–1992 were important in that the uncertainty and unpredictability about the future of peace and stability in the region became palpable and pragmatic; ideas and proposals on security cooperation were discussed enthusiastically inside and outside the region. Various of these ideas and proposals, including an Asian version of the Conference on Security and Cooperation in Europe, were relevant to what was eventually created: a security dialogue based on the existing ASEAN-PMC, to be chaired and managed by ASEAN. This body is ARF.

Regional security in the post–cold war era requires sufficient attention to both the military and nonmilitary aspects of security. Formal alliances, collective security formulas, or legally binding treaties are not suitable to the regional climate. Assuring peace and stability necessitates the same ideas that were prevalent during the cold war: promoting economic and social development, reducing tensions caused by political and social unrest in all nations, and avoiding the spread of such tensions to neighboring countries. The threat once posed by armed antigovernment movements in most of the countries in the region during the cold war has been largely removed. However, numerous possible sources of domestic tension and tension between nations still exist. Differences in ethnicity, social stratum, and local regional setting (especially the contrast between urban and rural areas) remain.

The earlier trend of governments in the region pursuing arms modernization programs may not be reversed easily. Even in terms of a strictly defensive military environment, security concerns have prevailed in the post–cold war Asia Pacific region. Some specialists argue that such arms modernization programs are not designed to project power, but are essentially defensive in nature. Moreover, even the large increases in defense spending by regional states are modest compared with defense spending in European and Middle Eastern countries (Dibb 1997, 349–353). In addition, the indigenous development of advanced technology in the regional states might be enhanced by modernization of the national defense.

However, Asia is the fastest-growing arms market in the world (Dibb 1997, 348). A few of the procurement programs, such as Malaysia's acquisition of MiG-29s and Indonesia's decision to purchase SU-30s, together with the naval and air force buildup in China, could alter the regional strategic balance significantly. A less costly security arrangement in terms of the expense and the allocation of natural, human, and social resources, as was the case during the cold war, should be encouraged. The current arrangements, however, have been largely successful, and such an approach is more persuasive with most countries in the region no longer overconfident in the myth of economic growth, a chimera that supported their defense modernization programs. Ironically, with the economic downturn some governments have had to cancel or postpone major arms contracts with Europe and the United States.

ARF as the Core of Regional Security

The ASEAN basis for the ARF approach to regional security began to unfold two decades ago. This approach addresses the ongoing structural change in international politics from a unipolar to a full-fledged multipolar—and thus multilateral—system, wherein several medium to large powers manage in concert the course of events in each region through consultation and mutual understanding.

Without doubt, an enlarged ASEAN becomes the core of the security consultation. The newcomers (especially Laos, Myanmar, and Cambodia, but also Vietnam) can themselves become issues brought up by ARF. In fact, the 1997 ARF meeting in Subang Jaya, Malaysia, focused on issues surrounding Myanmar and Cambodia, even though the latter had yet to acquire full membership. Thus, it is still necessary to distinguish the ASEAN-6 from the latecomers. The courses of action open to the new members are also quite limited.

ARF, which has convened in each of the past four years, seems to be entering a new stage. The chairman's statement issued by the ASEAN Secretariat following the 1997 meeting stated that although ARF's successful confidence-building arrangements should be continuously promoted, a preparatory study on preventive diplomacy by the track two group had already been made. The same statement also refers to the common recognition among the participants that the "positive relations among the major powers in the Asia-Pacific—China, Japan, Russia, and the United States" are important to "sustaining stability in the region." The statement further asserts that ASEAN will undertake the "obligation to be the primary driving force" for a successful ARF.

Two observations can be made from the chairman's statement. First, ARF is trying to be more than a mere forum. Preventive diplomacy has been a focus of its activities the past few years. Theoretically, one premise of preventive diplomacy is that "acts that require military action or the use of force" lay outside the scope of the concept (Tay and Talib 1997, 254). No coercive measures are required; preventive diplomacy seems quite suitable for the security cooperation formula that ASEAN and ARF could employ. However, if the participating countries work together on preventive diplomacy in earnest, they must show their determination and commit themselves to what is sometimes difficult to distinguish from interference in the internal affairs of a state (257). Such interference is unacceptable to most Asian governments.

Preventive diplomacy uses fact-finding missions and third-party mediation for confrontational parties. But the cases requiring such measures are not traditional types of conflicts (Tay and Talib 1997, 258). A territorial dispute that threatens to escalate is one such case. Another, more subtly, might be a serious mass-scale violation of human rights that could cause an exodus of refugees to neighboring countries. A third might be a clandestine arms buildup in border areas. In each of these cases, the governments concerned would probably not consent to inspection by a third-party, fact-finding mission. As was seen in Iraq in early 1998, coercive measures may be necessary to back up diplomatic efforts, but such an idea does not seem suitable in the ARF climate.

Second, a kind of tug-of-war exists between ARF's organizer—ASEAN —and the external powers involved. ASEAN is confident in its role as a driving force in regional security dialogue, but it recognizes that security cooperation arrangements such as those under ARF are possible only when the regional environment is stable and is maintained by positive relations among the major powers. Paragraph 4-(iv) of the 1997 chairman's statement plainly shows that ARF is subject to limitations ("Chairman's Statement" 1997). The chairman's statement can also be interpreted to imply that, without ASEAN initiatives, a comprehensive framework for security cooperation could not have been built by the major powers working alone.

Generally speaking, a politically integrated Southeast Asia under the banner of the ASEAN-10 will certainly provide the broader Asia Pacific region with more opportunities and potentialities to enhance security in the region. The possibilities of conflict arising between the member states, at the very least, have already been dramatically reduced. The norms and codes of conduct shared among the ASEAN-6 have now permeated the new member states.

External Powers

ASEAN has succeeded in bringing together through ARF diverse members from China to Europe. Indeed, as seen in the inception of ASEM, yet another ASEAN initiative, major restructuring in ASEAN's external relations has taken place. Moreover, although ASEAN's relationships with its traditional partners—the United States, China, and Japan—are still important, they have gone through some qualitative changes.

After withdrawing its armed forces from the Philippines, the United States has been engaged only moderately in this region. The sole remaining superpower has often tried to exert its influence arbitrarily in many parts of the world, but the Clinton administration has positively and patiently subscribed to the ASEAN-led multilateralism in Southeast Asia and the broader framework of the Asia-Pacific Economic Cooperation (APEC) forum. However, this positive development in U.S. attitudes does not mean that the United States sees no problems in the region. In the series of ASEAN meetings in 1997, some U.S. representatives, notably Secretary of State Madeleine Albright, confronted the ASEAN foreign ministers on human rights and democracy issues (*Mainichi Shimbun* 28 and 30 July 1997). On such occasions, China tends to side with ASEAN, which in turn irritates the Americans. China obviously has been playing an ASEAN card.

Although ASEAN should in no way be a subordinate variable in

U.S.-China diplomatic relations, China has definitely become involved; Beijing's political influence in the region may possibly outstrip that of ASEAN itself. The famous "China threat" argument (Jeshuran 1993; Gallagher 1994; Roy 1994; Bernstein and Munro 1997; Ross 1997; Whiting 1997), once hotly debated, seems to have calmed since Beijing has come to terms with the regional norm of striving toward peaceful solutions to problems between states. After the second ARF meeting in Brunei in August 1995, China assured that it would observe the ASEAN Declaration on the South China Sea, which ASEAN adopted in July 1992. China has begun tactfully using hard-line and soft-line approaches toward regional affairs.

Of course, no one is so optimistic as to believe that China has abandoned its territorial claims to the Paracels and the Spratlys. China certainly seeks to control what it historically regards as its own lake; Beijing views the tiny islands and reefs in dispute as the same irredenta as Hong Kong, Macau, and Taiwan. However, China has restrained its military activities around the Spratlys after it was observed that a military-type facility was built on Mischief Reef in early 1995. If ARF was devised primarily to solve the South China Sea territorial disputes peacefully (Tanaka 1995, 27), ASEAN's so-called constructive engagement approach toward China has been a moderate success. It seems all but impossible for Beijing to take any direct military action in the South China Sea (as it did in 1974 and 1988); such a move would destabilize the regional environment that is so crucial to sustainable economic and social development. China would lose its friends and political entente in what it considers a united front in challenging the human rights preachers of the West.

However, partly because of the constraints in the South China Sea, China has expanded its influence toward the Indian Ocean through Myanmar. Beijing's wooing of Yangon can be traced back well before the establishment of ARF and even before the Workshop on the South China Sea in 1990, but the potential Chinese presence in the Indian Ocean is a new factor to which "few governments have formulated consistent and clearly articulated responses" (Seekins 1997, 536). Myanmar now occupies a position similar to that of Pakistan vis-à-vis China in South Asia; because of geographic proximity, Myanmar may raise security concerns for India as well.

This does not necessarily imply that China poses a potential threat to its neighbors. China desperately needs to keep the regional environment benign. Progress in its economic reforms and liberalization programs is vital to securing superpower status in the next century. At least the new leaders in Beijing perceive and comprehend that any unilateral military action in the region would seriously undermine their long-term goals.

After the death of Deng Xiaoping in February 1997, Beijing's new leadership, led by party Secretary-General (and later President) Jiang Zemin, has followed the economic policy lines that Deng laid down in the late 1970s. At the 15th Communist Party Congress in mid-September 1997, the "Deng Xiaoping theory" was stipulated for the first time in the revised party platform as to what should be followed by his successors. In addition, Jiang's choice of Zhu Rongji as premier in March 1998 will surely accelerate reforms in all aspects, especially in light of the widely held hope among the Chinese that Zhu will "steer China toward economic stability and greater personal freedoms" (*Far Eastern Economic Review* 5 March 1998, 11). With the emergence of Zhu, a former Shanghai mayor, China will likely pursue policies that require a peaceful international environment as a backdrop.

The ASEAN-10 and Japan

A reform-oriented China should be welcomed not only by ASEAN but also by Japan. If, as Hans Maull puts it, "reconciling China with international order represents the biggest political challenge that the world is facing today" (1997, 466), then engaging China in regional as well as international affairs peacefully and incrementally benefits enormously both ASEAN and Japan. Both must take the lead in engaging China with the world, thereby building stable and constructive relationships not only in the bilateral context but also among all the Asia Pacific nations.

China is now well integrated into the security structures of the Asia Pacific region. Without China's participation, no major decision can be made regarding the future course of events in the region. In this respect, it is necessary to view Japan's role in an enlarged ASEAN in the much broader context of regional affairs. Moreover, Japan's relations with the United States—and the problems between the two—have significant implications for ASEAN and its enlargement because the security arrangements between the two countries are the keystone in the Pacific, especially after the U.S. withdrawal from the Philippines.

Japan now faces a difficult situation. With the economic downturn, Japan needs a new paradigm of national life. Relations among economic, political, bureaucratic, and social institutions, once thriving, have been structurally strained and are virtually on the verge of collapse. Therefore, Japan must recognize that coexistence and sharing the fruits of prosperity with neighboring countries are the keys to its revival. Meanwhile, Tokyo must eventually deal with the "Okinawa question" and the reduction of the U.S. military facilities there. Moreover, the U.S.-Japan Security Treaty itself—its reinforcement and the scope of its application—may prove to be a big source of concern for Beijing. The treaty could produce distrust or even outright hostility in Beijing.

However, looking at the politics and security of the region as a whole, it is clear that some positive developments have emerged for Japan. By contributing to ASEAN-led preventive diplomacy—despite shortcomings yet to be overcome—Japan will certainly win over the diverse members of ARF to promote mutual understanding on regional security. A successful formulation of the doctrine could even help Japan fulfill its aspiration for reform of the U.N. Security Council.

In the coming new century, the ASEAN-10 could become an experimental field—or possibly even a breakthrough—for Japan's diplomacy, which so far has been used mainly to extend financial and technical assistance to developing nations. Japan's participation in ARF causes little concern with regard to its determination to play a more active role in regional security. Together with ASEAN, Japan can allay the fears of its neighbors, even China and South Korea, which are also members of ARF.

Meanwhile, a continued constructive engagement approach toward some of the regional states, especially Myanmar and Cambodia, is essential. Japan, though it basically follows ASEAN's policies, has its own position in dealing with these countries. For example, Tokyo decided in 1998 to resume financial assistance to Yangon after ten years of suspension. Financial assistance of approximately US$20 million will be extended to Myanmar, criticism from inside and outside Japan notwithstanding. The financing is intended for repairs to the Yangon international airport to ensure safety and to bring it up to International Commercial Aviation Organization standards. The airport is antiquated, and the Japanese government once promised to have it repaired before suspending official aid in 1988.

Japan's decision invited criticism from Washington, but Foreign Ministry officials in Tokyo today seem to exhibit a strong defiance toward the inconsistencies and double standards the United States applies to issues concerning human rights. Although the impact of the aid might be small, it surely provides Japan with more possibilities to pursue an independent foreign policy.

For Cambodia, Tokyo played an active role in implementing the general election in July 1998 and in assisting the national reconciliation along with it. Japan offered a four-point proposal at the Manila conference on Cambodia in February 1998 that was supported by the countries present. The conference committed Japan to dispatching an envoy to mediate between then Second Premier Hun Sen and Prince Ranariddh, although the mediation was not quite successful. The Japanese proposal focused on the due process that would enable Prince Ranariddh to participate in the election, without whose participation the international community was unlikely to accept the result.

In this process of mediation, not only Foreign Ministry officials and the ruling Liberal Democratic Party figures had personal contact with both Hun Sen and Prince Ranariddh but also politicians, including Inoue Kazunari, a social democrat (*Mainichi Shimbun* 1 March 1998). Thus, Japan's diplomacy toward Cambodia has been nonpartisan. Moreover, it was Cambodia during the late 1980s and early 1990s that made Japan somewhat confident in its foreign policy implementation with its first-ever, full-scale dispatch of noncombatant Self-Defense Forces, and by its successful contribution to what U.N. Special Representative Akashi Yasushi called "peace-making [beyond just peace-keeping] operations" in the country. Japan will at least continue its efforts to engage Cambodia constructively with the countries of the region and the world, especially with the cooperation of ASEAN.

Conclusion

This chapter elaborated on the developments of the enlargement of ASEAN both in terms of institutions and regional politics, with an emphasis on the political and security dimensions. Southeast Asia and the surrounding Asia Pacific region have undergone a transition from the immediate post–cold war uncertainty to an emerging order arranged and constructed by the regional states themselves. However, a concerted effort by the external powers, premised on the amicable relationship among them, is indispensable for maintaining and enhancing this order. What is needed today is an incremental approach to regional security through consultation and trust building, together with such measures as enhancing the transparency in arms procurement, open information exchange, and holding seminars and study sessions for the leaders of the region.

ARF will certainly provide such opportunities, although it will take time to fully develop to the second stage, preventive diplomacy, and to the third, conflict resolution. But the concept of and approach to regional security that ASEAN has envisaged for the past 30 years is deepening its roots in the region. Mutual understanding between the extra-member states and the new members through their participation in the forum is crucial. Although it may sound too optimistic, the ASEAN way has, to some extent, won over China and even the United States, despite its defects and shortcomings. The possibility of a major armed conflict in the region has been remarkably reduced (again, with the possible exception of the Korean peninsula). We should accept this reality and take positive steps forward in enhancing regional security, a concept premised on the prosperity and social cohesiveness in each nation.

In this regard, the political turmoil that arose in Indonesia in mid-1998 in the wake of its economic crisis and the relinquishment of power by Suharto (whose reign over the country lasted nearly as long as ASEAN's entire history) may affect the institutional nature of ASEAN. Ironically, just as ASEAN was undergoing full-scale enlargement, the driving force of the organization was altered. Indonesia, a de facto regional leader due to its population, land area, abundance of natural resources, and behavior and influence in the developing world as a whole, may lose its centripetal role in the regional organization. Furthermore, the process of enlargement implies more diversity in membership and geographical components, which may bring about more centrifugal tendencies in the association.

Significant dichotomies may emerge in ASEAN: dichotomies between the mainland and the archipelago with plural regional centers, between rich and poor, between Muslims and non-Muslims, and between pro-China forces and anti-China forces, to name just a few. An institutional restructuring may also occur, especially around the role of ASEAN-PMC, as ARF deals with more issues that have so far been covered by the PMC. In the long run, even ARF may be incorporated into a broader framework for security cooperation such as an Asia Pacific

Regional Forum, which countries such as Australia and the United States are already demanding be formed. Considering all these factors, the enlargement of ASEAN may not necessarily be welcome without reservation, especially to those who wish to promote and consolidate Southeast Asian regional identity and cohesion. Through ASEAN enlargement, we should continue to watch carefully the ways in which Southeast Asia changes in the coming century. Since the establishment of ASEAN in 1967, the process of redefining the region has been ongoing.

Notes

1. In one of the earliest remarks on the subject, Nguyen Co Thach suggested Vietnam's entry into ASEAN unofficially at the January 1988 Asia Pacific Journalists' Roundtable Conference in Ho Chi Minh City.

2. For details on the procedures of Lao and Cambodian preparation for entry into ASEAN, see "Preparation for the Membership of Cambodia, Laos and Myanmar," ASEAN Secretariat, Jakarta. <http://www.asean.or.id/> (27 November 1996).

3. For details on the procedures of Myanmarese preparation for entry into ASEAN, see "Preparation for the Membership of Cambodia, Laos and Myanmar," ASEAN Secretariat, Jakarta. <http://www.asean.or.id/> (27 November 1996).

4. Reports in early 1998 asserted that the regional economic downturn would surely affect less developed regional countries as well. For instance, in Myanmar the currency, the kyat, dropped not only against the U.S. dollar but also against the Chinese renminbi. The exchange rate fell by nearly half in six months, whereas in the same period the amount of incoming Chinese consumer goods decreased by one-fifth or one-sixth (*Far Eastern Economic Review* 5 March 1998, 8). Meanwhile, Vietnam's leadership admitted that the country's growth rate slowed to 3 percent–4 percent.

Bibliography

Bernstein, Richard, and Ross H. Munro. 1997. "The Coming Conflict with America." *Foreign Affairs* 76(2): 18–32.

Buszynski, Leszek. 1983. *S.E.A.T.O.: The Failure of an Alliance Strategy*. Singapore: Singapore University Press.

"Chairman's Statement." 1997. The Fourth Meeting of the ASEAN Regional Forum, Subang Jaya, Indonesia. <http://www.asean.or.id/> (27 July).

Chalmers, Malcolm. 1996. *Confidence-Building in South-East Asia*. Trowbridge, Wiltshire, U.K.: Redwood Books, distributed by Westview Press.

Chin Kin Wah. 1995. "ASEAN: Consolidation and Institutional Change." *The Pacific Review* 8(3): 424–439.

Dibb, Paul. 1997. "Defence Force Modernization in Asia: Towards 2000 and Beyond." *Contemporary Southeast Asia* 18(4): 347–360.

Gallagher, Michael G. 1994. "China's Illusory Threat to the South China Sea." *International Security* 19(1): 169–194.

Jeshuran, Chandran, ed. 1993. *China, India, Japan, and the Security of Southeast Asia.* Singapore: Institute of Southeast Asian Studies.

Malik, J. Mohan. 1997. "Myanmar's Role in Regional Security: Pawn or Pivot?" *Contemporary Southeast Asia* 19(1): 52–73.

Maull, Hans. 1997. "Reconciling China with International Order." *The Pacific Review* 10(4): 466–479.

Mutalib, Hussin. 1997. "At Thirty, ASEAN Looks to Challenges in the New Millennium." *Contemporary Southeast Asia* 19(1): 74–85.

Narine, Shaun. 1997. "ASEAN and ARF: The Limits of the 'ASEAN Way'." *Asian Survey* 37(10): 961–978.

Nishihara Masashi and James Morley, eds. 1996. *Taitō suru Betonamu: Nichibei wa dō kakawaruka* (The emerging Vietnam: How should Japan and the United States engage?). Tokyo: Chūō Kōron-sha.

Oberdorfer, Don. 1997. *The Two Koreas.* Reading, Mass.: Addison-Wesley.

Peang-Meth, Abdulgaffar. 1997. "Understanding Cambodia's Political Development." *Contemporary Southeast Asia* 19(3): 286–308.

Ross, Robert S. 1997. "Beijing as a Conservative Power." *Foreign Affairs* 76(2): 33–44.

Roy, Denny. 1994. "Hegemon on the Horizon?: China's Threat to East Asian Security." *International Security* 19(1): 149–168.

Seekins, Donald M. 1997. "Burma-China Relations: Playing with Fire." *Asian Survey* 37(6): 525–539.

Tanaka Kyōko. 1995. "ASEAN shokoku to Chūgoku: Kensetsuteki engeijimento e" (ASEAN countries and China: Toward constructive engagement). *Kokusai mondai* (International affairs), no. 418: 17–29.

Tay, Simon, and Obood Talib. 1997. "The ASEAN Regional Forum: Preparing for Preventive Diplomacy." *Contemporary Southeast Asia* 19(3): 252–268.

Whiting, Allen. 1997. "ASEAN Eyes China: The Security Dimension." *Asian Survey* 37(4): 299–322.

Yamamoto Nobuto, Takano Takeshi, Kaneko Yoshiki, Nakano Ari, and Itaya Taisei. 1997. *Tōnan Ajia seiji-gaku: Chiiki, kokka, shakai, hito no jūsōteki dainamizumu* (A study of Southeast Asian politics: Multilayered dynamism of region, state, society, and people). Tokyo: Seibundō.

– 3 –

ASEAN in APEC

Yoshino Fumio

T HE ASSOCIATION OF SOUTHEAST ASIAN NATIONS has been called the most successful example of regional cooperation among developing countries. Set up more than 30 years ago with five original members—Indonesia, Malaysia, the Philippines, Singapore, and Thailand —ASEAN has played a significant role in the political stability and economic growth of Asia Pacific. The ASEAN members have come to be recognized as arbiters of peace and engines of growth for the region.

The Asia-Pacific Economic Cooperation (APEC) forum was born in 1989 via a catalyst from ASEAN. To entice all ASEAN members to join, APEC made some concessions on organization and decision making. APEC has steadily increased its membership, reaching 21 at the Kuala Lumpur meeting in November 1998. The agenda has shifted over time from economic cooperation to liberalization of trade and investment. As APEC has grown, its relationship with ASEAN has inevitably changed.

In 1997, ASEAN commemorated its 30th anniversary coincident with the beginning of the so-called Asian crisis. At the same time, it agreed to accept Cambodia, Laos, and Myanmar as members, although Cambodia's membership was later delayed. The role of ASEAN in the Asia Pacific region could change significantly over the next decade.

Liberalization Processes
The Birth of APEC and ASEAN's Role

APEC commenced as a consultative body of economic and trade ministers in the Asia Pacific region. Australian Prime Minister Robert Hawke strongly advocated a regional cooperative body, and he sent missions to the Pacific Rim countries to persuade them to join the new forum. Consequently, the ASEAN-6 (the original five members plus Brunei) and Australia, Canada, Japan, New Zealand, South Korea, and the United States participated in the first meeting in Canberra in November 1989.

In the early 1990s, several other proposals were put forth to promote regional economic cooperation. Malaysian Prime Minister Mahathir bin Mohamad proposed the East Asian Economic Group, later the East Asian Economic Caucus (EAEC), in December 1990. His proposal was restricted to the ASEAN-6, China, Japan, and South Korea. This proposal, sometimes called the "six plus three" initiative, was characterized by its omission of the United States, one of the regional superpowers, Australia, and New Zealand. Despite an appeal from ASEAN, Japan has not agreed to join the grouping.[1] In 1991, James Baker III, then U.S. secretary of state, recommended a grouping of the ASEAN economies, the East Asian economies, and North America that would exclude Australia and New Zealand. ASEAN rejected Baker's proposal.

For the ASEAN economies, joining APEC was one of the most substantial issues since the formation of ASEAN in 1967. Some members feared that ASEAN would lose its raison d'être if APEC successfully achieved economic cooperation and trade liberalization. ASEAN had not obtained substantial results despite extensively promoting trade liberalization and economic cooperation. This fear led ASEAN to urge other APEC members—initially the more advanced countries—to adopt the so-called ASEAN way as the APEC process. The ASEAN members gathered in Kuching, the capital city of Sarawak in Malaysia, and made the Kuching Consensus in September 1990, which can be summarized as follows:

- APEC should be based on the principles of equality, equity, and mutual benefit, taking into account the differences in stages of development and of sociopolitical systems among the countries in the region.
- APEC should provide a consultative forum on economic issues and should not lead to the adoption of mandatory directives for any participant to undertake or implement.
- APEC should not be directed toward the formation of an inward-looking economic or trading bloc, but should instead strengthen the open multilateral economic and trading systems in the world (Soesastro 1994).

The consensus shows ASEAN's desired prudence for the new regional forum. The advanced countries in APEC expressed overall agreement with the consensus. APEC was defined as a consultative forum without directives and proudly declared a motto of "open regionalism."

Liberalization in ASEAN

In the first half of the 1990s, the world economy swung between globalism and regionalism. The General Agreement on Tariffs and Trade's (GATT's) Uruguay Round of multilateral trade negotiations concluded in 1994, and subsequently the World Trade Organization (WTO) was formed in 1995. The North American Free Trade Agreement (NAFTA) also began in 1994, and the market integration of the European Union was completed in 1992. ASEAN's response to these events was the creation of the ASEAN Free Trade Area (AFTA), which was proposed by the Thai prime minister in 1992.

AFTA was not ASEAN's first attempt at trade liberalization. In 1977, the ASEAN Preferential Trading Arrangement (ASEAN-PTA) was implemented following the end of the Vietnam War and remains active. The ASEAN-PTA reduced each country's most-favored-nation tariff rates from zero to 50 percent. The items subject to tariff reduction are unilaterally and voluntarily determined by members.

The ASEAN-PTA has not worked well. Even though nearly 3,000 items are subject to tariff reduction, many of the items are insubstantial, some are nontradable goods within the region such as fur gloves and leather overcoats, and other products have small shares in regional trade. Furthermore, items are not consistent among countries. Even if the ASEAN economies had coordinated the items, the tariff reductions would not have significantly affected their trade volumes. That is because Singapore, which is a free trade port, has a considerable share of regional trade. In 1996, Singapore absorbed 5.6 percent of Indonesia's total exports and 48.6 percent of its exports to the ASEAN region. Similarly, for Malaysia, Singapore absorbed 20.5 percent of total exports and 72.0 percent of regional exports; for the Philippines, 6.0 percent of total exports and 41.5 percent of regional exports; and for Thailand, 12.1 percent of total exports and 62.2 percent of regional exports. These exports would not have been affected much by tariff reduction.[2]

AFTA could become analogous to the ASEAN-PTA. The small share of bilateral trade is a critical problem. For example, Malaysia's share of next-door neighbor Thailand's total exports in 1996 was only 3.6 percent, and, conversely, Thailand's share of Malaysia's total exports was 4.1

percent (International Monetary Fund [IMF], *Direction of Trade Statistics*). The situation has not changed much in recent years.

Although the effect of AFTA was not expected to be significant, ASEAN had little choice but to implement it. The Uruguay Round of global trade negotiations was nearing completion and NAFTA was about to get under way. ASEAN had to proceed with trade liberalization on its own. Furthermore, the world economy began to focus on emerging markets such as China, the countries of the former Soviet Union, and Eastern and Central Europe. ASEAN needed the new scheme to maintain links with investors and exporters.

AFTA was implemented in January 1993 and revised in 1994. The original AFTA scheme was to be completed by 2008 and its target was the formation of an integrated market with low tariffs ranging from zero to 5 percent and without nontariff barriers. Originally, AFTA did not cover raw materials, agricultural goods, and services. The AFTA process was strengthened through the Common Effective Preferential Tariff (CEPT) scheme.

In 1994, ASEAN agreed to complete the AFTA scheme by 2003 rather than 2008. Tariff reduction was categorized in two parts. The fast track applied to 15 categories: vegetable oils, cement, pharmaceuticals, chemical fertilizers, plastics, plastic products, rubber products, leather products, pulp, textiles, ceramic and glass products, gems and jewelry, copper cathodes, electronics, and wooden and rattan furniture. Other manufactured items were classified on a normal track.[3]

The AFTA-CEPT scheme has some problems. The exclusion of the automobile industry, which had been protected and fostered, has most annoyed non-ASEAN economies. For the automobile industry, AFTA adopted the ASEAN Industrial Complementation (AIC) and the Brand-to-Brand Complementation (BBC) schemes. These were set up to facilitate the purchase of locally produced parts by automobile manufacturers operating in the ASEAN economies. The schemes primarily reduced tariffs with respect to the trade of automobile parts within the region. Mitsubishi Motors of Japan, which had production sites in the region, played a major role in completing these schemes. However, neither the BBC scheme nor the AIC scheme is consistent with the AFTA-CEPT scheme.

The automobile-related companies that were excluded from both schemes appealed to ASEAN to set up yet another scheme. Consequently, the ASEAN Industrial Cooperation (AICO) scheme was implemented in November 1996. But the AICO scheme also has been ineffective. Participation requirements are strict (at least 30 percent of total capital from local investors and complementary local functions), the bureaucracy has been criticized for ambiguity and inefficiency, and the examination standards vary by country and lack transparency.

ASEAN's liberalization process in trade was converted from strengthening the extensive AFTA-CEPT scheme to completing the AICO scheme. About that time, the Asian currency crisis occurred. With the decline in exports in 1996, the ASEAN economies began to turn negative toward liberalization. From 1997, this tendency intensified. Policymakers began to discuss rescheduling the AFTA-CEPT scheme, raising tariff rates, and imposing nontariff barriers.[4]

Liberalization in APEC

The global movement toward liberalization has greatly affected APEC. In 1993, liberalization was APEC's primary task. Then, U.S. President Bill Clinton asked for an unofficial summit of the group's political leaders, and this summit later formed the base of APEC's liberalization process. In 1994, the Bogor Declaration was adopted at the second summit and official economic ministers' meeting. The primary content of the declaration was as follows:[5]

- Free and open trade and investment in the Asia Pacific region by no later than 2010 in the case of industrialized economies and 2020 in the case of developing economies.
- Expansion and acceleration of trade and investment facilitation programs.
- Intensified development cooperation to attain sustainable growth, equitable development, and national stability.

APEC recognized that "full and active participation in and support of the WTO by all APEC economies is key to our ability to lead the way in strengthening the multilateral trading system" ("APEC Economic Leaders' Declaration" 1994). Had ASEAN ignored the WTO process, it would have lost its raison d'être as a subregional group within APEC; ASEAN moved to implement trade liberalization ahead of APEC.

The Bogor Declaration progressed year by year. In 1995, the Osaka Action Programme set the schedule for the liberalization process. Policymakers were directed to prepare a concrete and substantive schedule of action to submit to the ministers' meeting in 1996 in Manila. Consequently, the ministers' meeting adopted a lengthy declaration including the Manila Programme of Action (MAPA). In MAPA, ministers agreed "to meet to reexamine individual plans of action in 1997, after taking into account the viewpoints of the private sector." The declarations adopted in Manila were the turning point of the APEC process. However, limitations in the APEC process have become apparent.

MAPA can be summarized as follows:

- With respect to tariff reduction, advancement to specific targets from the Bogor Declaration.
- Acceleration of the target year for some members relative to the Bogor Declaration.
- Enhanced commitment to the Uruguay Round.
- Broad support for completion of the Information Technology Agreement negotiations.
- Promotion of the abolition of nontariff barriers with specified items and deadlines.
- Improvement of transparency, implementation of the APEC database on customs and tariffs that became available from 1997, and the listing of present nontariff barriers until 1998 (Pangetsu 1997, 29).

Through the MAPA process, it became clear that all of APEC's members could not proceed together with liberalization. Brunei, Hong Kong, and Singapore had mostly achieved the targets set in Bogor by 1996. Chile, China, Indonesia, and the Philippines submitted plans with lower targets than were set in Bogor. Furthermore, at the WTO conference in Singapore in late 1997, APEC prioritized liberalization in information technology. The United States, the most influential advanced member of APEC, was thought to have a significant advantage in this area.

Two of the MAPA tenets reveal a change in course by APEC. Optimists contend that APEC has shifted from idealism to realism, whereas pessimists believe that APEC has succumbed to a common burden called liberalization. It is too early to determine the actual effects of trade liberalization.

Japan's Ministry of International Trade and Industry and other institutions have provided estimates as to the potential effect of APEC's liberalization process following the MAPA initiative. Table 1 shows that aggregate gross domestic product (GDP) in the region would increase 0.4 percent, or US$68.5 billion, permanently, in terms of 1995 prices. The aggregate GDP of the world economy would expand 0.2 percent, or US$70.9 billion. GDP was projected to rise for all APEC members (excluding Brunei and Papua New Guinea, for which information was unavailable). These projections are based on numerous assumptions,

Table 1. The Effect of APEC Liberalization on GDP

	Share of GDP (%)	Volume Increase (US$bn)
Australia	0.4	1.8
Canada	0.4	2.0
Chile	4.9	3.3
China	2.1	14.3
Hong Kong	0.4	0.6
Indonesia	2.4	4.9
Japan	0.1	7.2
Malaysia	7.4	6.3
Mexico	0.7	1.7
New Zealand	1.3	0.8
Philippines	4.3	3.2
Singapore	1.5	1.2
South Korea	0.8	3.8
Taiwan	1.3	3.3
Thailand	3.1	5.2
United States	0.1	8.9
APEC Total	0.4	68.5
Others	0.0	2.4
World Total	0.2	70.9

Source: Coordination Bureau, Economic Planning Agency (1997, Table B).

Note: Volume increase is calculated based on nominal GDP as of 1995.

including the homogeneity of production functions and perfect competition.

Comparative Liberalization

The trade liberalization process has been similar for both ASEAN and APEC. Both groups began with a comprehensive approach, then shifted to item-by-item negotiations when the former approach stalled. ASEAN shifted from the ASEAN-PTA to the AIC and the BBC, and from that to AFTA and AICO. APEC moved to develop a consensus on liberalizing information technology. Responding to these shifts, in both ASEAN and APEC the influence of their leaders strengthened. In ASEAN, Singapore is gaining dominance vis-à-vis Indonesia and the Philippines, where political leaders have changed, and Malaysia and Thailand, which suffer from an economic downturn. In APEC, the influence of the United States is increasing vis-à-vis Asia, which is experiencing economic stagnation.

The paths of these two regional cooperative groupings cannot be predicted easily. However, in ASEAN, protectionist pressures will likely rise because of economic hardship, and in APEC, developing consensus could become more difficult because of advanced negotiations in specific areas.

New Membership Problems

The year 1997 was a turning point for both ASEAN and APEC. Both experienced new membership problems. APEC was scheduled to include Peru, Russia, and Vietnam at the Kuala Lumpur meeting in 1998. Laos and Myanmar joined ASEAN in July 1997, but Cambodia's application was delayed.

Although other economies have applied to join APEC, only three countries were admitted in 1997. More important, membership was frozen for the next ten years. The international community viewed the freeze as APEC backing away from its motto of "open regionalism." Controversy surfaced over those countries admitted and those that were not. Chile and Mexico recommended Colombia and were reluctant for Russia to join. Mexico was strongly opposed to Russian membership. Vietnam's participation was broadly supported partly because it had already joined ASEAN in 1995.

Russia

The merit to Russia in joining APEC is not obvious. Some economists claim Russia has a psychological need to belong—that it is reluctant to be isolated in the international community given its previous status as a superpower in the cold war era. They cite Russia's eagerness to join the North Atlantic Treaty Organization (NATO) and to become the eighth member of the Group of Seven as supporting evidence. Therefore, Russia's reasons for joining APEC seem somewhat negative. Its motives do not seem geared toward tariff reduction and improved regional trade.

Russia's weak economic link with the Asia Pacific region can be seen from trade statistics. The ratio of Russia's exports to the ASEAN-5 of its total exports was only 1.3 percent in 1996. As for imports, ASEAN's share was a mere 1.0 percent. The ASEAN-5's exports to Russia were only 0.12 percent of their total exports. Russia's share of the ASEAN-5's total imports was only 0.15 percent (IMF, *Direction of Trade Statistics*). Russia's participation will likely have little impact relative to the ASEAN economies. Indeed, a Russian observer has noted that "only Vietnam is an intermediary country between Russia and ASEAN" (Voice of Russia radio broadcast, 15 May 1998).

For the ASEAN economies, Russia is a significant supplier of weapons but its economic relationships are weak. In fact, Russia's primary export goods to the ASEAN economies are weapons. In 1996, Russia was the second largest exporter of weapons worldwide after the United States. The ASEAN economies stand out as importers of weapons, ranking globally as follows: Thailand, 13th; Indonesia, 17th; Malaysia, 22nd; Myanmar, 33rd; Singapore, 36th; the Philippines, 43rd; and Vietnam, 45th (Stockholm International Peace Research Institute 1997, tables 9.1, 9.3). Russian weapons are especially attractive because of their cheap prices. However, Russia indirectly could be a countervailing power to China, which the ASEAN members view as a threat.

Russia's standing in APEC is a little more complicated. The ratio of Russia's exports to the region relative to its total exports is only 16.1 percent. This is extraordinarily low compared with other members. The Philippines has the second lowest dependency ratio in exports—at 45.2 percent. As for imports, Chile has the second lowest dependency ratio at 51.6 percent. Russia's import dependency ratio is 16.1 percent. Based on these statistics, it is difficult to justify Russia's participation in APEC.

Separating the Russian Far East (Siberia) from all of Russia, the ties to the Asia Pacific region become more apparent. In 1995, 48.3 percent of the Russian Far East's exports were destined for Japan, 10.5 percent for South Korea, 9.1 percent for the United States, 7.1 percent for China, and 6.1 percent for Vietnam, and these APEC members were the five largest exporters to the Russian Far East as well. The Russian Far East's export items consist primarily of foodstuffs—mostly marine products —which accounted for 46.6 percent of total exports in 1995. Coal, pe- troleum products, nonferrous metals, and fuel represented 22.6 percent of exports, and lumber accounted for 16.6 percent. As for imports, the U.S. share was 21.5 percent, followed by South Korea at 12.1 percent, Germany at 11.3 percent, and Japan at 10.7 percent. The Russian Far East's trade with APEC members accounts for 84.9 percent of its total exports and 61.8 percent of its total imports (*Roshia Kyokutō dēta bukku* 1996). These figures show the deep dependency of the Russian Far East on the Asia Pacific region. In recent years, this area has sought independence from the central government.

Some observers contend that support for Russia joining APEC de- rives from diplomatic considerations and the opportunity for the four regional superpowers—China, Japan, Russia, and the United States— to meet. In addition, APEC members may want to enhance their access to the vast energy resources in the Russian Far East. China, Japan, and South Korea, in particular, would likely reap advantages from discus- sions of regional energy issues through APEC. There also could be se- curity advantages in having Russia as a member. However, information about energy and security in Russia is insufficient and not transparent.

Peru

The economic relationship between Peru and the ASEAN economies is also weak. Even if the liberalization of trade and investment proceeds within APEC, it may not greatly affect the ASEAN economies vis-à-vis trade with Peru. Peru's exports to the ASEAN-7 (the original five members plus Brunei and Vietnam) in 1996 totaled US$182 million, or 3.1 percent of total exports. Exports to APEC members accounted for 50.4 percent of total exports. Peru imported US$53 million in goods from the ASEAN-7, or 0.8 percent of total imports in 1996, whereas imports from APEC members represented 53.2 percent of total imports. Because more than half of Peru's imports and one-third of its exports are with the United States, Peru apparently intends to use membership in APEC to strengthen ties with the United States.

Transitional Economies in Southeast Asia

The APEC members felt that the participation of Vietnam was necessary. In fact, Vietnam was qualified given that its imports and exports with APEC members had reached nearly two-thirds of its total trade volume. However, with the addition of Laos and Myanmar to ASEAN, not all of the ASEAN economies are members of APEC. Therefore, ASEAN is no longer a subset of APEC and APEC must therefore reconsider the appropriateness of regarding ASEAN as a subregional group. ASEAN might now face dual policy decisions concerning the seven APEC members and the two nonmembers. In addition, the economies of Laos and Myanmar, as well as Vietnam's, are in transition and income levels are far below those of the other ASEAN economies. ASEAN's cooperative economic projects may no longer be applicable to all member economies. This diversity could weaken ASEAN's centripetal force.

Both ASEAN and APEC will find it increasingly difficult to deal with countries denied membership in their respective "clubs." ASEAN delayed the membership of Cambodia, whereas APEC has postponed membership for Colombia, Ecuador, India, Macao, Mongolia, Pakistan, Panama, and Sri Lanka until at least 2008. APEC's central premise of open regionalism took a step backward when the group granted membership to Russia without the customary ten-year waiting period following application (see Ashayagachat 1998). APEC is entering a new stage as an integrated organization with exclusivity and power. The process of trade liberalization has shown that voluntary inputs from member countries only go so far; at some point, the organization must pressure its members to liberalize at the same speed.

Interregional Relationships

Both ASEAN and APEC recognize the necessity of mutual coordination with other regional groups. ASEAN encourages members to establish

Table 2. Major Economic Indicators of APEC Members

Country/Region	Population (million)	Area (1,000 sq. km.)	Per Capita Income (US$)	GNP (US$bn)
Brunei	0.3	5	17,872	5.5
Indonesia	197	1,812	1,080	213.4
Malaysia	21	329	4,370	89.8
Philippines	72	298	1,160	83.3
Singapore	3	1	30,550	93.0
Thailand	60	511	2,960	177.5
Vietnam	75	325	290	21.9
ASEAN-7 Total	428	3,281	1,598	684.4
Japan	126	377	40,940	5,149.2
South Korea	46	99	10,610	483.1
Taiwan	22	36	12,838	274.6
Hong Kong	6	1	24,290	153.3
China	1,215	9,326	750	906.1
Australia	18	7,682	20,090	367.8
New Zealand	4	268	15,720	57.1
Papua New Guinea	4	453	1,150	5.0
Russia	148	16,889	2,410	356.0
Canada	30	9,221	19,020	569.9
United States	265	9,159	28,020	7,433.5
Mexico	93	1,909	3,670	341.7
Peru	24	1,280	2,420	58.7
Chile	14	749	4,860	70.1
APEC Total	2,443	60,730	6,414	16,910.5
ASEAN-7/APEC	17.5%	5.4%	24.9%	4.0%
APEC/World	45.8%	46.7%	125.0%	57.3%

Source: *World Development Indicators 1998*, *Brunei Darussalam Key Indicators 1997*, and *World Almanac '98* (in Japanese).

Note: Per capita income and GNP data as of 1996; population data as of mid-1996, except the end of 1996 for Taiwan. Brunei is per capita GDP and GDP instead of per capita income and GNP.

ties with nonmember nations; Thailand and Myanmar, for example, are promoting a regional economic cooperative among countries on the Indian Ocean. Similarly, APEC members other than the ASEAN participants are also promoting interregional relationships. The 1994 Summit of the Americas agreed to establish the Free Trade Area of the Americas by 2005. APEC members in North America have created a vast free trade area. Such regional groups will certainly have some effect on Asia's APEC and/or ASEAN members.

The more the interregional relationships are tightened, the more globalism proceeds. The increase in interregional relationships may eventually weaken the raison d'être of organizations such as ASEAN and

Table 3. Trade Intensity Indexes

Exporter \ Importer	Japan	China	Hong Kong	Taiwan	South Korea	Singa-pore	Brunei	Indo-nesia	Malay-sia
Japan		2.06	1.68	2.62	2.57	2.08	0.96	2.77	2.59
China	3.03		5.68	0.00	1.72	0.98	0.25	1.14	0.61
Hong Kong	1.01	13.36		0.99	0.58	1.13	0.30	0.70	0.65
Taiwan	2.01	5.48	3.77		0.85	1.88	0.00	2.35	2.36
South Korea	1.89	3.42	2.33	1.27		2.03	2.89	3.07	2.31
Singapore	1.27	1.06	2.42	1.61	1.09		472.62	0.00	12.49
Brunei	5.17	0.05	0.01	0.80	0.00	2.03		0.03	0.08
Indonesia	4.47	1.68	0.84	1.48	2.72	2.33	0.65		1.62
Malaysia	2.07	0.94	1.60	1.70	1.09	8.41	10.40	1.96	
Philippines	1.57	0.35	0.66	0.76	0.37	1.40	0.06	0.50	1.32
Thailand	2.60	1.30	1.58	1.05	0.65	4.97	33.28	1.91	2.51
Papua New Guinea	3.32	1.37	0.33	0.10	1.94	0.50	0.00	0.64	0.73
Australia	3.05	1.93	1.04	1.81	3.37	1.53	4.34	5.04	1.95
New Zealand	2.38	1.00	0.86	1.12	1.70	0.58	0.05	2.04	1.58
Canada	0.58	0.40	0.12	0.21	0.35	0.08	0.01	0.39	0.13
United States	1.68	0.75	0.61	1.22	1.53	1.10	4.50	0.80	0.95
Mexico	0.22	0.12	0.12	0.02	0.07	0.10	0.00	0.02	0.02
Chile	2.51	0.89	0.17	1.69	2.02	0.23	0.00	1.18	0.31
Peru	1.03	2.80	0.26	1.10	1.01	0.08	0.00	0.64	0.88
Vietnam	4.08	1.57	0.70	1.72	0.45	2.35	0.00	1.69	1.37
Russia	0.55	2.23	0.07	0.25	0.29	0.29	0.00	0.05	0.10

Source: International Monetary Fund, *Direction of Trade Statistics,* and various governmental statistics.
Note: Data as of 1996.

APEC. But such a development also could be seen as progress favorable to both the regional and the world economies.

ASEAN's Economic Relationships within APEC

ASEAN's Economic Status

Table 2 illustrates the major economic indicators of APEC members. APEC accounts for more than half of the total gross national product (GNP) of the world economy. Nearly half of the world's population resides in the APEC region, and the living standards are somewhat higher than the world average.

The ASEAN-7 account for 17.5 percent of the APEC population but only 4.0 percent of its GNP. The GNP of the ASEAN-7 is unexpectedly

Philip-pines	Thai-land	Papua New Guinea	Aus-tralia	New Zea-land	Can-ada	United States	Mex-ico	Chile	Peru	Viet-nam	Russia
3.47	3.27	1.33	1.58	1.50	0.40	1.82	0.54	0.64	0.47	1.09	0.29
1.10	0.59	0.63	0.93	0.54	0.33	1.12	0.08	1.02	0.62	2.11	1.34
2.03	0.74	0.67	1.19	0.65	0.44	1.40	0.12	1.04	0.17	1.32	0.34
2.34	2.01	0.46	1.52	1.19	0.58	1.78	0.47	0.60	0.34	4.45	0.08
2.51	1.50	0.41	1.22	0.77	0.29	1.10	0.55	1.53	1.05	4.85	0.45
3.12	4.17	4.39	2.01	1.13	0.10	1.22	0.19	0.19	0.09	5.42	0.22
0.00	3.79	0.00	0.33	2.29	0.02	0.08	0.00	0.00	0.00	0.00	0.00
1.99	1.31	1.84	2.45	0.99	0.30	1.09	0.31	0.57	0.07	1.94	0.25
2.04	3.01	1.95	1.36	1.13	0.22	1.20	0.41	0.27	0.06	1.79	0.08
	1.59	0.49	0.39	0.20	0.18	1.28	0.06	0.11	0.08	1.36	0.04
1.92		1.27	1.32	0.65	0.34	1.19	0.07	0.22	0.43	3.39	0.12
5.58	1.84		31.88	5.59	0.01	0.21	0.00	0.00	0.00	0.00	0.00
2.01	1.56	45.22		26.13	0.53	0.42	0.09	0.71	0.24	1.06	0.14
2.02	0.95	16.06	17.94		0.46	0.61	0.45	1.22	3.06	1.18	0.79
0.16	0.15	0.09	0.31	0.27		5.44	0.26	0.36	0.39	0.07	0.21
1.67	0.85	0.39	1.69	1.02	6.76		5.50	2.06	2.01	0.39	0.45
0.02	0.04	0.00	0.05	0.01	0.39	5.55		2.23	1.56	0.00	0.07
1.14	0.56	0.46	0.43	0.50	0.29	1.10	0.58		14.77	0.08	0.32
0.93	0.44	0.00	0.28	0.06	0.86	1.32	0.99	6.59		0.20	0.30
3.70	0.64	0.00	3.90	0.64	0.33	0.30	0.00	0.31	1.43		0.58
0.30	0.20	0.00	0.01	0.01	0.04	0.37	0.02	0.06	0.05	0.59	

low when taking into consideration their political clout. But this is the reality of ASEAN.

Table 3 shows trade intensity indexes. The ASEAN index[6] for Singapore, a hub country for trade, shows that the indexes for both imports and exports are high. The index also shows that Brunei does not have tight trade relationships with most ASEAN economies because its exports are concentrated in mineral resources. However, Brunei imports from a few neighboring countries, including Singapore, Malaysia, and Thailand. Also, among the ASEAN economies Indonesia and the Philippines have significant trade imbalances with some regional countries.

It is interesting to examine the relationship between the ASEAN economies and their trade partners. Except for Brunei, all the ASEAN economies' import and export indexes to Japan exceed 1.0. Relative to

Table 4. Direct Investment Matrix (%)

Outflow ＼ Inflow	Indonesia	Malaysia	Philippines	Singapore	Thailand	Vietnam
Indonesia		0.3	5.8	NA	0.3	NA
Malaysia	4.7		0.6	NA	0.6	1.0
Philippines	0.0	0.0		NA	0.0	NA
Singapore	10.5	28.4	3.0		14.2	32.5
Thailand	5.4	0.0	0.6	NA		0.0
ASEAN-5	20.5	28.7	10.1	0.0	15.0	33.5
Japan	25.6	27.4	5.8	34.3	47.2	7.0
South Korea	4.1	3.8	1.1	NA	6.7	9.7
Taiwan	1.8	4.6	0.7	NA	20.9	9.2
Hong Kong	3.7	0.1	29.0	NA	1.3	9.2
China	0.1	0.2	NA	NA	0.6	NA
Australia	1.5	0.8	0.2	NA	0.4	0.6
New Zealand	0.2	0.1	0.0	NA	NA	NA
Canada	0.1	0.3	0.0	NA	0.0	NA
United States	2.1	17.2	3.4	39.6	21.1	1.1
APEC	59.7	83.2	50.5	73.9	113.3	70.3
World	100.0	100.0	100.0	100.0	100.0	100.0

Source: Japan External Trade Organization (1998, Table 1-14) and Ogiwara (1998).

Note: Data as of 1996. Matrix organized based on inflow statistics. Thailand's statistics have some double counting.

trade with the United States, the export intensity indexes for Indonesia, Malaysia, Thailand, and Vietnam fall below 1.0, whereas the import indexes exceed 1.0. The indexes indicate that these countries are relatively important to the United States.

Table 4 shows a direct investment matrix that is derived from each country's investment flow statistics. Specifically, it shows the share of investment from APEC members in total foreign direct investment (FDI) for the ASEAN-5 plus Vietnam. A low dependency on APEC members is observed in the Philippines; this occurred because investment from the United Kingdom increased rapidly since 1995, whereas that from the United States fell 94.6 percent year-on-year in 1996.

APEC has three recognized superpowers—China, Japan, and the United States. Japan has the largest economy in Asia. China, of course, is the most populous nation in the world with a population of well over one billion. China also has significant influence on regional diplomacy. The developed countries have tread lightly with China in regard to human rights concerns and unfair trade practices for fear of offending the government of such a potentially large market. The United States is the only country that has proven capable of playing a dual leadership role, both economically and politically, in the region since the end of the cold war. Although its per capita income trails that of Japan, the United States' economic influence definitely dominates. All three superpowers are also dialogue partners with ASEAN.[7]

JAPAN   Japan and the United States are the primary advanced markets for the ASEAN economies. Japan is the biggest trade partner for many ASEAN economies. In 1996, the ratio of exports to Japan relative to total exports was 33.5 percent for Brunei, 28.9 percent for Indonesia, 13.4 percent for Malaysia, 10.2 percent for the Philippines, 8.2 percent for Singapore, 16.8 percent for Thailand, and 26.4 percent for Vietnam. For the ASEAN-7 combined, the ratio was 14.4 percent, compared with 19.2 percent in 1989, the year APEC commenced. ASEAN's dependency on Japan has gradually declined (IMF, *Direction of Trade Statistics*).

In turn, the share of Japan's exports to the ASEAN economies has risen annually. In 1985, the ASEAN economies experienced a primary commodity depression and economic growth rates declined. Also in 1985, the Plaza Accord ushered in a period of recovery and economic boom times for the ASEAN economies. In 1986, as Japan's exports to the United States increased rapidly owing to yen appreciation, the ratio of Japan's exports to the ASEAN-7 was only 5.9 percent; by 1996, it had risen to 17.8 percent.

Thus, the significance of the ASEAN market to Japan has risen, whereas the importance of the Japanese market to the ASEAN economies has declined. Japan's exports to the ASEAN economies have risen because of increased demand for consumer goods owing to increased income levels and expanded imports of intermediate and capital goods generated by Japan's direct investment. Conversely, the factors causing ASEAN's declining exports to Japan include the diversification of their export markets because of the emergence of big markets such as China and the improvement in their terms of trade with Japan.

The ratio of Japan's imports from the ASEAN-7 to total imports was relatively stable from 1988 to 1996, excluding 1995, during which the total was unusually low.[8] Similarly, the ratio of ASEAN's imports from Japan to their total imports also has changed little.

However, the content of imports has changed dramatically over the years. From 1988 to 1996, the ratio of manufactured goods in Japan's imports from the ASEAN economies increased, probably because of the rise in Japan's investment in them. For instance, the ratio of manufactured goods in Japan's imports from Indonesia rose from 9.7 percent in 1988 to 29.1 percent in 1996 (IMF, *Direction of Trade Statistics*). This tendency is common in the other ASEAN economies as well. As their industrial structures matured, the weight in ASEAN exports shifted from primary goods to high-value-added manufactured goods. Japan played a role in absorbing such products. In the late 1980s, Thailand and Indonesia recorded extreme increases in direct investment from Japan. In 1988, Japanese investment in Thailand was four times larger than the previous year, whereas total FDI in Thailand was three times larger. In 1990, when FDI in Thailand peaked, Japanese investment accounted for almost half of the total. Japanese companies that invested in the ASEAN economies created new demand for capital goods and parts. The lack of suppliers for these products in the region inevitably caused Japanese companies to import them from their home country. Thailand's imports from Japan, for example, grew 32.5 percent in 1989 and 33.5 percent in 1990 (IMF, *Direction of Trade Statistics*).[9]

Japan's direct investment in Indonesia increased from US$1.48 billion in 1987 to US$8.75 billion in 1990. In 1991, it exceeded US$10 billion, and in 1995 it reached US$39.92 billion. Japan was the largest investor in the early 1990s, but the biggest investors in the mid-1990s were Singapore in 1993, Hong Kong in 1994, and the United Kingdom in 1995. Trade between Indonesia and Japan reveals the same trends as that between Thailand and Japan. In 1990, Japanese investment was nearly three times larger than the previous year. In the same year, Indonesia's imports from Japan increased 52.7 percent from the previous year. In the following four years, Japan's investment did not exceed the 1990 level. Correspondingly, the growth rates of Indonesia's imports from Japan were 11.4 percent in 1991, -0.6 percent in 1992, 8.0 percent in 1993, 27.4 percent in 1994, and 30.0 percent in 1995. The increase coincided with the rapid rise in Japan's investment in Indonesia.[10]

By analyzing trends in Thailand and Indonesia, we can conclude that Japan's investment in the ASEAN economies was closely connected to its exports to them. As Japan's investment to those countries increased, its exports of capital goods and parts to them also expanded.

Japan has the closest economic relations with the ASEAN economies in APEC (tables 3 and 4). In this sense, the ASEAN economies have suffered from Japan's recession since the early 1990s. Similarly, Japan has been seriously affected by the recession that surfaced in the ASEAN economies in 1997.

THE UNITED STATES   The United States also has a strong relationship with the ASEAN economies in APEC. For the major ASEAN economies, the ratios of exports to the United States to their total exports in 1996 were 18.4 percent for Singapore, 16.5 percent for Indonesia, 18.2 percent for Malaysia, 19.3 percent for the Philippines, and 18.0 percent for Thailand. Although the ratios for Brunei and Vietnam were low, at 1.2 percent and 4.5 percent, respectively, the ASEAN-5 had a combined ratio of nearly 20 percent. Exports to the United States from Singapore, Malaysia, the Philippines, and Thailand exceeded those to Japan. The ratio of each ASEAN economy's imports from the United States to its total imports exceeded 10 percent. The ASEAN economies' trade with the United States has not changed significantly since the formation of APEC in 1989.

The nature of U.S. trade with the ASEAN economies is gradually changing. As for U.S. exports, 4.4 percent were destined for the ASEAN-7 in 1989, rising to 7.0 percent in 1996. The share of U.S. imports from the ASEAN-7 was 5.2 percent in 1989 and 8.4 percent in 1996 (IMF, *Direction of Trade Statistics*). The ASEAN economies are increasingly significant to U.S. trade.

U.S. direct investment differs by country (table 4). U.S. investment in Singapore exceeds that from Japan. However, U.S. investment in Indonesia, the Philippines, and Vietnam is relatively small. The U.S. presence in ASEAN reflects not only economic concerns but also regional security considerations. Its influence on the region through international organizations such as the United Nations and the WTO exceeds that of Japan.

The U.S. relationship with ASEAN through APEC was formed at the first stage of APEC. Both ASEAN and the United States conceded and eventually participated in APEC in 1989. The second stage began in July 1993 when U.S. President Bill Clinton defined his Asia Pacific policy. When visiting Japan and South Korea, Clinton suggested the New Pacific Community initiative. The initiative called for an increased diplomatic and military influence in Asia Pacific to strengthen the U.S. commitment to the region.

In 1994, reflecting Clinton's intention, APEC held its first unofficial summit in Seattle, Washington. Malaysian Prime Minister Mahathir, who had criticized the summit, was absent attending a friend's wedding.

At this summit, the United States seemed to want to make APEC like NAFTA. It suggested that trade liberalization follow the guidelines of the recently established WTO. A majority declined the U.S. proposal. However, the Bogor summit in 1994 and the Osaka summit in 1995 acceded to U.S. leadership. Clinton missed the Osaka summit because of domestic problems. Vice President Al Gore attended instead and succeeded in getting security issues onto the agenda. This was a victory for U.S. diplomacy. Clinton's absence from the Osaka summit could have reflected a change in the U.S. attitude toward APEC.

The third stage is the period since the Manila summit in 1996. The United States became passive toward Asia Pacific diplomacy partly because of a concentration on domestic issues. In APEC, the U.S. interest shifted to the early liberalization of specific areas such as information technology. For the ASEAN economies, excluding Singapore, information technology is an area with comparative disadvantages, and therefore they are not positive toward such liberalization.

The Asian economic crisis since 1997 has changed dramatically the relationship between the United States and the ASEAN economies. Indonesia and Thailand requested financial support from the International Monetary Fund (IMF), and they felt that the IMF response would be matched by U.S. interest. This conclusion seemed reasonable because the United States is the IMF's biggest contributor. However, domestic concerns prevented the United States from stepping up. Disputes over the role of the IMF were raised on both sides of the Pacific.

The relationship between the United States and the ASEAN economies in APEC is greatly affected by China. China, like the ASEAN economies, is an exporter of labor-intensive goods to the United States and, in this sense, competes with the ASEAN economies in the U.S. market. Furthermore, China figures significantly in security issues.

CHINA   ASEAN was originally set up by the anticommunist powers in Southeast Asia. Therefore, China was a potential enemy. More recently, China and the ASEAN economies have specialized in labor-intensive products, so they compete in the advanced markets. But this situation is changing.

In the autumn of 1990, Indonesia and Singapore restored diplomatic relations with China. This period was characterized by the aftereffects of the Tiananmen Square massacre in June 1989. Therefore, the strengthening of relations with China on the part of Indonesia and Singapore held special significance. At the same time, the United States had placed economic sanctions on trade with China. In 1992, Deng Xiaoping delivered an address supporting China's open-door policy, which quickened China's transition to a socialist market economy. At that time, China and the ASEAN economies were said to be economically substitutable in the world market. In fact, FDI to China decreased following the Tiananmen Square massacre, whereas FDI to Indonesia, Malaysia, and Thailand increased. After Deng's speech, FDI to China recovered but that to the ASEAN economies decreased.(Soesastro 1997).

In trade relations, Japan's imports from China accounted for only 3.9 percent of total imports in 1989. In 1996, the ratio rose to 8.8 percent. In the United States, China's share rose from 0.8 percent to 3.3 percent during the same period. Despite economic sanctions, China's penetration into advanced markets was significant. By comparison, in the same period, Japan's imports from the ASEAN economies rose from 11.8 percent to 15.0 percent. In the U.S. market, ASEAN's share rose from 5.2 percent to 8.4 percent. China's growth in trade with the advanced economies has matched that of the ASEAN economies.

What are the direct economic relationships between the ASEAN economies and China? In 1989, only 1.9 percent of the ASEAN-7's total exports were to China, but the ratio rose to 2.8 percent in 1996. The share of the ASEAN-7 in total Chinese exports was 5.7 percent in 1989 and 6.2 percent in 1996. Trade relations between China and ASEAN have not greatly expanded. But direct investment is different. For example, Malaysia sent an economic mission led by its prime minister to China to promote its direct investment. Singapore's investment in China represented 6.6 percent of its total investment at the end of 1995, and 12.3 percent of Thailand's investment flowed into China in 1996. China received US$42.14 billion in FDI in 1996, of which Singapore supplied US$2.25 billion; Malaysia, US$459.95 million; Thailand, US$328.18 million; Indonesia, US$93.54 million; the Philippines, US$55.51 million; and Vietnam, US$1.45 million. The aggregate of the ASEAN contributors was US$3.19 billion, or 7.6 percent of China's total FDI (China Yearbook 1997).

Since the mid-1990s, the ASEAN economies and China have enhanced their mutual dependency and the relationship has changed from substitutable to complementary. However, the Asian crisis could change these relationships. China's yuan is fixed to the U.S. dollar, whereas the ASEAN currencies depreciated and, as a consequence, Chinese exports are losing their international competitiveness. Judging from Japan's trade statistics, the influence of exchange rate variation has yet to feed through. Furthermore, Chinese exports can be more or less substituted by ASEAN exports in the markets in advanced countries. For the ASEAN economies, the increase in exports could drive their economic recovery. But if China were to devalue its currency, ASEAN products would lose their relative competitiveness. Therefore, China and ASEAN's economic ties are more closely related than can be grasped from trade and investment statistics.

CLOSER ECONOMIC RELATIONS   Australia and New Zealand partially agreed to a free trade agreement in 1965. Subsequently, in 1983, a further liberalization process began and in 1990 all restrictive measures on trade in commodities between them were completely abolished. Tariffs were abolished in 1988 and export subsidies were abolished in 1987. In 1995, the restriction on quality (whereby low-quality commodities are subject to import restrictions to protect unskilled labor in the importers) was abolished.

The Closer Economic Relations (CER) pact differs from AFTA in that it is an agreement between only two countries, both of which have similar economic structures. The trade intensity index is 26.13 when Australia is an exporter and New Zealand is an importer, and in the reverse case it is 17.94. Both figures show a high degree of interdependence. AFTA and the CER have met frequently to negotiate and enhance mutual connections. Thus, the CER/AFTA relationship complements the relationship of Australia and New Zealand as dialogue partners with ASEAN.

Using the trade intensity index, we can analyze the economic relations between ASEAN and both countries in the CER. When Australia is an exporter, the indexes exceed one vis-à-vis the ASEAN-7. Similarly, the New Zealand indexes exceed one vis-à-vis the ASEAN-7 excluding Singapore, Brunei, and Thailand.

Conclusion

In this chapter, we discussed ASEAN as a regional cooperative institution in APEC from an economic viewpoint. In the near future, transfers of power in some of the ASEAN members and other domestic political problems could affect international relations. In APEC, regional security issues are also discussed, and members must work to ensure that their ties extend beyond solely economic concerns.

In the first section, we discussed the trade liberalization processes of both ASEAN and APEC. A common path began with comprehensive and voluntary negotiations, and then shifted to specific negotiations following stagnancy. In ASEAN, voluntary actions were restrained because of the Asian crisis. In APEC, the United States has become irritated that its leadership was not structured into the forum.

In the second section, we dealt with new membership problems from an economic viewpoint. ASEAN, based as it is in Southeast Asia, is essentially a closed institution. However, APEC has supported open regionalism, and it was a great conversion for APEC to institute a ten-year moratorium on new participation. Some analysts contend that APEC has strayed from its motto. We cannot easily predict what Russia's membership will mean for APEC. At present, the economic significance of Russia's participation is not large, but it will affect APEC if the issues shift to energy and security matters. For ASEAN as a subregional group in APEC, the effect of APEC's economic diversity through increased membership is not negligible. Furthermore, having both members and nonmembers of APEC complicates ASEAN's interdependence relationships.

In the third section, we dealt with the ASEAN economies' bilateral relationships with the non-ASEAN economies in APEC. ASEAN's economic dimensions are rather small compared to its influence in APEC. The economic interdependency between Japan and ASEAN has deepened, and Japan's dependence on the overall ASEAN economy is getting higher. Japan's commitment to the ASEAN economy is characterized by the close connection it places on direct investment and trade. The U.S. dependency on the ASEAN economies is also expanding. The ASEAN economies, still suffering from the economic crisis that began in 1997, expect much from the U.S. economic presence in APEC. However, the United States impatiently demands that the ASEAN economies open their markets in APEC and the WTO, which the ASEAN economies are not yet prepared to do. China and the ASEAN economies have competed in the export markets of the advanced countries and the investor countries, but recent economic growth in the ASEAN economies has led to increased investment in China from these countries. Moreover, the economic ties between China and the ASEAN economies go beyond trade and investment. Although ASEAN and both Australia and New Zealand have a close relationship in regional cooperative institutions, their interdependency is not currently significant.

The ASEAN economies are facing an economic crisis, and we cannot predict how this crisis will affect the unity of ASEAN as a regional cooperative institution. The role of ASEAN in APEC will inevitably change. Both ASEAN and APEC stand at the crossroads in addressing what they, as institutions, can do to mitigate the crisis.

Notes

1. Ajanant points out that "Japan remained very passive as she was not certain whether the U.S. would see her involvement in APEC as an irritant" (1997, 6). Japan's position on this issue has been used as an example of its lack of independence in diplomacy.

2. In this paragraph, the "ASEAN economies" refer to the ASEAN-10, excluding Laos and Cambodia, for which statistics are not available. Trade statistics are based on data from the International Monetary Fund's *Direction of Trade Statistics* and each country's government statistics.

3. Items with tariff rates of 20 percent or less were classified as fast track and were scheduled to be liberalized no later than 1998; normal track items were scheduled for liberalization by the year 2000.

4. At the 11th AFTA council in October 1997, a consensus was reached to strengthen the AFTA scheme, despite currency instability and the participation of Laos and Myanmar in the CEPT scheme, and to adopt the 1998 CEPT package.

5. This is the summary in the declaration to common targets issued by the APEC economic ministers in Osaka on 19 November 1995.

6. The index does not include data on Indonesia's imports from Singapore as these figures are not available.

7. ASEAN has appointed dialogue partners since 1976. They include Australia, Japan, New Zealand, and the United Nations Development Program (1976); the United States (1977); the European Union (then the European Community) (1980); Canada (1981); South Korea (1991); and China, Russia, and India (1996).

8. Because of yen depreciation relative to the U.S. dollar, the value of Japan's imports decreased. Japan's total imports were US$225.9 billion in 1995, compared with US$274.1 billion in 1994 and US$349.5 billion in 1996.

9. For Thailand, the investment statistics are based on data from the Bank of Thailand and the trade statistics are based on data from the IMF.

10. Indonesia's investment statistics are based on data from BKPM (Investment Coordinating Board), and the trade statistics are based on data from the Central Bureau of Statistics.

Bibliography

Ajanant, Juanjai. 1997. *Global, Regional and Sub-regional Trading Arrangements.* Mimeo. Bangkok, Thailand: Chulalongkorn University.

Akaha Tsuneo, ed. 1997. *Politics and Economics in the Russian Far East.* London and New York: Routledge.

"APEC Economic Leaders' Declaration of Common Resolve." 1994. ASEAN Second Summit and Official Economic Ministers' Meeting, 15 November, Bogor, Indonesia.

Ashayagachat, Achara. 1998. "Vietnam Upbeat about Early Entry to Regional Forum." *Bangkok Post* (24 January).

Baker, James A., III. 1991. "America in Asia: Emerging Architecture for a Pacific Community." *Foreign Affairs* 70(5): 1–18.

China Yearbook 1997. 1997. Beijing: China Statistical Publishing House.

Coordination Bureau, Economic Planning Agency, ed. 1997. *APEC bōeki jiyūka no keizai kōka* (The impact of trade liberalization in APEC). Tokyo: Economic Planning Agency.

Hagiwara Ayako. 1998. "Azia shokoku no chokusetsu tōshi tōkei" (Direct investment statistics in Asian countries). *Kaigai tōshi kenkyūjohō* (April): 26–107.

International Monetary Fund. Various issues. *Direction of Trade Statistics.* Washington, D.C.: International Monetary Fund.

Japan External Trade Organization. 1998. *JETRO Annual Report 1998.* Tokyo: Japan External Trade Organization.

Lim Chee Peng and Robert R. Teh, Jr. 1996. "Linkages between AFTA and Other Regional Trading Arrangements such as CER." In Chia Siow Yue and Joseph L. H. Tan, eds. *ASEAN in the WTO: Challenges and Responses.* Singapore: Institute of Southeast Asian Studies.

Pangetsu, Mari. 1997. "Assessing APEC Trade Liberalization." In C. Fred Bergsten, ed. *Whither APEC?: The Progress to Date and Agenda for the Future.* Washington, D.C.: Institute for International Economics.

Roshia Kyokutō dēta bukku 1996 (Russian Far East data book 1996). 1996. Tokyo: Institute of Russian and East European Economic Studies.

Smith, Anthony L. 1998. "The AFTA-CER Dialogue: A New Zealand Perspective on an Emerging Trade Area Linkage." *ASEAN Economic Bulletin* 14(3): 238–252.

Soesastro, Hadi. 1994. "The International Framework for APEC: An Asian Perspective." In Chia Siow Yue, ed. *APEC: Challenges and Opportunities.* Singapore: Institute of Southeast Asian Studies.

———. 1997. "APEC: An ASEAN Perspective." In Donald C. Hellmann and Kenneth B. Pyle, eds. *From APEC to Xanadu: Creating a Viable Community in the Post–Cold War Pacific.* New York: M. E. Sharpe.

Stockholm International Peace Research Institute (SIPRI). 1997. *SIPRI Yearbook 1997.* Stockholm: Stockholm International Peace Research Institute.

– 4 –

International Capital Movements and Financial Networks

Okuda Hidenobu

THE ECONOMIES of the Association of Southeast Asian Nations achieved rapid growth for approximately ten years from the latter half of the 1980s, with a combination of exports and investment expansion as the driving force (see table 1). In an age of globalization, they implemented "foreign-capital-led industrialization" (Okuda 1998), under which export-oriented industrialization was promoted by actively inviting in foreign capital and foreign enterprises. At the same time, financial reforms were undertaken in these countries with a financial liberalization policy as the pillar, and a system of channeling domestic and overseas funds into the growth sector was developed based on the market mechanism. In response to foreign-capital-led industrialization and financial liberalization, large amounts of outside funds have flowed into Southeast Asia since the end of the 1980s, and intraregional capital movement has also become active.

In 1997, however, a currency crisis occurred in Thailand, which had been regarded as a typical success case of foreign-capital-led industrialization until then. Its impact escalated into an economic crisis and spread to practically all of East Asia, forcing industrialization through the active utilization of foreign capital in an extensive adjustment process. As in Thailand's crisis, where a management crisis in the financial sector acted as the trigger, the major cause of the crisis in the other ASEAN economies was the fragility of their financial sectors. This fragility and the recent rapid inflows of overseas funds are interrelated. International

Table 1. Resource Balance in East Asian Countries (% of GNP)

	Indonesia	Malaysia	Philippines	Singapore	South Korea	Taiwan	Thailand
				Trade Balance			
1975	8.0	3.2	−10.0	−48.0	−10.5	−4.3	−7.2
1985	9.9	10.5	−2.7	−18.9	−0.9	16.7	−5.6
1995	2.5	−1.3	−14.2	−7.4	−2.2	3.0	−9.0
				Current Account Balance			
1975	−3.8	−5.5	−6.0	−10.2	−9.1	−3.8	−4.2
1985	−2.3	−2.1	−0.3	0.0	−1.0	14.6	−4.0
1995	−1.7	−8.8	−2.5	13.3	−2.0	2.0	−8.0
				Share of Manufacturing Sector			
1975	8.9	16.8	25.7	23.9	26.2	30.9	18.7
1985	16.0	21.3	25.2	23.6	29.3	37.6	21.9
1995	24.3	35.1	22.9	26.7	26.9	28.2	29.2
				Per Capita GNP (US$)			
1985	520	1,970	570	7,620	2,160	n.a.	800
1995	990	3,900	1,020	27,090	9,680	12,720	2,710
				Gross Domestic Saving			
1975	21.0	23.8	26.8	29.0	18.1	27.1	20.6
1985	29.8	32.7	18.8	40.6	31.4	32.9	24.8
1995	35.8	37.2	14.7	52.0	36.7	26.1	36.5
				Capital Formation			
1975	20.3	23.4	30.9	39.9	27.1	30.4	26.7
1985	28.0	27.6	14.3	42.5	29.6	19.1	28.2
1995	37.8	40.6	22.3	33.2	37.1	23.8	43.1
				Resource Gap			
1975	0.7	0.4	−4.1	−10.9	−9.0	−3.3	−6.1
1985	1.8	5.1	4.5	−1.9	1.8	13.8	−3.4
1995	−2.0	−3.4	−7.6	18.8	−0.4	2.3	−6.6

Source: Asian Development Bank (1997).

capital movements in the ASEAN region in the 1990s must be understood against this general background. Clarification of this interrelationship is essential to understanding recent international capital movements in the ASEAN region, and it is also necessary in assessing the future structure of capital movements and financial networks in the region.

The objective of this chapter is to investigate the financial networks in the ASEAN region that have been formed since the latter half of the 1980s through foreign-capital-led industrialization, to explain hypothetically their basic structures, and to describe their future prospects. A number of surveys and studies have been conducted concerning recent international capital movements in the ASEAN region.[1] Research is also emerging with regard to the originating process and the causes of the recent financial crisis. The themes of these studies are discussed here, as are the characteristics of recent capital movements in the ASEAN economies as they relate to the structural changes in financial networks. The main concern of the present examination is how the financial networks, formed through foreign-capital-led industrialization and financial liberalization, relate to changes in the recent international capital inflow into the region, as well as in the nature of the structural factors that have caused the crisis since 1997.

In the first section of the chapter, ASEAN-type development finance paradigms corresponding to foreign-capital-led industrialization and financial liberalization, which have been promoted under globalization, are conceptualized, and the financial mechanism on the basis of which international capital movements took place is hypothesized.

In the second section, actual changes in and characteristics of international capital movements in the ASEAN economies from the latter half of the 1980s until the mid-1990s are surveyed. During this period, the capital flows into the ASEAN economies increased rapidly, and their weight also shifted from official to private funds; the form of capital diversified from loans to include direct investment and securities investment. From the mid-1990s onward, a great change took place in capital movements; the inflow became excessive, and the weight of short-term funds became greater, thereby threatening the stability and soundness of funds.

How did the changes in the content of funds and the subsequent Asian financial crisis occur? In the third section, a hypothetical explanation is presented with reference to the structure of the interregional financial networks, and the changing process of international capital movements is examined from the viewpoint of differences in the structure of financial systems in the ASEAN economies and in the recipients of overseas funds. In the fourth section, the same question is dealt with from a broadened viewpoint including industrialized countries and providers of funds.

In the final section, a brief survey is presented on the financial networks that have been built in East Asia from the three aspects of domestic, regional, and international finance, enlarging on the earlier arguments.

Globalization and Change in Development Finance Paradigms

The Development Finance Paradigm before Globalization

From the 1950s until the 1970s, official funds from government development assistance and international financial agencies, such as the International Monetary Fund and the World Bank, constituted the pillar of capital movement from industrialized to developing countries. The movement of private funds to developing countries was limited, and the recipients in developing countries were mostly public-sector bodies, such as governments and government-related agencies. Developing countries have often assumed a cautious attitude toward direct investment by foreign enterprises and the borrowing of private funds for fear of economic control by foreign capital.

The development strategies of the ASEAN economies vary from country to country, and the development process of the financial system in each country is far from uniform. Generally speaking, however, the policies adopted by the countries in the 1970s featured import substitution and low interest rates.

Figure 1 shows a model of development patterns. Because capital inflow from overseas was limited, investment in developing countries essentially relied on domestic funds, and due to a sense of wariness toward foreign enterprises, local businesses were the main investors. Under the financial systems in developing countries, however, domestic funds were not sufficient to support rapid economic growth by local enterprises. Because the investment risk was high for inexperienced local businesses, and given that small domestic investors, being sensitive to risks, refrained from placing money in local businesses, local companies suffered from a shortage of funds. Generally in developing countries, moreover, the

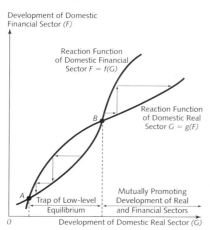

Figure 1. The Paradigm of Financial Development before Globalization

Development of Domestic Financial Sector (F)

Reaction Function of Domestic Financial Sector $F = f(G)$

Reaction Function of Domestic Real Sector $G = g(F)$

B

A

Trap of Low-level Equilibrium

Mutually Promoting Development of Real and Financial Sectors

0   Development of Domestic Real Sector (G)

Source: Okuda and Kuroyanagi (1998, 33).

degree of disclosure is low with respect to business information and information on political and economic conditions. This lack of information constituted a serious impediment to capital intermediary activities.

The experience of industrialized countries shows that there is a mutually promoting relationship between the development of the financial sector and the real economy.[2] In developing countries that are not achieving much economic growth, the financial system and the real economy tend to conflict, thereby restraining development. A policy of keeping interest rates artificially low could be a device to break through such a mutually restraining relationship between the real economy and the financial sector. If the development of the real sector is promoted by the generation of a large amount of long-term funds required for industrialization through an artificial device, and if the real sector then shifts to an independent development process, the development of the financial sector can be promoted as a consequence. Funds from abroad may be said not only to have made up for a quantitative shortage of policy-oriented funds but also to have qualitatively supplemented funds that were difficult to raise domestically, such as long-term capital.

The Development Finance Paradigm in a Globalizing Economy

In all the ASEAN economies, a policy change was effected in the latter half of the 1980s toward foreign-capital-led industrialization and financial liberalization. The economic growth experienced by these countries in the 1990s was brought about by the development finance paradigm in the current globalizing economy, in which goods and services markets became combined on a global scale. Figure 2 illustrates this paradigm. First, the new industries constituting the core of economic development are borne not by local businesses but by what I call foreign-affiliated enterprises; some are joint ventures with foreign companies, whereas others are subsidiaries of foreign companies. They do not require policy-oriented fund procurement. Investment risks are greatly reduced with foreign-affiliated enterprises, which generally have great capital power, advanced technology, and long experience. Moreover, because foreign-affiliated enterprises are often well known and have a high degree of disclosure, they can absorb funds even from the small investors in

Figure 2. The Paradigm of Financial Development after Globalization

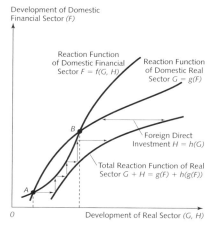

Development of Domestic
Financial Sector *(F)*

Reaction Function
of Domestic Financial
Sector $F = f(G, H)$

Reaction Function
of Domestic Real
Sector $G = g(F)$

B

Foreign Direct
Investment $H = h(G)$

Total Reaction Function of Real
Sector $G + H = g(F) + h(g(F))$

A

0   Development of Real Sector *(G, H)*

Source: Okuda and Kuroyanagi (1998, 34).

developing countries sensitive to risks. Because these businesses can procure funds overseas, the underdevelopment of financial systems in developing countries is not that much of a business problem for them.

For foreign-affiliated enterprises to play the core role in the development of a leading sector, a financial system for the smooth procurement of investment funds at home and abroad is necessary. It is desirable that funds be freely procured at home and abroad. It is easier to raise funds using free-market mechanisms than to create funds within a developing country through artificial devices. Deregulation of foreign exchange, interest rates, and businesses, along with market entry by foreign financial institutions, facilitates fund procurement. These are natural policies if the goal is the creation of a financial system consistent with such objectives.

Foreign-Capital-Led Industrialization and the Financial System

In Southeast Asia's foreign-capital-led industrialization in the 1990s, the main role in the introduction and development of the industries indispensable for economic development was played by foreign-affiliated enterprises. Although local businesses continue to have a majority share of the economy, they mostly belong to the nontradable sector, such as service and traditional manufacturing industries, and are unable to constitute the core of new industries.

According to research by a think tank of a large Japanese commercial bank, fund procurement by Japanese businesses in Southeast Asia is highly reliant on Japanese banks. Where market entry by Japanese banks is restricted, Japanese businesses sometimes have to rely on local banks for domestic funds, but even in such cases the involvement of Japanese

66   Okuda

Figure 3. The Financial System under FDI-Led Industrialization

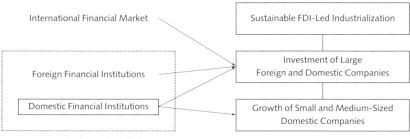

Source: Okuda (1998).

banks is often extensive. They may, for instance, introduce the business
to a local bank. The think tank found that a pattern of fund procurement
by foreign-affiliated enterprises that is closely related to banks in the
home country generally applies to U.S. and European affiliates as well.
Figure 3 illustrates the financial systems in the ASEAN economies as they
developed with the aid of foreign direct investment (FDI).

The Dai-Ichi Kangyō Research Institute (1997) determined that foreign-affiliated enterprises have close relations with international financial markets and foreign financial institutions and essentially have no
problems raising foreign-currency funds. At the same time, because
these enterprises are excellent clients for local financial institutions, they
can procure local-currency funds as well. In the case of foreign-currency
funds, however, there can be obstacles to procurement due to restrictions
under foreign-exchange legislation, and in the case of local-currency
funds, there tend to be problems of high procurement costs and a shortage of funds due to the underdeveloped local financial system. Because
local enterprises, with the exception of a limited number of major businesses, have no access to overseas financial markets and foreign financial
institutions, they basically rely on local financial institutions for fund
procurement. The funds procured by them are limited to the local currency. Just as with foreign-affiliated enterprises, they tend to be bothered
by high fund-raising costs and a shortage of funds.

For foreign-affiliated companies to play the key role in the development of a leading sector, the financial system must enable them to
smoothly procure investment funds locally and overseas. The policies
introduced toward this end in the 1990s were aimed at facilitating fund

procurement by foreign-affiliated enterprises and creating a financial system that supports foreign-capital-led industrialization.

International Capital Movements in the 1990s

What international fund movements actually emerged under the financial systems created since the latter half of the 1980s? In the first half of the 1990s, the industrialization process progressed satisfactorily, and in the latter half industrialization gradually became inefficient and a financial crisis spread throughout the region.

International capital movements in Southeast Asia underwent a sea change because of the policy switch to foreign-capital-led industrialization and financial liberalization. First, as shown in figure 4, the capital inflow into the ASEAN region increased rapidly. Such a change was caused not only by financial reforms in the region's countries but also by factors in the industrialized countries that lend to developing countries. In the United States, Japan, and Western Europe, savings usually exceeded investment and surplus funds accumulated. Competition among financial institutions and markets intensified in these countries as a result of financial liberalization policies, and surplus funds tended to flow into developing countries in pursuit of investment opportunities with higher profitability. There was also a factor on the side of the ASEAN borrowers of such funds: rapid economic growth led by FDI. This growth gained momentum in the latter half of the 1980s and turned the region into an internationally recognized investment target. These countries had been wary of receiving investments from abroad, but they shifted to a stance of financial liberalization and deregulation of foreign exchange and overseas investment with a view to actively accepting funds from foreign countries. With such factors reinforcing each other, a significant amount of funds flowed into Southeast Asia in the late 1980s and early 1990s.

Second, the composition of the funding changed. Initially, official funds from government agencies of industrialized countries and international financial institutions took a large share, but in the latter half of the 1980s the share of private funds greatly increased. According to table 2, the composition of funds flowing into Southeast Asia has varied substantially from country to country. In those countries where the income level is high, the macroeconomic performance is good, the growth rate is fast, and inflation is low, or where there are many enterprises with

Figure 4. The Foreign Capital Inflow to ASEAN Economies (US$ billion)

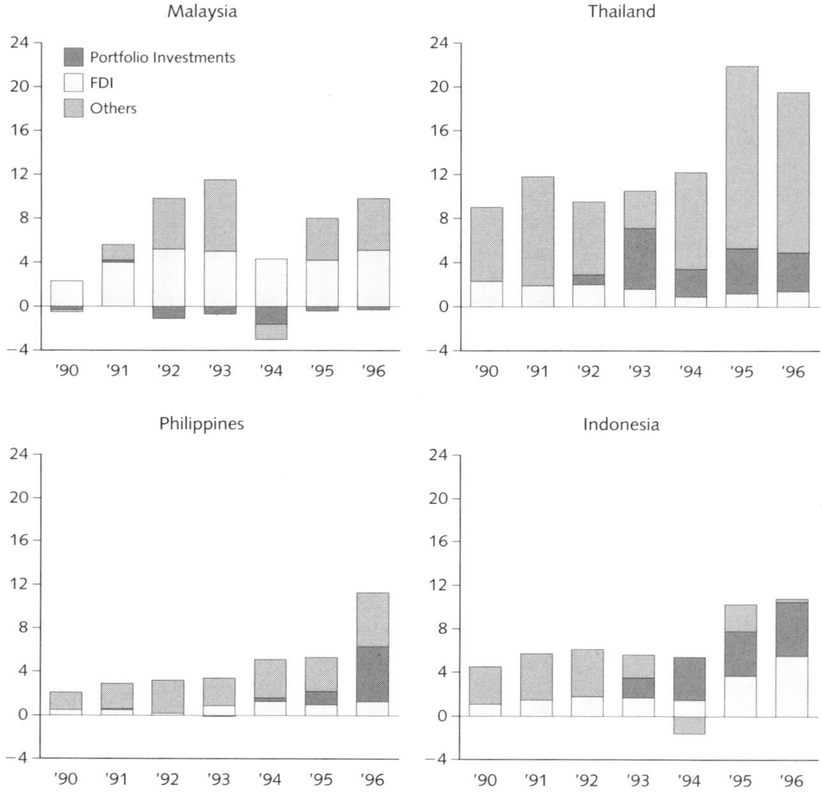

Malaysia

Thailand

Philippines

Indonesia

Legend: Portfolio Investments / FDI / Others

Source: World Bank, *World Tables 1998.*
Note: Others = capital account surplus − portfolio investments − FDI.

high international creditworthiness, such as foreign-affiliated companies and domestic blue-chip companies, the ratio of private funds in the inflow from abroad tends to be high. Conversely, in countries where the income level is low and the macroeconomic performance is poor, there are generally few businesses with high international creditworthiness, and therefore the amount of private funds from abroad tends to be small. Despite the differences by country, however, the ratio of private funds flowing into the ASEAN economies in the latter half of the 1980s moved higher than the ratios recorded until the 1970s.

Third, although credit from banks used to be the main source of

Table 2. Measurements of External Finance in East Asian Countries (% of GNP)

	Indonesia	Malaysia	Philippines	Singapore	South Korea	Taiwan	Thailand
			Total External Debt				
1975	36.7	22.3	28.1	11.4	40.3	12.4	12.5
1985	44.3	69.9	89.1	23.4	51.7	14.5	45.9
1995	64.6	42.5	51.8	9.8	22.2	10.3	50.4
			FDI Received				
1980s	2.4	4.6	1.0	3.3	0.5	1.0	8.0
1990s	12.5	8.5	1.9	3.8	0.4	0.9	6.8
			International Market Borrowing				
1975	5.3	4.6	1.6	0.2	1.5	n.a.	0.0
1985	0.1	6.6	3.0	1.9	5.1	n.a.	3.5
1995	3.7	3.5	1.7	1.2	3.1	0.7	4.0

Source: Asian Development Bank (1997).

finance, funds now entered in diversified forms, such as direct investment, securities investment, and even fund procurement through offshore markets. FDI surged, in particular from the latter half of the 1980s to the early 1990s. This FDI started with a rapid increase in investment from Japan, induced by the high yen after the Plaza Accord of 1985 on realigning exchange rates. Later, investment from such Asian newly industrialized economies (NIEs) as South Korea and Taiwan increased. Subsequently, investment from Western countries also went up. In the early 1990s, there was a sudden expansion of the inflow of short-term funds from industrialized countries and international financial markets, mainly in the form of bank lending and securities investment, induced by the rapid growth and high interest rates in the ASEAN region. Offshore financial markets set up in Thailand and Malaysia to promote the inflow of funds accelerated this trend. Overseas institutional investors briskly increased their investment in the rapidly growing stock markets in the region.

Fourth, the entry of funds accelerated in the mid-1990s. Having promoted foreign-capital-led industrialization and financial liberalization since the latter half of the 1980s and achieved sizzling growth as a result, Southeast Asian countries toward the middle of the 1990s came to be regarded as relatively safe, profitable investment targets by investors in industrialized countries. An even larger amount of funds flowed in from them and from international financial markets, and the ratio of this inflow relative to the economic size of each country increased.

The composition of the foreign funds underwent a change at the same time. In the late 1980s, the share of long-term funds going directly into production, typically in the form of direct investment, was large. Toward the mid-1990s, however, funds that were apt to be withdrawn and might not constitute productive investment, such as securities purchases and short-term bank credit, increased. The fact that the ASEAN economies maintained a policy of essentially pegging their exchange rates to the U.S. dollar encouraged this trend. The pegs to the dollar functioned to bring in FDI for quite awhile. But when sustained over a long period of time, these rates began to draw in short-term investment aimed at profits from high domestic interest rates, thereby altering the nature of currency policy.

Changes in International Capital Movements and ASEAN's Crisis

The currency crisis started in Thailand in the summer of 1997 and soon spread throughout East Asia. Some observers argue that the foreign capital introduced in the past several years was the key to the crisis. That is, much of the capital inflows were not used efficiently and productively. This problem became evident when economic growth decelerated. Plunging currencies created turmoil, first in the financial sectors and later throughout the East Asian economies. The scale of the crisis was smaller among those countries that had used foreign capital productively. Apart from the impact of some currency volatility overlap from neighbors, such countries suffered relatively little damage.

Good Financial Systems for Foreign-Capital-Led Industrialization

Whether it is possible to use foreign capital efficiently and productively depends to a large extent on the capability of the financial system in a country. To use this money truly productively, there must be domestic financial institutions capable of systematically providing funds to domestic sectors. The existence of such financial institutions has accentuated the differences in the use of foreign capital, and this affected the scale of the damage from currency, financial, and economic turmoil.

The rapidly expanding FDI starting from the late 1980s transferred capital and management resources into recipient countries and accelerated their growth through the expansion of exports and domestic demand. But the mere expansion of investment using solely foreign capital should inevitably lead to a bottleneck in growth (Krugman 1994). The endogenous economic growth theory, espoused by Krugman and others, posits that a quantitative increase in capital causes its marginal utility to diminish and the growth rate to decline. To maintain a high growth rate over a long period, the marginal utility of capital must be stable so that the inflow of foreign funds will keep expanding. For this purpose, efforts must be made to expand social investment, such as investment in education, to get an economic infrastructure in place, and to develop modern supporting industries, such as the parts industry.

It is difficult to use foreign funds for these efforts. The benefits of investment in education and the installation of infrastructure come mainly in the form of externalities, and it is difficult to procure funds for them on a market basis. Moreover, because these activities cannot generate foreign currency, an exchange risk will arise if overseas funds are used for them. Also, even if an attempt is made to develop local supporting industries, the companies in them will hardly be creditworthy and will find that they cannot raise foreign funds. Fund procurement operations for these activities inevitably depend on domestic funds and the local financial system.

The enormous inflow of FDI into the ASEAN economies that began in the latter half of the 1980s shows that foreign capital can be secured over a short period in a favorable investment environment. The accumulation of local capital progresses through investments based on bank credit, and the economic growth rate is dependent on the growth rate of local capital. Because this capital materializes only through the intermediary role of local banks, the route of economic growth will differ depending on banks' capability to finance smaller local businesses. To accelerate the growth rate, measures are needed to expand finance activities for local businesses.

For the ASEAN-type industrialization led by foreign capital to be successful, the funds that have flowed in from abroad must be used efficiently and productively. To this end, local resources must be accumulated that cannot be introduced from abroad but are nonetheless indispensable for enhancing production efficiency.[3] Because it is difficult to introduce funds directly from overseas financial markets and institutions for the development of local resources, the local financial system needs to play an intermediary role in providing funds to this area. It may sound paradoxical, but the success of foreign-capital-led industrialization may well depend on the capabilities of the local financial system.

Financial Systems in the ASEAN Economies

In the absence of close, interrelated networks between local and foreign financial institutions, unproductive financial activities will proliferate and international capital movements will be distorted. How, then, can an interrelationship be formed between local finance and foreign financial markets? Here, the case of the ASEAN-4 (Indonesia, Malaysia, the Philippines, and Thailand) is examined. The differences in the formation of domestic financial networks in these countries may have affected the inflow of overseas funds and led to the differences in their subsequent financial performance.

Two questions are important as regards the regional financial systems. First, what is the government's stance on macroeconomic financial policy, in particular on the exchange rate and interest rates? In the late 1980s, a policy of essentially pegging the local currency to the dollar was adopted by the ASEAN economies to promote inflows of investment funds. This system induced the expected inflows by the governments but also probably caused an excessive inflow of funds by artificially removing exchange risks and thus making the original investment risks appear smaller than they actually were. Nominal exchange rates continued to be pegged to the dollar over a long period. In Thailand, an excessive inflow of funds occurred in the mid-1990s, and a similar phenomenon occurred in Malaysia at the beginning of the decade. In the Philippines, by contrast, the nominal exchange rate was not stable against the dollar until the mid-1990s, and fund inflows until then were small. Once the exchange rate against the dollar became stable, however, the inflow of funds increased rapidly.

Second, what routes do inflowing funds move through? This particularly concerns the policy the authorities adopt toward using offshore markets and assigning roles to foreign financial institutions in the domestic market. Just like other developing countries, the ASEAN-4 were wary of investment from abroad until the early 1980s and adopted restrictive measures with respect to direct investment. Moreover, except for Thailand, these countries had only relatively recently achieved independence from colonial control, and in the first days of independence, foreign financial institutions were dominant in their markets. Under the circumstances, their governments adopted a policy of restricting the economic activities of foreign financial institutions from the viewpoint of developing domestic ones. On the changeover to a policy of foreign-capital-led industrialization, acceptance of direct investment was promoted, and restrictions on foreign exchange were relaxed to induce an inflow of funds. With respect to the entry into the domestic market of foreign financial institutions, however, the response varied greatly from country to country.

In Indonesia, deregulation of foreign exchange began in the 1970s, and the number of foreign banks entering the market increased. Foreign banks engaged mainly in transactions with foreign-affiliated enterprises, however, and were not keen on transactions with local businesses. But because domestic banks were small in size and weak in capital power, Indonesian companies often procured funds from abroad without having recourse to domestic banks. This practice made it difficult for the policy-making authorities to control fund flows.

After achieving independence, Malaysia adopted restrictive policy measures with respect to the activities of foreign financial institutions. Tight government control on inflows of funds from overseas was also maintained, and when short-term foreign funds surged in the 1990s, measures were taken to restrict deals involving them. Subsequently, responding to measures for the introduction of foreign capital taken by Thailand and other neighboring countries, Malaysia opened an offshore market on the island of Labuan, but a strict attitude was maintained toward the entry of foreign financial institutions. As a result, the inflow of short-term funds into Malaysia has been relatively tightly controlled, and the ratio of long-term funds, such as direct investment, is high.

In Thailand as well, a restrictive policy was taken toward foreign financial institutions with a view to fostering domestic ones. In the 1990s, however, due to the necessity to introduce capital more aggressively, an offshore market was set up. But this market turned into a route for the procurement of cheap funds by weak domestic financial institutions. Moreover, most of these funds were short term, and they were often used for investment in real estate and other purposes that were not necessarily productive. Even domestic financial institutions without sufficient capabilities to manage funds acquired access to a large amount of overseas funds, and an excessive inflow of short-term funds resulted.

In the Philippines, structural reforms were undertaken in the financial sector in the late 1980s with the support of international financial institutions, and the building of a financial system based on market principles was promoted. The entry of foreign financial institutions also increased extensively in the forms of branch offices and investments. An offshore market that opened in the 1970s served as an access point for remittance from Philippine workers overseas in the 1990s. Because there were few Philippine companies that could procure funds directly from overseas without going through banks, it was relatively easy to monitor the inflow of funds. As a result, although overseas funds flowed in rapidly in the 1990s, they were used relatively productively and caused no great problems.

Capital Movement and Geographical Linkage

The distortions and changes in inflows of overseas funds into the ASEAN economies were related to the relationship between these countries and overseas funds. From the late 1980s to the mid-1990s, huge amounts of overseas funds flowed into the region. In the same period, the ASEAN economies deregulated international capital movements, so it is natural to assume that finance in the region became more integrated. If international capital movement is completely liberalized and all artificial barriers are removed, and if, at the same time, symmetry of information is maintained throughout the global economy, there can be no regional bias in capital flows. In actuality, however, biases exist in specific regions and economies.

Feldstein and Horioka (1980) have put forth a home bias. If the world's financial markets are completely linked and no asymmetry is present in international information, countries' savings will be distributed in a geographically indiscriminate manner, so that all will enjoy the same rate of profitability in different markets in the world. According to a metrical analysis, however, the rates of investment and savings in a country do not change indiscriminately; investment has a bias to its own country. The home bias suggests that it is easier for a domestic saver to invest domestically than to invest internationally because asymmetry is weaker for domestic than for international investment.

If asymmetry in information affects the route of investment, a country bias in international capital movement can be predicted. When specific regions (or countries) have a strong interrelationship in transactions among their real economies, mutual information must be exchanged between them. In the process of frequent information exchanges, asymmetry in mutual information should become weaker in comparison with that of other regions (or countries). Therefore, regions (or countries) with a strong transactional relationship between them in terms of the real economy have a strong mutual linkage in international capital movements as well.

Tables 3, 4, and 5 show the geographical interrelationship in physical terms and the geographical interrelationship in financial terms in East Asian countries. Looking at the correlation between the two interrelationships, we see that there are countries where the two are relatively consistent and those where there is quite a gap between the two. In Thailand and the Philippines, the geographical interrelationship in physical and financial terms is relatively consistent. On the other hand, in South Korea and Indonesia, a significant difference is observed between the two. Characteristically, in countries where a difference is observed, the geographical interrelationship in financial terms with Europe exceeds that of the physical terms.

Table 6 summarizes the consistency between international capital movement and real economic activities. If the consistency were perfect, the figures in the table would all be equal to unity. The gap between the geographical interrelationships in physical and financial terms suggests the existence of international capital movement isolated from activities in real economies. Moreover, if a bias from asymmetry in information in international capital movement exists, this may mean that international capital movement occurs in contradiction to asymmetry in information.

In South Korea, for example, the interrelationships with Japan and the United States are strong in both trade and direct investment in terms of the real economy. The balance of bank credit to South Korea shows that a great share is taken by borrowings from Europe, with which South Korea's interrelationship in physical terms is weak. Moreover, given that bank credit from Europe increased in the early 1990s and most funds were for short-term lending, it may be inferred that these funds did not necessarily represent capital movement based on information about the real economy.

Future Financial Networks in ASEAN

Through financial reforms in recent years, the market environment surrounding local banks has gradually become competitive in every ASEAN economy. Sound market competition contributes to the enhancement of the management efficiency of financial institutions. However, the

Table 3. Direction of Trade in East Asian Countries (% share)

	Indonesia	Malaysia	Philippines	Singapore	South Korea	Taiwan	Thailand
	United States						
Exports	15.9	20.7	35.3	18.3	19.3	23.7	17.8
Imports	9.1	16.3	18.4	15.1	22.5	20.1	8.7
Average	12.5	18.5	26.9	16.7	20.9	21.9	13.3
	Japan						
Exports	28.4	12.7	15.8	7.8	13.6	11.8	16.7
Imports	26.9	27.3	22.4	21.2	23.7	29.2	29.2
Average	27.7	20.0	19.1	14.5	18.7	20.5	23.0
	Western Europe						
Exports	10.6	9.0	11.0	8.3	9.0	7.6	8.5
Imports	14.4	11.4	7.7	9.8	9.7	10.3	11.0
Average	12.5	10.2	9.4	9.1	9.4	9.0	9.8
	NIEs-3						
Exports	19.1	28.4	12.4	11.3	13.8	29.6	20.5
Imports	17.3	18.6	14.2	7.6	2.2	8.8	9.8
Average	18.2	23.5	13.3	9.5	8.0	19.2	15.2

Source: Asian Development Bank (1997).

NIEs-3: Newly industrializing economies, including Hong Kong, South Korea, and Taiwan.

Table 4. Source of Foreign Direct Investment in East Asian Countries (% share)

	Indonesia	Malaysia	Philippines	Singapore	South Korea	Taiwan	Thailand
United States	5.6	13.2	23.6	41.8	31.6	25.7	15.6
Japan	10.9	20.4	13.3	23.3	25.0	28.3	39.3
Western Europe	17.2	14.6	12.0	22.9	34.8	13.0	21.3
Other	66.3	51.8	51.1	12.0	8.6	32.9	23.7
Total	100.0	100.0	100.0	100.0	100.0	100.0	100.0

Source: Economic Planning Agency (1997).

Table 5. Source of Bank Loans in East Asian Countries (% share)

	Indonesia	Malaysia	Philippines	Singapore	South Korea	Taiwan	Thailand
United States	7.8	9.6	8.3	20.0	10.0	5.8	2.5
Japan	39.4	22.9	36.4	14.9	12.0	54.4	30.8
Western Europe	30.0	29.0	41.8	41.5	52.2	25.3	45.5
Italy	0.3	1.3	1.1	0.7	2.7	0.6	4.0
Germany	9.4	10.4	19.8	14.1	11.9	10.9	18.2
Netherlands	4.8	1.7	3.7	7.2	4.4	2.4	4.1
United Kingdom	7.4	5.9	7.0	7.6	12.6	4.1	12.0
France	8.2	9.7	10.2	11.9	20.5	7.3	7.3
Total	100.0	100.0	100.0	100.0	100.0	100.0	100.0

Source: Bank of International Settlements, Annual Report 1997.

Table 6. Bank Loan Linkage versus Trade and FDI Linkage in East Asian Countries

	Indonesia	Malaysia	Philippines	Singapore	South Korea	Taiwan	Thailand
				United States			
Trade*	0.6	0.5	0.7	0.1	0.5	0.5	0.4
FDI†	1.4	0.6	0.8	0.1	0.3	0.4	0.4
				Japan			
Trade	1.4	1.8	0.8	2.1	1.2	0.6	2.4
FDI	3.6	1.8	1.1	1.3	0.9	0.4	1.4
				Western Europe			
Trade	2.4	4.1	4.4	5.0	3.1	5.8	2.6
FDI	1.7	2.9	3.5	2.0	0.8	4.0	1.2
				Others			
Trade	1.2	0.6	1.8	2.2	4.8	1.3	1.0
FDI	0.3	0.3	0.5	1.8	4.5	0.8	0.6

Source: Bank of International Settlements, Annual Report 1997; Economic Planning Agency (1997); Asian Development Bank (1997).

*Trade is the ratio of the share in bank loans/the share in trade.
†FDI is the ratio of the share in bank loans/the share in FDI.

experience of the ASEAN economies in recent years has shown that unsound market competition encourages an inefficient financial system and entails the danger of eventually causing a financial or economic crisis. The disproportionate development of domestic financial networks induced distorted, unproductive utilization of overseas funds, and this constituted an important factor in causing the financial and economic crisis in the ASEAN economies in the late 1990s. To respond to globalization while at the same time avoiding these problems, what characteristics should a financial network have? Two aspects of this are domestic financial networks in the ASEAN economies and international financial networks.

Determining Factors in Financial Networks

Continuous and efficient provision of funds cannot be carried out in international financial business if it is not based on appropriate information, just as in domestic financial activities. For information production to proceed efficiently, two factors are important. The first is a comparative advantage in the regional information peculiar to each market. Let us compare, for example, the markets in Hong Kong and Singapore. The Hong Kong economy has a strong linkage in its real economy with its hinterland, China, so it can be assumed that Hong Kong has a comparative advantage over the markets in Singapore and other countries in information production with respect to financial transactions with China. Similarly, the offshore markets in the ASEAN economies can have an advantage in a certain financial territory, depending on the degree of comparative advantage in their information production.

Efficient production of information does not depend on the strength of the linkages in physical economic activities alone. The second factor in information production is the degree of development in financial infrastructure. Hong Kong and Singapore have functioned as regional financial markets, apart from providing financial services to their hinterlands. An important factor behind this is that in both markets, many legal and financial experts are concentrated, and communications facilities and other infrastructure are well developed. Due to the provision of financial and economic infrastructure, benefits of the concentration of financial institutions in both markets have been generated.

Future Images of Financial Networks within Each Country

The basic role of the financial system is to procure funds both at home and abroad and play an intermediary role in distributing them to various sectors. To conduct efficient financial activities in both fund-raising and investment, the financial system must be able to produce information on the real economy efficiently. In financial intermediary activities, an advantage in information production on the real economy will be crucial for the structure of a financial network. For instance, in information on fund procurement by local enterprises in Thailand, the financial market located in Thailand is likely to have a comparative advantage over Hong Kong's financial market despite the benefits of accumulation that the latter enjoys. In each country, accordingly, domestic financial markets will continue to play a decisive role in financial activities.

In considering the future image of domestic financial markets, we need to examine the degree of penetration and the role of foreign financial institutions. As long as the ASEAN economies continue to allow foreign capital to lead industrialization, foreign-affiliated enterprises will play a central role in leading business sectors. Therefore, it is desirable to incorporate foreign-affiliated enterprises and their networks in the real economy into the financial system. A gap in this respect apparently existed between the real sector and the financial sector in the ASEAN economies in the 1990s, and the halfway opening of the financial sector to the outside world caused an excessive inflow of unproductive short-term funds. Conducting appropriate information gathering through sufficient entry of foreign-affiliated financial institutions will produce a durable financial market for large-scale international capital movements in this age of globalization.

In this respect, the share of foreign-affiliated financial institutions in various countries is of great interest. In the United States, the opening of both the real economy and the financial sector to the outside world has greatly advanced, and the share of foreign-affiliated financial institutions is considerable. In Japan, where the entry of foreign firms has been lagging in the domestic market, the share of foreign-affiliated financial institutions is small by contrast. In the rest of East Asia, such shares vary greatly from country to country. Compared with the linkage with foreign countries in the real sector, the foreign share in the financial sector is not always large. Although it is not possible to name an appropriate foreign entry share in concrete terms, it is necessary to examine future domestic financial networks with the question of appropriate share proportions in mind.

The introduction of foreign capital not only strengthens the capital power of local banks but also contributes to the introduction of new financial techniques and expanded access to foreign-affiliated enterprises. Moreover, if corporate governance of banks is to improve through the diversification of bank investors, it can greatly contribute to the removal of corrupt relations with specific business groups and to the sound management of banks. To strengthen the financial system for foreign-capital-led industrialization, foreign capital must be actively used not only in the real economy but also in the financial sector.

ASEAN's Future Role in International Financial Networks

In capital movements, the ASEAN economies will continue to be regarded as capital demanders for the near future. In step with their rapid growth, the savings rate in these countries has moved to a high level in recent years. If the potential growth rate continues to be high and, therefore, brisk investment also continues, the international balance of payments in these countries will continue to be on the deficit side. Southeast Asia will be regarded as a capital-deficient region in the world's capital movements, and inflows of funds from industrialized countries will continue.

Singapore and Hong Kong have functioned as international financial markets in East Asia. In the 1990s, countries in the region started to develop offshore markets, and their interest in international financial business became stronger. The key to the examination of future networks will be how to treat the impact of the entry of foreign financial institutions into the region.

First, the role of offshore markets for the purpose of preventing the direct participation of foreign financial institutions in domestic markets will be reduced with the entry of foreign institutions. The function of such offshore markets has concentrated on "foreign-to-local" transactions, a function somewhat anomalous for an offshore market. This function will diminish when the introduction of funds from abroad is liberalized. In this sense, the fact that an offshore market was never introduced in Indonesia, a country where the restriction on foreign exchange transaction was abolished early, provides food for thought.

For Hong Kong and Singapore, where markets concentrate on "overseas-to-overseas" transactions—the essential function of an offshore market—not much direct damage will be caused by the penetration of foreign financial institutions into countries in the region. If the penetration becomes more intense, however, causing the importance of interregional locations in information production to decline, the circumstances may undergo a change. Should the advantage in information production of international financial markets shift from interregional locations to the benefits of accumulation, transactions will go to outside international financial markets that are larger than Singapore or Hong Kong.

Notes

1. The surveys and studies can be grouped into two broad categories. One seeks to grasp directly the capital movements with respect to the countries in the region through statistical data. The other examines changes in financial integration by observing changes in interrelationships among interregional financial parameters.

2. There is both a push theory that the development of the financial sector induces growth of the real economy and a pull theory that the development of the real economy induces the development of the financial system.

3. Among the needed local resources are economic infrastructure, such as transport and communications facilities; social infrastructure, such as education and legislation; and supporting industries, such as parts manufacturing.

Bibliography

Asian Development Bank. 1997. *Key Indicators of Developing Asian and Pacific Countries*. Oxford: Oxford University Press.

Dai-Ichi Kangyō Research Institute. 1997. *Ajia kinyū shijō* (Financial markets in Asia). Tokyo: Tōyō Keizai Shinpō-sha.

Economic Planning Agency. 1997. *Ajia keizai 1997* (The Asian economy 1997). Tokyo: Economic Planning Agency.

Feldstein, M., and C. Horioka. 1980. "Domestic Savings and International Capital Flows." *Economic Journal* 90: 314–329.

Institute of International Monetary Affairs. 1998a. *Firipin no kinyū mondai* (Financial problems in the Philippines). Tokyo: Institute of International Monetary Affairs.

———. 1998b. *Tai no kinyū mondai* (Financial problems in Thailand). Tokyo: Institute of International Monetary Affairs.

Kobayashi Toshiyuki. 1997a. *ASEAN 4 e no shikin ryūnyū no kakudai to sono eikyō* (The expansion of financial flows to the ASEAN-4 and their impact). Research Report No. 12. Tokyo: Fuji Research Institute Corporation.

———. 1997b. *Tai no tsūka fuan hassei no yōin to sono eikyō* (The factors causing currency instability in Thailand and their impact). Research Report No. 17. Tokyo: Fuji Research Institute Corporation.

Krugman, Paul. 1994. "The Myth of Asia's Miracle." *Foreign Affairs* 73(6): 62–78.

Okuda Hidenobu. 1998. "The Role of Domestic Banks in the FDI-Led Industrialization." *EXIM Review* 18(1): 1–26.

Okuda Hidenobu and Kuroyanagi Masayoshi. 1998. *Nyūmon kaihatsu kinyū* (Introduction to development finance). Tokyo: Nihon Hyōron-sha.

Taniuchi Mitsuru. 1997. *Ajia no seichō to kinyū* (Economic growth and finance in Asia). Tokyo: Tōyō Keizai Shinpō-sha.

World Bank. 1997. *Global Development Finance 1997*. Washington, D.C.: World Bank.

– 5 –

Intraregional Trade:
Transitions and Outlook

Takeuchi Junko

TRADE among member economies of the Association of Southeast Asian Nations has increased steadily since the late 1980s. Such intraregional trade consists of traditional primary goods exports, intra-industry trade in intermediates, and materials and other goods. However, the driving force behind the expansion of intraregional trade has been intra-industry trade, which is led by investment in the electrical and electronic equipment industry. This industry, in particular, attracted large sums of direct investment from outside the region. Furthermore, the electrical and electronic equipment industry has proven highly suitable to international divisions of labor and the export promotion policies adopted by the ASEAN governments.

Intraregional Trade among the ASEAN-5
The Structure of Intraregional Trade

To indicate the share of intraregional trade among the ASEAN-5 (Indonesia, Malaysia, the Philippines, Singapore, and Thailand), I have compiled a trade matrix. The matrix, which uses exports of each country, shows that intraregional trade did not change significantly for the ASEAN-5 in the first half of the 1980s. However, the proportion of intraregional trade thereafter began a steady rise, from 17.7 percent in 1986 to 19.1 percent in 1990 and 23.2 percent in 1996. Two periods are compared in this matrix: 1986 to 1990 (the first half) and 1990 to 1996 (the second half). A comparison of average annual growth rates for nominal

Table 1. Average (Nominal) Rate of Export Growth for Selected Countries and Regions (%)

To From		NIEs	ASEAN-5	China	Japan	United States	European Union	World
NIEs	1986–1990	29.8	32.5	28.1	21.9	8.5	25.4	18.1
	1990–1996	17.1	16.5	24.0	8.3	6.1	7.9	13.9
ASEAN-5	1986–1990	26.0	23.2	19.9	16.4	19.3	25.6	21.0
	1990–1996	19.9	19.3	24.3	10.5	13.9	13.2	15.5
China	1986–1990	30.0	19.6	–	16.0	19.2	10.9	19.0
	1990–1996	7.6	14.9	–	22.3	30.9	21.2	15.7
Japan	1986–1990	15.7	28.3	−11.3	–	2.7	14.6	8.1
	1990–1996	9.8	13.9	23.5	–	3.7	1.2	6.1
United States	1986–1990	21.8	22.5	11.5	15.9	–	16.7	16.0
	1990–1996	10.3	14.6	16.4	5.6	–	3.5	8.0
European Union	1986–1990	25.4	27.5	3.6	28.5	9.0	18.7	17.0
	1990–1996	14.2	14.7	16.5	6.5	5.6	4.0	5.4
World	1986–1990	22.3	26.0	7.8	17.2	8.7	18.7	13.7
	1990–1996	12.7	15.4	21.3	8.6	8.4	4.4	7.7

Source: International Monetary Fund (annual).

trade values (in U.S. dollars) among selected regions and countries of the world indicates that in the first half the ASEAN-5 was the fastest-growing group in both exports and imports (table 1). In the second half, China supplanted the ASEAN-5 as the leader in both exports and imports, but the region's export growth rate continued on par with China's. The ASEAN-5's exports grew most sharply to the newly indus-trializing economies (NIEs) of Hong Kong, South Korea, and Taiwan in the first half and to China in the second half; imports advanced most sharply from the NIEs in the first half and intraregionally in the second half. As a result, exports to Asia—intraregional, the NIEs, and China—went from 28.6 percent of total ASEAN-5 exports in 1986 to 39.5 percent in 1996. During the same period, exports to Japan declined from 21.5 percent to 14.2 percent of the total and those to the United States from 21.2 percent to 18.5 percent.

The value of intraregional exports rose US$15.0 billion in the first half and US$49.9 billion in the second half. During both periods, more than 40 percent of the growth was due to an expansion of intraregional exports by Singapore. Directly behind Singapore was Thailand in the first half and Malaysia in the second half. The largest absorber of their expanded intraregional exports was Singapore. Indeed, most of the so-called intraregional trade was with Singapore (table 2). Thailand, Malaysia, Indonesia, and Myanmar were particularly dependent on exports

Table 2. Changes in Export Market Share

Percent of ASEAN-5	ASEAN-5 = 100%					NIEs-3	China	Japan	United States	European Union	Total Value (US$mn)
	Singapore	Thailand	Malaysia	Indonesia	Philippines						
1986											
Singapore	–	15.3	62.0	18.1	4.6	10.2	2.5	8.6	23.4	11.6	22,501
Thailand	62.7	–	30.4	4.6	2.3	8.3	3.1	14.2	18.1	22.2	8,864
Malaysia	78.1	11.9	–	1.8	8.2	9.8	1.2	23.3	16.4	14.8	13,977
Indonesia	81.9	5.5	5.4	–	7.1	6.9	0.9	44.9	19.6	9.5	14,810
Philippines	44.5	19.4	28.0	8.1	–	9.5	2.1	17.7	35.6	18.7	4,807
Brunei	39.3	47.9	8.2	0.3	4.3	9.1	0.0	66.9	6.1	0.1	1,798
Vietnam	0.0	9.5	71.4	19.0	0.0	28.4	NA	22.3	0.0	10.6	341
Myanmar	50.0	3.6	10.7	35.7	0.0	14.2	1.4	8.3	0.7	9.0	288
Laos	NA	NA	NA	NA	NA	NA	64.3	7.1	NA	NA	14
Cambodia	NA	NA	NA	NA	NA	NA	NA	NA	33.3	NA	3
1996											
Singapore	–	20.4	64.7	8.3	6.6	15.8	2.7	8.2	18.4	13.0	125,126
Thailand	65.9	–	19.7	8.3	6.2	10.2	3.4	16.8	18.0	16.0	55,743
Malaysia	74.9	15.0	–	5.7	4.4	13.0	2.4	13.4	18.2	13.7	78,246
Indonesia	63.5	11.5	15.4	–	9.6	13.1	4.1	25.8	13.6	15.3	49,914
Philippines	43.4	27.6	24.4	4.6	–	9.2	1.6	17.9	33.9	15.9	20,543
Brunei	50.5	48.3	1.0	0.2	0.0	3.2	NA	53.5	1.9	17.6	2,374
Vietnam	42.6	6.5	14.7	19.9	16.3	6.5	3.9	25.6	4.3	23.5	7,156
Myanmar	63.9	NA	12.0	10.0	14.0	7.3	10.5	7.9	8.9	8.6	1,189
Laos	1.0	99.0	0.0	0.0	NA	0.6	0.3	0.6	0.9	22.7	321
Cambodia	44.8	44.8	7.3	3.1	NA	7.0	2.0	2.0	1.3	37.2	301

Source: International Monetary Fund (annual).

Note: Includes some estimates from the statistics of trading partners. For the 1996 statistics for Myanmar, Laos, and Cambodia, the total for the four countries not marked "NA" has been deemed 100.

to Singapore. Dependence on Singapore was even more pronounced with imports. Singapore accounted for more than half of all intraregional imports from the ASEAN-4 (the ASEAN-5 excluding Singapore). Indeed, Singapore accounted for almost 80 percent of Malaysia's imports.

The contribution of Indonesia and the Philippines to the expansion of intraregional exports was small, although the degree of contribution was higher for both countries in the second half than in the first. Comparisons of the destination mix for intraregional exports in 1986 and 1996 show expansion in the shares of trading partners in mutual exports between Thailand and the Philippines, Thailand and Indonesia, and Malaysia and Indonesia. Thus, the expansion in intraregional trade during this period was mainly an increase in interdependence on the Malay Peninsula, in which Singapore served as the core. However, there were signs of more active trading among the ASEAN-4, where levels of complementation were traditionally low.

Investment-Led Expansion

In 1995, the largest item in intraregional exports was machinery and electrical equipment at 52.3 percent of the total,[1] followed by mineral fuels (9.4 percent), basic metals and metal products (5.2 percent), and chemicals (4.9 percent) (table 3). A high percentage of intraregional trade is in heavy industrial and chemical products.

To gauge the nature of trade between individual countries, the top five export categories were extracted (table 4). Thus, the high level of transactions in electrical and electronic equipment is immediately obvious. Indeed, machinery and electrical equipment accounted for more than half of intraregional exports by value. A comparison of exports and imports shows that intra-industry trade in information equipment and parts and in electronic tubes (e.g., semiconductors and cathode-ray tubes) accounted for a large proportion of the trade between Singapore and Malaysia, Singapore and Thailand, and Malaysia and Thailand. "Special trade products" (Standard International Trade Classification [SITC] 93) for the Philippines included consigned production, primarily of semiconductors, in which raw materials were imported for processing and reexport. Other than exports from Indonesia to Thailand and to the Philippines, electrical and electronic equipment was deeply entwined in all intraregional trade.

In the late 1980s, the ASEAN economies began accepting massive amounts of incoming direct investment from other countries. Most such

Table 3. Value of Intraregional Trade in 1995

HS Code	Item	CEPT Cover-age (US$mn)	Total (US$mn)	Coverage Rate (%)	Share (%)
01–05	Animals, meat, etc.	394.4	849.6	46.4	1.2
06–14	Vegetables	480.1	1,302.9	36.9	1.9
15	Animal and vegetable oils	703.6	846.5	83.1	1.2
16–24	Processed foods	934.7	1,679.7	55.6	2.4
25–27	Mineral fuels	3,390.1	6,442.8	52.6	9.4
28–38	Chemicals	2,969.7	3,347.4	88.7	4.9
39–40	Plastics	2,496.5	3,541.8	70.5	5.2
50–63	Textiles and textile products	1,938.1	2,355.3	82.3	3.4
64–67	Footwear, umbrellas, etc.	98.7	277.8	35.5	0.4
71	Gems	1,070.1	1,099.8	97.3	1.6
72–83	Basic metals and metal products	3,387.0	3,606.3	93.9	5.2
84–85	Machinery and electrical equipment	32,759.0	35,914.3	91.2	52.3
86–89	Transportation equipment	1,322.9	1,715.5	77.1	2.5
90–92	Precision equipment	1,286.5	1,326.0	97.0	1.9
	Total	56,279.7	68,720.8	81.9	100.0

Source: ASEAN Secretariat.

Note: Share figures indicate share of total trade.

HS: Harmonized Commodity Description and Coding System; CEPT: Common Effective Preferential Tariff.

investment went to the machinery sector, particularly the electrical and electronic equipment and transportation equipment industries, and the weighting of the machinery sector within the manufacturing industry grew rapidly. The export mixes of the ASEAN economies reveal a rapid decline in the share of primary products (food, fuel) from 1986 to 1996 and a rapid rise in the share of machinery. By 1996, more than 80 percent of machinery was electrical and electronic equipment in all countries (table 5).

The expansion of trade in electronic equipment on the Malay Peninsula was driven by a division of processes made possible by the supply of intermediate goods. Japan's Ministry of International Trade and Industry (MITI) conducts regular surveys of the foreign business activities of Japanese companies, and MITI (1998) indicates that the major motivation for electrical equipment manufacturers setting up operations in the ASEAN-4 was cost factors, followed by market factors, specifically, the desire to expand local sales channels or relationships with customers locally (suppliers following their Japanese customers overseas). Supplies of intermediate goods between countries in the region not only move between finished goods manufacturers and parts manufacturers but also actively trade within companies. The MITI survey breaks down sales for the Japanese electrical equipment manufacturers located in the ASEAN-4. Sales to the local market accounted for 29.4 percent of total sales in fiscal year 1995, whereas sales elsewhere in the Asian region were 20.3 percent of total sales. However, about 60 percent of sales to Asia was actually intrafirm trade between the local subsidiaries of group members. Corporate behavior and investment patterns therefore have a significant impact on intraregional trade.

The potential for intrafirm trade exists in areas other than electrical and electronic equipment. For example, the following items in table 4 could potentially be traded internally by companies: (a) automobile parts in Thailand and the Philippines and (b) vegetable oils (e.g., palm oil) in Indonesia and Malaysia. Although it is impossible to verify, the former could use the Brand-to-Brand Complementation (BBC) scheme for regional economic cooperation, whereas the latter could return products in conjunction with investments in palm cultivation by Malaysian companies.

Also significant is the trade in petroleum and primary goods (including processed goods). Rice and sugar in Thailand, crude oil in Indonesia, and crude oil and wood products in Malaysia are major intraregional export items. Singapore exports petroleum products to all of the ASEAN-4. The ASEAN-4 are increasing their petroleum refining capacity but remain dependent on refining services in Singapore, a vestige of traditional intraregional trade.

ASEAN's intraregional trade has been greatly influenced by the trade and investment policies adopted by member economies over the past 30 years. Faster countries began in the 1960s and slower countries in the 1980s to switch the focus of their industrialization strategies from import substitution to export promotion, but the region was slow to lower its tariff barriers. For example, Malaysia switched to an export-oriented policy in the early 1970s, but it did not begin to reduce import tariffs in earnest until the late 1980s. Even slower was Thailand, which into the 1990s still had average tariff rates (income from import duties divided by import values) in excess of 10 percent. Furthermore, some industries still maintain nontariff barriers in the form of local content requirements. However, countries usually waive tariff and nontariff barriers for imports of capital and intermediate goods for their export industries. Governments generally want to promote the export of manufactured goods and often create export-processing zones with exemption from import duties for export industries. As a result, intraregional trade has

Table 4. Major Trade Items of the ASEAN-5 in 1996 (%)

To From		Singapore Item	Share	Indonesia Item	Share	
Singapore	1			Petroleum products	44.1	1
	2			Hydrocarbons, etc.	4.9	2
	3			Metrology equipment	2.6	3
	4			Petroleum additives	2.6	4
	5			Telecommunications equipment	2.5	5
				Total	56.8	
Indonesia	1	Crude oil	10.0			1
	2	Gem products	9.6			2
	3	Petroleum products	6.0			3
	4	Telecommunications equipment and parts	5.8			4
	5	Tin	4.8			5
		Total	36.2			
Thailand	1	Information equipment and parts	38.0	Sugar	21.5	1
	2	Integrated circuits	7.8	Rice	15.8	2
	3	Radios and television sets	3.6	Chemicals	6.0	3
	4	Motors, etc.	3.1	Videocassette recorders and parts	3.4	4
	5	Rice	2.0	Petrochemicals	2.8	5
		Total	54.5	Total	49.4	
Malaysia	1	Electronic tubes	23.2	Crude oil	8.9	1
	2	Parts for information and office equipment	11.2	Aircraft parts	8.4	2
	3	Telecommunications equipment and parts	7.5	Electronic tubes	8.2	3
	4	Electrical equipment and parts	4.3	Air conditioners and parts	4.1	4
	5	Petroleum products	2.6	Vegetable oils	3.9	5
		Total	48.8	Total	33.4	
Philippines	1	Special trade products	41.3	Vegetable oils	30.3	1
	2	Electrical equipment and parts	37.1	Chemical fertilizers	16.9	2
	3	Petroleum and petroleum products	3.3	Automobiles and parts	8.5	3
	4	Telecommunications and audio equipment	2.9	Special trade products	8.5	4
	5	Office and information equipment	2.0	Vegetables and fruits	2.8	5
		Total	86.6	Total	66.9	

Source: Compiled from trade statistics of individual countries.

Note: Compiled from exporting country statistics. However, Singaporean exports to Indonesia were compiled from Indonesian import statistics. For the Philippines, SITC 2-digit titles were used; for Singapore, Indonesia, and Malaysia, SITC 3-digit

Thailand

Item	Share
Electronic tubes	12.8
Petroleum products	10.5
Office equipment	9.3
Telecommunications equipment	6.9
Parts for information and office equipment	5.1
Total	44.6
Crude oil	14.7
Frozen fish	13.1
Petroleum products	5.8
Ships	4.0
Fiber	3.2
Total	40.8
Crude oil	26.8
Parts for information and office equipment	15.4
Electronic tubes	10.9
Railroad ties and other wood products	10.0
Telecommunications equipment	2.4
Total	65.5
Special trade products	76.2
Automobiles and parts	8.1
Nonferrous metals	3.6
Electrical equipment and parts	1.9
Lumber	1.8
Total	91.5

Malaysia

Item	Share
Electronic tubes	21.4
Telecommunications equipment	8.1
Petroleum products	6.0
Electrical circuits	5.0
Electrical equipment	4.8
Total	45.3
Vegetable oils	8.1
Parts for information and office equipment	7.6
Paper and cardboard	7.1
Coal	5.9
Unprocessed metal sheets	3.9
Total	32.5
Information equipment and parts	15.3
Rice	8.7
Rubber	7.6
Integrated circuits	5.9
Sugar	4.6
Total	42.1
Special trade products	80.1
Electrical equipment and parts	6.7
Office and information equipment	1.3
Raw rubber	1.2
Natural gas	1.0
Total	90.2

Philippines

Item	Share
Electronic tubes	13.8
Parts for information and office equipment	8.9
Telecommunications equipment	5.4
Petroleum products	4.8
Information equipment	4.6
Total	37.5
Copper	32.4
Coal	8.7
Inorganic chemicals	7.0
Crude oil	4.8
Chemical fertilizer	4.4
Total	57.3
Sugar	13.5
Rice	7.7
Information equipment and parts	6.4
Automobile parts	4.4
Plastics	3.3
Total	35.2
Electronic tubes	17.3
Railroad ties and other wood products	8.0
Crude oil	7.3
Minerals	3.8
Plywood	3.1
Total	39.5

titles. In all cases, the top five items were selected. Thai statistics do not note the digit of titles. Share means item's share to total exports.

Table 5. Changes in Export Structures (%)

SITC		Singapore		Thailand		Malaysia		Indonesia		Philippines	
		1986	1996	1986	1996	1986	1996	1986	1996	1986	1996
0	Foods	5.4	1.8	43.3	18.9	5.5	2.4	12.0	7.6	18.1	6.8
3	Fuels	20.7	7.9	0.8	0.7	22.8	7.9	56.1	25.8	1.4	1.9
5	Chemicals	5.8	5.5	1.6	3.8	1.7	3.2	1.8	3.5	5.0	1.7
6	Basic manufactures	7.4	5.7	16.3	11.9	7.2	9.4	13.4	21.9	9.0	6.3
7	Machines	38.6	65.9	10.9	33.6	25.2	55.3	0.4	10.0	8.9	56.6
	Electrical machinery*	29.7	57.4	8.7	26.7	21.8	49.2	0.1	7.9	7.8	53.5
8	Miscellaneous manu-										
	factured goods	8.3	7.5	16.6	24.0	5.0	9.0	4.6	17.3	12.1	20.0
9	Unclassified	6.4	2.8	0.9	1.0	0.3	1.1	0.2	0.2	27.0	1.1
Share of manufactured goods											
	to total export	66.4	87.4	46.3	74.3	39.4	78.0	20.4	52.8	62.1	85.6

Source: U.N. trade statistics.

*Total of SITC 75, 76, and 77.

grown tremendously in those export industries that have avoided barriers. The expansion of intraregional trade since the late 1980s was in
large part due to the growth of the electrical and electronic equipment
industry in the ASEAN economies as export industries took advantage
of this business environment.

However, the same trend has not been observed in all export-processing-zone industries. Intraregional trade is lackluster in another typical
example of an export-processing-zone industry: apparel. There could be
several reasons for this. First, the production process for apparel is short
so there is limited opportunity to divide processes between countries.
Second, the region relies heavily on extraregional textile suppliers, such
as Italy, Japan, South Korea, and Taiwan, because most apparel industries
in the ASEAN economies are supported by demand from the developed
countries, and this usually takes the form of licensed production or consignment processing. In such transactions, the buyer specifies the intermediates to be used in production.

Third, weak midstream (cloth) sectors are a problem shared by all the
ASEAN economies. For example, some analysts have pointed to the in-
ability of Thailand to provide stable supplies of quality cloth to export
manufacturers as the reason for the competitive decline of its apparel industry (Suehiro 1998, 181). Among the many factors behind the failure
of the midstream sector to develop are the technical challenges posed
by dyeing and the linkage between the upstream and downstream sectors. Fourth, the fierce competition in apparel exports makes growth

difficult for intraregional and domestic textile suppliers. The onslaught from China, Vietnam, and others has forced the ASEAN-4 to turn to higher-priced segments of the apparel market, but the higher the price of the finished product the better the intermediates required. On the other hand, the forerunner countries in textile exports are expanding the gaps in nonprice competition by using innovative technologies and refined production systems to provide small-lot/high-variety production, shorter delivery times, and better quality and color.

Outlook for Intraregional Trade
Intraregional Trade Liberalization

An ASEAN summit meeting held in Hanoi in December 1998 adopted an emergency economic program, part of which called for the ASEAN-6 (the ASEAN-5 plus Brunei) to accelerate the reduction of intraregional tariffs so that 90 percent of the items covered by the CEPT (Common Effective Preferential Tariff) scheme would have tariffs between zero and 5 percent by the year 2000. Relative to the tariff-rate goals for the year 2003 that countries had already submitted, the new goal requires the greatest concessions from Thailand (which has the fewest goods exempted from tariff reductions) and Indonesia. Reductions will be needed faster than originally scheduled for processed foods (HS [Harmonized Commodity Description and Coding System] 16–24) and footwear (HS 64–67) among manufactured goods, and also for unprocessed agricultural goods.

The CEPT coverage rate is the percentage of a given product area accounted for by the trade value of CEPT-eligible goods as found on the lists of tariff reductions submitted by a country. Coverage rates are highest for gems, precision equipment, metals, and machinery and electrical equipment, and lowest for footwear and umbrellas, vegetables, and animals and meat[2] (table 3). The Asian recession will make it more difficult to reach the tariff reduction targets agreed to at the summit, but should the target reductions be realized there would be three major changes.

The first would be an expansion in exports of goods that are major exports of individual countries but are not exported in large quantities to other countries in the region, such as apparel, food, furniture, footwear, and other light industrial goods. These are industries in which each country has a degree of competitiveness. However, in the apparel and footwear industries, for example, there are (a) companies that are promoted as export-oriented and therefore able to sell only a limited percentage of their output in the domestic market and (b) companies that specialize in serving the domestic market. If tariff and nontariff barriers are lowered but no changes made to this structure, the export companies will be unable to increase their sales to the domestic market but will be able to export to neighboring countries. When the Thai economy was booming, its retail sector had what was essentially a mismatch in supply and demand for apparel, which some analysts believe inflicted opportunity costs (Takeuchi 1995, 225) because manufacturers were unable to fully anticipate the rise in the level of products demanded by consumers. The economy may be in a slump now, but consumer tastes have grown more sophisticated, and it seems obvious what the impact will be if products made to international export standards are allowed on the market. If countries tolerate this situation, the companies serving the domestic market will fall by the wayside not because of domestic competition but because of competition from imports.

The second change would be in the industries in which intra-industry trade develops. As in the electrical and electronic equipment versus apparel industries, the division of labor depends on the nature of the manufacturing process and the specific character of the industry. Intraregional trade will not expand even with low tariffs if there are no strong substitutes available in the region. The industry with the greatest potential for expansion in intraregional trade is the assembly industry, and within it, the automotive industry, which has been forced by industrial policies to establish multiple bases of operation within the region.

Automobile sales volumes have been in decline throughout the region since the currency crisis. In the fourth quarter of 1998, Thailand and Malaysia showed signs of a slight rebound, but more time will be required before sales return to their peak 1996 levels. There is, undoubtedly, a strong latent demand among manufacturers with several bases of operation in the region to concentrate their production to improve capacity utilization rates. Meanwhile, parts manufacturers are attempting to export part of their products to counter the contraction of local markets and in the process are gaining more expertise in serving export markets. Reductions in tariff and nontariff barriers will greatly encourage these trends.

Third would be the potential for expanded exports of chemicals, steel, and other materials. The materials industry in the region has made steady increases in capacity during the 1990s, though many of these

Table 6. Overview of Trade for Individual Countries

	Vietnam	Myanmar	Cambodia
Export value (US$billion)	7.26	0.89	0.86
Import value (US$billion)	11.14	1.92	1.19
Export by SITC section (%)			
Food	33.4	51.3	NA
Beverages	0.1	0.0	
Crude materials	6.9	30.2	
Fuel	21.7	0.6	
Animal and vegetable oils	0.5	0.0	
Chemicals	0.9	0.0	
Basic manufactures	5.3	6.4	
Machines	5.7	1.0	
Miscellaneous manufactured goods	25.5	6.5	
Unclassified	0.1	4.0	
Major export items (US$million)	Rice (855)	Timber (193)	Rubber (41)
	Coffee (420)	Beans (214)	Timber (187)
	Frozen shrimp (325)	Rice (21)	

Source: Asian Development Bank (annual).

Note: Data based on the 1995 calendar year except Myanmar, which is based on the 1995–1996 fiscal year.

projects are not yet fully operational. Although some chemical and metal products are in the top ranks of intraregional exports, many more might supplant extraregional products, at least in part, if they were to achieve appropriate price levels. Such an opening is exactly what is required to boost capacity utilization rates. These areas would likely enjoy the benefits of intraregional liberalization in advance of full liberalization.

Trade Relations with the New ASEAN Members

Although the scale of new members' trade is small (table 6), new members' entry into ASEAN adds another dimension to intraregional trade. The current trade structures of new members Vietnam, Myanmar, and Cambodia[3] are reviewed below.

VIETNAM   The start-up of full-fledged oil production in the 1990s led to a rise in the export value of mineral fuels. In 1995, this sector accounted for 21.7 percent of exports and was Vietnam's largest export item. Vietnam has no domestic refining capacity, so all oil is exported as crude oil and some is reimported as petroleum products for the domestic market. The manufactured goods export rate climbed from 29.2 percent in 1986 to 37.5 percent in 1995, about 70 percent of which was accounted for by "miscellaneous manufactured goods" (SITC 8), mostly apparel

and other light industrial products. Major primary goods exports included rice (11.8 percent of total exports), coffee (5.8 percent), and
shrimp (4.5 percent). Over the past decade, rice exports rose sharply with
a corresponding increase in share, whereas exports of shrimp sagged and
the share declined steadily.

In 1996, Vietnam's largest trading partners were Japan (25.6 percent), the European Union (23.5 percent), and the ASEAN-5 (13.0 percent). Among the ASEAN-5, Singapore was the largest trading partner at
5 percent. Singapore indicates that 42.4 percent of its imports from
Vietnam were of crude oil. Vietnam's dependence on intraregional trade
increased markedly in the late 1980s. From 1986 to 1990, Vietnam's share
of intraregional trade rose from 6.2 percent to 12.8 percent. Growth has
slowed since then, however, and Vietnam has the loosest trade relations
of any new ASEAN member with the rest of the region. Vietnam imported primarily from the ASEAN-5 (23.2 percent), the European Union
(13.0 percent), and South Korea (12.9%). More than half of all imports
from the ASEAN-5 came from Singapore, and about 30 percent of those
were of petroleum products, indicating that Vietnam uses Singapore as
a consignment refiner.

MYANMAR   According to Myanmar's trade statistics, food, primarily
rice, accounted for 51.3 percent of total exports in fiscal 1995–1996, followed by raw materials, primarily timber, at 30.2 percent. The bulk of
Myanmar's rice was exported to Asia and Africa, mostly in spot trading,
which results in large fluctuations in the destination breakdown from
year to year. In fiscal 1988–1989,[4] about 60 percent of rice exports was to
Africa, but in fiscal 1995–1996 about 70 percent was to the ASEAN region. Manufactured goods accounted for a low 17.9 percent of exports
in fiscal 1995–1996.

Myanmar's trading partner statistics[5] show Myanmar's clear trend
away from China in favor of the ASEAN economies for both imports
and exports since fiscal 1988–1989. A comparison of fiscal 1995–1996
against fiscal 1988–1989 shows that exports to China fell from 43.5 percent to 3.9 percent of the total, whereas exports to the ASEAN economies rose from 17.2 percent to 42.0 percent. For imports, China's share
fell from 27.0 percent to 13.9 percent, whereas ASEAN's rose from 11.0
percent to 40.0 percent. In fiscal 1995–1996, timber accounted for about
30 percent of intraregional exports and rice about 15 percent.

CAMBODIA[6]   Timber exports have expanded in the 1990s, accounting for 21.7 percent of total exports in 1995. In addition, the absolute value of rubber exports continues to rise, but the pace is slowing, and in 1995 rubber accounted for only 4.8 percent of exports. The manufactured goods export rate is unclear, but the total of the 1995 export values for the 17 apparel manufacturers listed in the *Cambodia Business and Investment Handbook 1996* (Ministry of Commerce, Cambodia) was equivalent to 3.1 percent of the year's exports. Although still frail, processing-style export industries are beginning to develop. Cambodia's exports in 1996 were primarily to the European Union (37.2 percent) and intraregional trade (31.9 percent) (table 2). The top intraregional trading partners were Singapore and Thailand, each with 14.3 percent of overall exports.

Myanmar and Cambodia currently serve as the timber suppliers to the ASEAN-5, and there is little threat to the ASEAN-5 in opening their markets to them. On the other hand, the absolute values involved are small when these countries are viewed as export markets. They do look favorable as future markets for final consumer goods because they are located close to the region, have similar lifestyles, have low penetration levels for durable goods, and do not have any strong consumer goods manufacturers of their own. However, any growth in this market depends on the emergence of a consumer class with stable jobs and income, and that seems unlikely over the short term. If anything, when infrastructure development gears up, these countries could serve as absorbers of cement, steel, and other materials for which the ASEAN economies have excess capacity.

Conclusion

Intraregional trade has expanded from a core of Singapore and Malaysia, both of which are major producers of electronic parts, to Thailand, the Philippines, and Indonesia, and the percentage of intraregional trade has risen. However, this expansion does not mean that the region is any less dependent on outside demand. Several surveys taken since the currency crisis (e.g., see Inoue 1998; Tejima 1998; Japan External Trade Organization 1998)[7] indicate that the effects on the electrical and electronic equipment industry—the driving force behind intraregional trade —of the slump in intraregional demand caused by the currency crisis have been relatively slight; indeed, the industry could benefit from falling foreign exchange rates. Thus, intraregional trade is large at the level of parts, but the region still depends on outside markets for sales of the finished goods that incorporate these parts.

Notes

1. The data for this section came from the Web site of the ASEAN Secretariat; therefore, intraregional trade includes the ASEAN-6 (the ASEAN-5 plus Brunei). I have used data for 1995 because, unlike 1996, there were clear trade values listed for Common Effective Preferential Tariff (CEPT) scheme items. The breakdown of trade did not change significantly in 1996.

2. At the 1994 meeting of economic ministers, it was agreed to apply the CEPT scheme to vegetables, meat, and other unprocessed agricultural products, setting 2003 as the deadline for removing exemptions for specific products, which is somewhat later than the deadline for industrial goods.

3. The limitations of the data used must be underscored. The basic data for trade results and destinations came from the International Monetary Fund's (IMF's) *Direction of Trade Statistics,* and for the goods mix from the Asian Development Bank's (ADB's) *Key Indicators.* Where local statistics were available, local figures were compared against the IMF/ADB figures and if the gaps between the two were large or if a breakdown of trade by trading partner and item was available, the local statistics were used as well. Any discussion of Laos is omitted owing to the absence of adequate trade data.

4. The data begins with fiscal 1988–1989 because that was the period when border trade began to be included in trade statistics.

5. Trading partner statistics were basically drawn from IMF data, but large gaps existed between the IMF's statistics and Myanmar's own reporting on its trading partners; therefore, Myanmar's statistics were used for data on that country (see table 2 for the IMF data).

6. There is little in the way of item-by-item breakdowns available for Cambodian trade. Even the ADB's *Key Indicators* (1998) provides only export trends for rubber and lumber.

7. All of these surveys cover only Japanese companies, but they are referred to because of the enormous presence that Japanese companies have in the electrical and electronic equipment industry in the ASEAN economies.

Bibliography

Asian Development Bank. Annual. *Key Indicators of Developing Asian and Pacific Countries.* Oxford, U.K.: Oxford University Press.
Inoue Kazuko. 1998. "Higashi Ajia kinkyū ankēto (2)" (Emergency survey of

East Asia 2). *The Compass* (August). Published by the Mitsui Trade Research Center.

International Monetary Fund. Annual. *Direction of Trade Statistics.* Washington, D.C.: International Monetary Fund.

Japan External Trade Organization (JETRO). 1998. "Ajia tsūka kiki no genchi Nihon kigyō ni ataeta eikyō" (Impact of the Asian currency crisis on local Japanese companies). Press release, August 1998, JETRO, Tokyo.

Ministry of International Trade and Industry (MITI). 1998. *Dai 26 kai waga koku kigyō no kaigai jigyō katsudō* (26th survey of overseas business activities by Japanese companies). Tokyo: Ministry of Finance, Printing Bureau.

Suehiro Akira, ed. 1998. *Tai keizai būmu, keizai kiki, kōzō chōsei* (Boom, crisis, and structural adjustment in the Thai economy). Tokyo: Japan Thailand Association.

Takeuchi Junko. 1995. "Ajia shijō no tenbō" (Outlook for Asian markets). Sakura Institute of Research, ed. *Shinseiki Ajia no sangyō o yomu* (Reading Asian industry in the new century). Tokyo: Diamond, Inc.

Tejima Shigeki. 1998. "Ajia kiki ga Nihon no chokusetsu tōshi ni ataeru eikyō" (The impact on Japanese direct investment of the Asian crisis). *Kaigai tōshi kenkyūjo hō* (Journal of overseas investment) (September/October). Published by the Export-Import Bank of Japan.

– 6 –
Foreign Direct Investment and Economic Cooperation

Takeuchi Junko

FOREIGN DIRECT INVESTMENT (FDI) has become increasingly important to the Association of Southeast Asian Nations economies[1] on two levels. The first is the FDI that flows *into* those economies. Massive investment inflows since the late 1980s have changed ASEAN's industrial structures and made a major contribution to the growth of the region's export-oriented industries. Today, however, the ASEAN economies are experiencing a slowdown in the growth of their labor-intensive export industries and will be forced to modify their industrial structures. FDI plays a vital role in the development of more sophisticated industrial structures. The focus of inward foreign investment policies in the region is to attract investment into high-value-added industries to expand those industries.

The second level is the direct overseas investment *from* the ASEAN economies. Since the early 1990s, rapid increases in investment into other economies have come from Singapore, Malaysia, and Thailand. They have become major investors both within ASEAN and in the Indochinese economies. This trend reflects the expansion of domestic enterprises in a high-growth environment and the creation of business opportunities as regulations loosen in recipient countries.

ASEAN is moving toward regional economic integration through trade and investment liberalization. One aim of this process is to attract a continuing inflow of FDI by offering the prospect of a single market with a population of approximately 480 million people. Another goal is to implement regional trade liberalization ahead of the World Trade Organization (WTO) and the Asia-Pacific Economic Cooperation (APEC) forum so that regional industries can achieve coordination and enhance their competitiveness against industries in other regions.

This chapter will

- ascertain the characteristics of FDI inflows and the subsequent changes in industrial structures since the late 1980s.
- argue that the ASEAN economies have reached turning points in the 1990s from the perspectives of competition with China in trade and investment, and the role of the ASEAN economies themselves as exporters of capital.
- consider the economic significance of changes in the nature of ASEAN as a regional community in terms of moves toward economic integration and the emergence of an expanded ASEAN.
- examine the relationship between economic integration and direct investment in ASEAN on the basis of the preceding analyses.

FDI and Changes in the Regional Economy
Direct Investment Inflows in ASEAN

Since the late 1980s, FDI has flowed into the ASEAN economies on an unprecedented scale. With the exception of Singapore, which has registered constant growth in its direct investment inflows, the other economies can be divided into two groups, defined by the amounts of foreign investment approved. The leading group in terms of foreign investment received consists of Thailand and Malaysia. Investment flowing into these two economies began to expand conspicuously during the late 1980s and peaked in 1990. Investment expanded again in 1994–1995, forming a second peak. The second group, the late starters, consists of Indonesia and the Philippines. The expansion of investment in these economies was gradual during the late 1980s, but there has been a dramatic increase since 1994.

The 1985 Plaza Accord triggered a significant rise in the value of the yen. This caused a rapid increase in overseas expansion by Japanese companies, many of which began to expand dramatically into the other Asian economies. The recipient countries, in turn, began to promote manufactured exports as a way of earning foreign currency. They also worked to improve their investment environments by easing regulations and enhancing incentives. Having experienced a recession of unprecedented severity in 1985–1986, the ASEAN economies began to make significant moves toward structural adjustments.

These efforts exhibited two common features. First, regulations were eased with the aim of achieving economic growth led by the private sector. Second, there was an increasing tendency to look outward, the manifestations of which included export promotion and the introduction of foreign investment. However, there was some variation in the timing and extent of these measures. Aspects of the basic investment environment, such as the state of infrastructure and the political situation, have a key influence on investment decisions. Decisions also appear to have been influenced by the timing of deregulation and by moves to provide an environment in which business would enjoy a high degree of freedom.

In the leading group, Thailand enhanced its investment incentives in 1983, including exemption from foreign ownership restrictions for investment in export and labor-intensive industries. The devaluation of the baht in 1984 accelerated export-oriented industrialization, which had previously been approached half-heartedly.[2] Similarly, Malaysia passed the Investment Promotion Act in 1986 and eased restrictions on the ownership of companies that were contributing to exports or employment. It also enhanced incentives, including the extension of periods of exemption from corporate tax. The easing of ownership restrictions was a bold move for Malaysia, where the need to correct economic gaps between ethnic groups has made the ownership of businesses, including ownership by domestic capital, a sensitive issue.

Since 1986, Indonesia has implemented policy packages that have included continuing tariff reductions and the easing of restrictions on foreign investment. Two measures in particular appear to have contributed to the improvement of Indonesia's investment environment. First, in the 1989 package, Indonesia reduced the number of sectors in which participation was restricted by switching from a positive list to a negative list of industries subject to restrictions on investment and participation. Second, in the 1994 package, Indonesia liberalized the mode of operations by foreign capital and eased capital localization regulations.[3] The easing of restrictions concerning equity ownership ratios has implications for management control, considered by many to be the most basic aspect of business management. Changes in this area have an even greater influence on foreign investment decisions than do tax holidays or other incentives.

From 1983, the Philippines faced a period of political instability, natural disasters, and other problems; much time was required before it could return to a growth path. In 1991, it passed the Foreign Investment Act, enhanced investment incentives, and stepped up efforts to promote exports. However, views of the Philippine investment environment did not consistently improve until the inauguration of the Ramos administration in 1992. In 1994, regulations were loosened through amendments to the Foreign Investment Act, and an electric power shortage was overcome. These and other changes appear to have brought the Philippines up to the same level as its neighbors in terms of investment environments (see Takeuchi 1995a).

In the 1990s, perceived shortages of labor and infrastructure due to concentrated investment inflows have caused production environments in the leading group to deteriorate due to wage rises and other factors. Inflows of investment began to slow or even decline after 1991, in part because of increased selectivity toward foreign investment on the part of host governments. This was one factor that caused the flow of investment to shift toward Indonesia and the Philippines.

The first prominent feature of foreign investment inflows from 1986 to 1996 was the possibility of maintaining high levels of investment over the long term, thanks to the expansion of investment by the newly industrializing economies (NIEs)—South Korea, Taiwan, Hong Kong—and to the emergence of new sources of investment to replace the old. When the yen first began to strengthen, South Korea and Taiwan enjoyed rapid export growth due to improvements in the relative competitiveness of their products. After 1987, however, the export environment of those countries started to deteriorate because of external trade friction and a variety of domestic factors, including rising wage levels. Currency values rose markedly in 1988 and 1989, and a sharp rise in overseas investment occurred as companies, like their Japanese counterparts, began to adjust their overseas and domestic production activities. Production of highly labor-intensive items, such as apparel, footwear, and electronic goods, was shifted to the ASEAN economies.

An analysis of investment in the ASEAN economies by source shows that the countries in which investment from the NIEs accounted for the biggest shares of total cumulative investment from 1986 to 1996 were Indonesia, Malaysia, and the Philippines (table 1). However, if the investment boom that brought massive inflows of foreign investment is divided into early (1986–1990) and late (1991–1996) phases, we find

Table 1. Approved Foreign Direct Investment by Country and Region (%)

		Japan	United States	European Union	NIEs-3	ASEAN-5	Others	Total
Indonesia	1986–1990	14.9	5.1	13.9	17.8	3.2	45.1	100.0
	1991–1996	13.5	5.0	17.4	17.6	10.8	35.6	100.0
	1986–1996	13.8	5.0	16.8	17.7	9.4	37.4	100.0
Malaysia	1986–1990	25.6	4.7	7.2	33.2	11.2	18.0	100.0
	1991–1996	21.0	16.4	4.9	20.8	14.1	22.8	100.0
	1986–1996	22.4	12.9	5.6	24.5	13.3	21.3	100.0
Philippines	1986–1990	25.4	16.5	9.3	35.6	2.5	10.8	100.0
	1991–1996	14.9	21.1	13.1	16.5	12.0	22.3	100.0
	1986–1996	17.5	19.9	12.2	21.2	9.7	19.4	100.0
Singapore	1986–1990	37.0	38.9	21.1	NA	NA	2.9	100.0
	1991–1996	27.5	44.7	26.8	NA	NA	1.1	100.0
	1986–1996	29.5	43.5	25.6	NA	NA	1.5	100.0
Thailand	1986–1990	32.4	8.0	14.0	35.4	6.0	4.3	100.0
	1991–1996	35.6	14.9	18.1	15.4	9.5	5.1	100.0
	1986–1996	34.5	12.6	16.7	22.2	9.2	4.8	100.0

Source: Compiled from data of investment agencies of each country.

Note: Investment figures are paid-up capital + loans. Figures for Singapore and Malaysia include only investment in the manufacturing sector.
NIEs-3: Hong Kong, South Korea, and Taiwan.

that the contribution from the NIEs declined during the late phase. Figures for Japan, which was the first to expand its investment in ASEAN, show a similar pattern. The deceleration of investment from the NIEs and Japan has been offset by increased investment from the United States and Europe and from within the region (the ASEAN-5). Inflows from Europe and the United States have been characterized by massive investment in the chemical sector. With a few exceptions, a sharp increase in the shares of the United States and Europe in investment inflows into the ASEAN economies was observed.

A second feature is the high percentage of investment in heavy and chemical industries, especially during the late phase (table 2).[4] In Indonesia and the Philippines, there has been a significant decline in the percentage of investment channeled into light industries. The downtrend is especially dramatic in textiles. The distribution of investment among the heavy and chemical industries varies from country to country, but the concentration of investment in the petroleum, chemical, and machinery sectors has been a common pattern.

The order of foreign investment inflows can be summed up simply. During the first stage, there was increased investment in industrial

Table 2. Approved Foreign Direct Investment by Sector (%)

		Light Industries			Heavy Industries			Total
		Total	Food	Textiles	Total	Chemical	Machinery	
Indonesia	1986–1990	39.8	3.2	16.8	60.2	42.3	7.6	100.0
	1991–1996	30.6	5.3	3.9	69.4	52.0	12.7	100.0
	1986–1996	31.7	5.1	5.4	68.3	50.9	12.1	100.0
Malaysia	1986–1990	33.2	6.8	4.1	66.8	9.8	20.0	100.0
	1991–1996	30.4	2.3	3.4	69.6	11.2	24.8	100.0
	1986–1996	31.2	3.5	3.6	68.8	10.8	24.0	100.0
Philippines	1986–1990	46.9	3.4	29.2	53.1	12.4	22.0	100.0
	1991–1996	11.1	2.4	3.4	88.9	33.0	11.5	100.0
	1986–1996	17.9	2.6	8.0	82.1	29.3	13.5	100.0
Singapore	1986–1990	14.0	5.0	0.3	86.0	9.5	60.1	100.0
	1991–1996	9.0	1.9	0.2	91.0	25.3	50.7	100.0
	1986–1996	10.2	2.6	0.2	89.8	21.6	52.9	100.0
Thailand	1986–1990	31.2	7.1	6.1	68.8	12.6	42.1	100.0
	1991–1996	30.2	7.8	6.1	69.8	20.6	48.6	100.0
	1986–1996	30.7	7.5	6.1	69.3	16.9	45.6	100.0

Source: Compiled from data of investment agencies of each country and the Bank of Thailand.

Note: Investment figures for Singapore include local investment; figures for Thailand are based on net inflows; figures for Indonesia exclude oil and gas.

adjustment with a view toward exporting. The main targets for investment at this stage were light industries and processing/assembly industries, such as electronics. By the second stage, export-oriented businesses were already operating successfully, and investment began to focus on the siting of production nearer to markets with a view toward sales at home or in neighboring countries. This shift reflected the expansion of domestic markets for consumer goods due to export-driven economic growth and the growth of markets for intermediate goods due to production expansion in export industries. The latter trend was especially significant because the expansion of domestic markets to a certain scale brought an upsurge of investment in facility-intensive industries, which had achieved the minimal appropriate scale of production.

This pattern was typified in the petrochemical industry. Work began on a series of major projects in the 1990s, and a sharp increase in the chemical sector's share of cumulative investment approvals[5] in the late phase was observed. During this phase, production of ethylene, the upstream part of the petrochemical industry, began in Malaysia and Indonesia. In Thailand, too, approvals were obtained for several private-sector ethylene projects.[6]

A third feature is the prevalence of projects with high export ratios. In Indonesia, the percentage of export-oriented projects (projects with export ratios of 65 percent or higher) rose from 31.2 percent in 1987 to 72.4 percent in 1988. The percentage of export-oriented projects continued to rise, reaching 78.7 percent in 1987–1990 and 82.1 percent in cumulative terms in 1991–1996. In Malaysia, the ratio of export-oriented projects (projects with export ratios of 80 percent or higher) increased

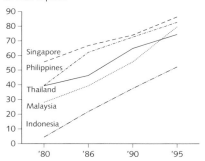

Figure 1. Change in Ratio of Manufactured Goods to Total Exports

Source: Asian Development Bank.
Note: "Manufactured goods" are the sum of SITC (Standard International Trade Classification) 5–9.

from 29.3 percent in 1986 to 51.7 percent in 1987. In cumulative terms, the ratios were 18.4 percent in 1982–1985 and 64.4 percent in 1986–1990. These increases are indicative of a shift in investment toward export-oriented projects. However, in 1991 the ratio fell to 46.7 percent. As with sector trends, this appears to indicate increased investment in the siting of production operations close to markets.[7] In Thailand also, the ratio of export-oriented projects (projects with export ratios of 80 percent or higher) decreased from 68.6 percent in 1986–1990 to 30.5 percent in 1991–1996 in cumulative terms, but over the total period the ratio was higher than 50 percent. In all the economies surveyed, a conspicuous increase in the ratio of manufactured exports can be seen since the late 1980s (fig. 1).

Changes in Industrial Structures

These trends in foreign investment inflows from 1986 to 1996 indicate that the influence of foreign investment on investment activity has strengthened in many economies. Foreign investment accounted for only 24.4 percent of cumulative total investment approvals in Indonesia from 1986 to 1996, but ratios for other economies were much higher: 77.3 percent for Singapore, 69.1 percent for Thailand, and 57.6 percent for Malaysia.[8] Even the Philippines registered a figure of 37.7 percent. Some investments are not included in statistics prepared by investment approval agencies, but it appears that the manufacturing sector, especially industries targeted for promotion by governments, have captured

Table 3. Structural Changes in the Manufacturing Industries (%)

		Light Industries		Heavy Industries				
		Total	Food	Total	Machinery			
					Total	Machinery	Electronics	Transport
Indonesia	1986	61.7	26.3	38.3	14.0	0.8	3.0	6.1
	1990	60.9	27.5	39.1	14.8	1.3	3.0	7.6
	1994	57.6	20.2	42.4	20.3	1.3	4.0	11.4
Malaysia	1986	46.9	20.6	53.1	23.9	2.1	15.3	2.9
	1990	39.7	13.2	60.3	35.3	3.8	21.5	5.4
	1994	34.1	9.3	65.9	39.4	4.8	29.8	4.8
Philippines	1986	58.1	41.7	41.9	7.9	0.8	4.7	1.0
	1990	63.9	38.8	36.1	14.5	0.9	8.7	2.9
	1994	59.2	34.7	40.8	16.6	1.0	9.5	4.2
Singapore	1986	19.5	5.7	80.5	52.5	6.3	35.8	8.5
	1990	17.5	4.4	82.5	54.8	5.9	39.8	7.5
	1994	15.4	4.1	84.6	59.5	26.3	24.1	7.2
Thailand	1986	66.9	26.0	33.1	12.6	2.4	3.0	4.6
	1990	60.7	19.1	39.3	23.4	5.2	5.8	9.9
	1994	51.4	18.9	48.6	23.2	6.6	8.8	7.8

Source: Compiled from the *National Accountant of Thailand* and industrial statistics of each country.
Note: Data on a value-added basis.

a significant share of investment. These trends in foreign investment thus seem to have had a considerable influence on the progress of industrialization and on changes in industrial structures during this period.

One change in industrial structures over the past ten years or so has been the growing importance of heavy and chemical industries, and especially the machinery industries, in the manufacturing sector. This pattern has occurred in all the economies surveyed, albeit to differing degrees (table 3).

Contributions to growth within the machinery sector vary somewhat from country to country. In some cases, growth has been led by the transportation equipment sector, especially the automobile industry, due to the expansion of domestic markets, whereas in other cases the main contributor has been the electronics industry, in which growth has been driven by exports. The machinery industry should also be included among industries that have achieved export-led growth, as evidenced by the increasing contribution within that sector from data processing equipment, such as computers and computer peripherals, which have high export ratios.

The contribution of the electronics industry to the growth of the machinery sector since 1986 has been high in Malaysia and the Philippines: around 70 percent and 60 percent, respectively; Indonesia's transportation equipment industry has contributed almost 70 percent. In Thailand, the electronics and transportation equipment industries have each contributed close to 40 percent, but the machinery industry has also made a significant contribution of more than 20 percent. In Singapore, the machinery industry has contributed 60 percent, and the electronics industry slightly more than 20 percent. Moreover, the major contributor within the transportation equipment sector in that country has been the shipbuilding and repair industry, not the automobile industry. Here, too, a close linkage with external demand is evident. In all the economies surveyed except Indonesia, it would be reasonable to conclude that the growth of exports played a major role in the expansion of the machinery sector.

There have also been changes in comparative advantages. This can be analyzed by the revealed comparative advantage (RCA) index, which is calculated by dividing the percentage contribution of a specific item to a country's exports by the contribution of the same item to world exports. If the RCA index is greater than 1.0, a comparative advantage exists; the higher the index, the greater the comparative advantage.[9]

One characteristic trend has been the proliferation and leveling of comparative advantage industries. A comparison of the numbers of comparative advantage industries in each economy in 1986 and 1995 shows a marked increase in all countries except Singapore (table 4). In general, when industries in each country are shown on a graph in ascending order of RCA indices, the curve tends to level out in step with progress toward industrialization (Japan External Trade Organization [JETRO] 1989, 90–98). A shallow curve indicates that the country has a balanced industrial structure and has achieved mature industrialization. This is because industrialization in its early stages is limited to industries that produce exportable manufactured goods, and production factors tend to be concentrated in comparative advantage industries. As industrialization proceeded, however, interindustry linkages began to form, leading to the correction of gaps between industries. When RCA indices for 1986, 1990, and 1995 are compared in this way, it becomes apparent that the graph curves for all the economies surveyed except Indonesia have rapidly flattened out. This pattern confirms that although the overall index tends to fall, a transition from specialization based on a minority of comparative advantage industries with high RCA indices to a

Table 4. Comparative Advantage Industries in ASEAN Economies

	Singapore	Indonesia	Thailand	Malaysia	Philippines
	Number of CA industries				
1986	30	12	24	15	17
1990	31	18	33	23	24
1995	23	25	38	25	20
	Structure of CA industries by sector in 1986 (%)				
Chemical and metal	13.3	25.0	4.2	13.3	17.6
Electronics	63.3	0.0	12.5	33.3	5.9
Textiles	13.3	58.3	41.7	33.3	41.2
Resource based	3.3	16.7	8.3	20.0	23.5
Other light industries	6.7	0.0	33.3	0.0	11.8
	Structure of CA industries by sector in 1995 (%)				
Chemical and metal	4.3	4.0	5.3	8.0	5.0
Electronics	73.9	12.0	39.5	48.0	25.0
Textiles	0.0	44.0	26.3	12.0	35.0
Resource based	8.7	16.0	2.6	20.0	10.0
Other light industries	13.0	24.0	26.3	12.0	25.0

Source: Compiled from U.N. trade statistics.

Note: Comparative advantage (CA) industries are those for which the revealed comparative advantage indices exceed 1.0.

flatter pattern made up of numerous comparative advantage industries is evident (fig. 2).

However, there is a limit to growth in the number of comparative advantage industries, and not all domestic industries can have a comparative advantage. Indeed, production factors such as labor that are available within a single country are finite. Over the past ten years, a considerable shift in comparative advantage in the ASEAN economies has taken place. In particular, there has been a marked shift from textiles to electronics.[10] A comparison of lineups of comparative advantage industries in 1986 and 1995 reveals that in Indonesia there was dispersal to nontextile light industries before the emergence of the electronics industry, but that in Thailand, Malaysia, and the Philippines, the distribution of comparative advantage industries shifted from textiles to electronics. A comparison of the top five items in terms of RCA indices from 1986 to 1995 shows that in Singapore radios and televisions were replaced by recorders and office and data processing equipment, and that in Indonesia underwear and fertilizers were ousted by footwear and synthetic textiles. These changes are indicative of the increasing sophistication in each country's lineup of comparative advantage industries.

Having strengthened its comparative advantage domestically, the

Figure 2. Changes in the Structure of Comparative Advantage Industries*

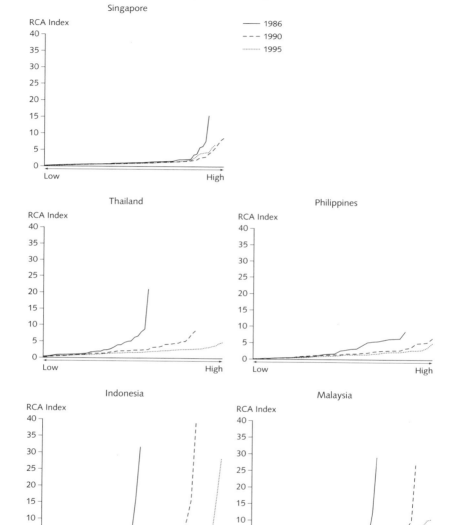

Source: Compiled from U.N. trade statistics.

* Comparative advantage industries are those for which the revealed comparative advantage indices exceed 1.0. See note 9.

electronics industry has expanded its share of exports in each country and gained a bigger share of world export markets. From 1986 to 1995, the industry's share of exports rose from 29.7 percent to 57.0 percent in Singapore, from 21.4 percent to 48.5 percent in Malaysia, from 8.5 percent to 26.7 percent in Thailand, and from 7.3 percent to 23.0 percent in the Philippines. In 1995, the ASEAN-5 accounted for more than 20 percent of world export markets for data processing equipment, televisions, radios, recorders, and electronic tubes.

Growth of Regional Economic Links

Another change that has occurred over the past decade is the formation of increasingly close regional economic links through trade. In terms of the export matrix, intraregional trade has increased from 17.7 percent overall in 1986 to 22.2 percent in 1995. Malaysia accounted for 38.1 percent of the increase in intraregional trade during this period, Singapore for 36.3 percent, and Thailand for 17.2 percent. The expansion of trade by the three countries on the Malay Peninsula was thus responsible for most of the rise in intraregional trade. This pattern reflects the growth of the existing division of labor between Singapore and Malaysia in the electronics industry, as well as the formation of new divisions of labor between Singapore and Thailand and between Malaysia and Thailand. Electronic goods contributed significantly to the growth in trade among these countries (64.1 percent between Singapore and Malaysia, 65.4 percent between Singapore and Thailand, and 41.1 percent between Malaysia and Thailand).

In the 1960s, the expansion of foreign electronics companies into the ASEAN economies was concentrated mainly in the electrical appliance category, a development that reflected import substitution policies. The foreign companies established small-scale production bases in each ASEAN economy to manufacture goods for sale in local markets.

This behavior changed radically in the 1970s. Singapore, which had few restrictions on foreign investment, and Malaysia and the Philippines, which gave export-oriented companies considerable freedom in such areas as ownership ratios and import of intermediate goods by establishing export-processing zones, were turned into the offshore production bases of those companies. Political troubles in the Philippines subsequently caused companies to retrench their operations or to withdraw entirely, but Singapore and Malaysia continued to attract FDI due to trade friction and other problems affecting the advanced economies.

Singapore's labor market began to tighten during this period, and its government adopted policies designed to create a more advanced industrial structure. These changes triggered a period of adjustment, during which companies relocated their production operations from Singapore to Malaysia, leading to the formation of a complementary relationship between these two economies. The range of products covered by these divisions of labor has expanded since the late 1980s, and their complexity has been further increased by the participation of Thailand. These relationships appear to have promoted trade among the three countries.

An analysis of 1995 statistics concerning the three-nation trade in electronic goods shows that it is dominated by intermediate goods. Semiconductors and electronic tubes (cathode-ray tubes, or CRTs, for example) accounted for more than 30 percent of exports of electronic goods from Singapore and Malaysia to the other two countries. Parts for office machines and data processing equipment accounted for more than 40 percent of Thailand's total exports of electronic goods to Singapore and Malaysia.

A second feature is the high reexport ratio. Reexports account for 34.2 percent of Singapore's total exports of electronic goods, but the ratios for Malaysia and Thailand are much higher, at 50.6 percent and 51.3 percent, respectively. Categories in which only small percentages of items exported to Malaysia and Thailand are reexported (i.e., in which many items are produced in Singapore) include parts and circuit boards for office machines and data processing equipment. This suggests that production operations in Singapore are increasingly acting as supply bases for intermediate goods. These patterns reveal intense activity through process-based divisions of labor involving the reciprocal supply of intermediate goods among electronics companies located on the Malay Peninsula.

Singapore has also developed excellent telecommunications and transportation infrastructures, and its government has implemented policies designed to attract regional operational headquarters (OHQs) and international purchasing offices. These factors have helped to turn Singapore into a hub for regional distribution systems. Some companies not only integrate their physical distribution systems but also manage exchange risk centrally by selling products from regional bases and by purchasing capital goods through their OHQs. The aforementioned characteristic of the electronics trade is reflected in this type of corporate behavior.

Rising production costs in Malaysia and Thailand and the improvement of investment environments in Indonesia and the Philippines have compelled foreign electronics companies to establish production operations in Indonesia and the Philippines. As a result, trade between Indonesia and Singapore and between Indonesia and Malaysia will likely expand. Direct investment has induced increasingly close trading relationships within the region; these relationships may well spread throughout the entire region, led by the machinery sector.

A Turning Point for ASEAN

The ASEAN economies, by accepting direct investment, have become exporters of manufactured goods and have achieved high economic growth. However, an increasing number of countries have used foreign investment as a lever for entry into export markets, and competition in world markets is intensifying. Moreover, the competitiveness of manufactured goods changes over extremely short periods. Countries in the region now compete for both investment and exports. China, meanwhile, by pursuing reform and open-door policies in the 1990s, has become a major threat to the ASEAN economies both as an absorber of direct investment and as an exporter of manufactured goods.

Competition for Direct Investment and Pressure for Industrial Advancement

Foreign investment in China (contract basis) surged from US$12 billion in 1991 to US$58.1 billion in 1992, and broke through the US$100 billion barrier in 1993. A comparison of direct investment inflows on an international balance-of-payments basis similarly reveals a clear contrast between the rapid growth of investment in China and the stagnation of investment in the ASEAN-5 from 1992 onward (fig. 3). China has been viewed with caution due to the high risks associated with policy changes and other factors. Its vast market with a population of 1.2 billion, however, has long been the focus of keen interest among foreign companies. Confidence in government policy strengthened when Deng Xiaoping proclaimed in February 1992 that the pace of reform would be stepped up. Investors also reacted favorably to the sustained rise in China's economic growth rate over a period of several years. The rapid expansion of investment in China appears to have been triggered by these factors. In particular, there has been a rapid shift from ASEAN to China as the

Figure 3. Direct Investment Inflows in the ASEAN-5 and China (US$ billion)

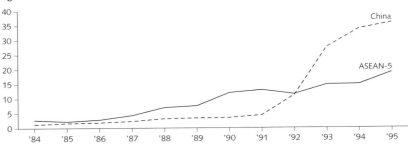

Source: International Monetary Fund, *Balance of Payments* annual.

target for investment by Hong Kong and Taiwan, which can take advantage of their common language, personal contacts, and other factors. In the 1990s, there has been a decline in the NIEs' share of investment approvals in the ASEAN economies, especially those in the leading group (Thailand, Malaysia).

Similarities in the industries targeted by China and ASEAN to attract foreign investment are striking. In 1994, the Chinese government announced its industrial policy guidelines for the 1990s, in which it identified machinery, automobiles, electronics, and petrochemicals as mainstay industries for the future. These are also growing industries or industries targeted for promotion in the ASEAN economies. Like the ASEAN members, China has a policy of using foreign investment to foster these industries. ASEAN and China will thus be competing to attract investment in these areas.

Also significant is China's shift to domestic production of key component parts, such as tape deck devices for videocassette recorders (VCRs) and compressors for air conditioners, at a relatively early stage of development. This relates in part to the problem of foreign currency shortages, but it can also be seen as evidence of the government's strong negotiating power backed by China's large domestic market. For example, the Chinese government centralized the supply of tape deck devices: A single foreign-affiliated company supplies all VCR factories in China. This would be unimaginable in the ASEAN economies, which are seeking to attract investment by liberalizing restrictions on the activities of foreign companies. The ASEAN governments are also eager to raise local content ratios and need to reduce their dependence on imported intermediate goods to improve their trade balances and to enhance the competitiveness of their finished products. However, it is difficult to exercise policy guidance; most ASEAN members have taken steps to reduce or exempt import tariffs on intermediate goods used in the production of export goods.

The effect of China's economic development on the ASEAN economies will depend on how they build complementary relationships with China. If China creates highly integrated production structures domestically, China could increase its advantage in terms of investment environment from the viewpoint of competitiveness at the finished product level, too. At the same time, the scope for complementary relationships between ASEAN and China could be reduced, causing China to emerge increasingly as a threat to the ASEAN economies.

China is now formidably competitive in exports. A comparison of market share in world export markets for the key export items of China and the ASEAN-5 in 1986 and 1995 shows that the shares of the ASEAN-5 have fallen in absolute terms in only a few categories, such as cotton fabrics. However, China had a bigger market share than the ASEAN-5 in such areas as household goods, clothing, underwear, watches and clocks, and toys in 1995 (table 5). From virtually zero in 1986, China increased its share of world exports in many of those categories to 10 percent–20 percent in 1995.

Changes in China's domestic comparative advantage mix are also evident. The number of comparative advantage industries soared from 11 in 1986 to 39 in 1990 and to 46 in 1995. Moreover, China's comparative advantage mix is becoming increasingly similar to that of the ASEAN economies, including a tendency to shift from textiles to electronics. These changes are reflected in the growing competition between China and ASEAN and are affecting the exports of the ASEAN economies, for which export growth rates slowed significantly in 1996. Singapore, Malaysia, and Thailand all achieved dollar-based export growth rates of almost 20 percent from 1990 to 1995, but in 1996 the year-on-year growth rate fell to 5.9 percent for Singapore and Thailand's retracted to minus 1.5 percent. This deceleration is attributable in part to cyclical economic factors, including market stagnation affecting the key products, such as semiconductors, of those three nations. However, there has also been an underlying downtrend in exports of such items as clothing, synthetic fibers, furniture, and watches and clocks. These industries have entered a downward phase in terms of comparative advantage.

Changes in comparative advantage are a natural consequence of

Table 5. Changes in Share of the World Export Market (%)

	1986		1995	
	ASEAN-5	China	ASEAN-5	China
Total exports	3.1	1.5	6.3	3.0
Wood products	3.8	0.0	10.9	6.4
Textile yarn	1.7	1.5	6.8	6.4
Cotton fabrics	3.7	14.6	2.8	16.5
Man-made fabric	4.6	4.6	8.1	7.6
Pottery	0.0	6.6	4.1	18.2
Office machines	1.3	0.0	7.9	5.5
Automatic data processing equipment	4.1	0.0	20.2	1.9
Office and data processing machine parts	2.6	0.0	18.8	1.8
Television receivers	7.9	0.0	22.2	3.6
Radio broadcast receivers	11.8	0.0	28.0	11.5
Sound recorders	1.6	0.0	28.8	4.6
Telecom equipment	2.2	0.0	11.4	3.5
Household-type equipment	1.7	0.0	4.2	6.4
Transistors and valves	15.6	0.0	20.2	0.7
Furniture and furniture parts	2.1	0.4	6.8	3.9
Travel goods and handbags	1.2	0.1	3.9	19.8
Men's outerwear	4.6	0.0	7.4	18.4
Women's outerwear	5.8	0.0	6.6	15.6
Undergarments	11.3	0.0	8.7	16.5
Outerwear, knitted	5.2	0.0	8.4	11.7
Undergarments, knitted	5.8	0.0	8.7	11.9
Footwear	0.8	1.6	10.5	15.5
Watches and clocks	1.6	0.0	7.0	8.9
Toys and sporting goods	2.6	1.7	5.7	15.1
Gold, silver, and jewelry	4.3	0.0	11.6	6.7

Source: Compiled from U.N. trade statistics.

industrial advancement. However, problems can occur if comparative advantage shifts over a short period of time because not all management resources and assets, such as machinery and labor skill, are interchangeable. Employment problems are an extreme example of this. As their business performances deteriorated, local apparel manufacturers in Thailand laid off large numbers of workers. Jobless people with only elementary education cannot immediately find work in the electronics industry because most foreign-affiliated electronics companies employ high school graduates even as line workers, and only 5.1 percent of Thai workers had completed higher education in 1995. Moreover, because only 19 percent of students proceeded to higher education in 1992, there will be no rapid rise in the number of graduates. Because of the labor supply-demand situation, workers who have completed higher education tend to receive relatively high wages, regardless of their quality. This is a disadvantage for the electronics industry.

Since the late 1980s, during the process of industrialization through the introduction of foreign investment, most exporting industries in the ASEAN economies have achieved growth through participation in the global strategies of foreign-affiliated companies. In such a situation, a comparative advantage gained over five years brings with it the prospect of further dramatic change, including the loss of that advantage over the next five years. Relentless efforts to raise the level of industries are necessary to maintain industrial competitiveness. Moreover, during transitional periods, adjustment costs are likely.

Industrial advancement can be interpreted as having two aspects. The first aspect is an emphasis on high-tech industries, as illustrated by Singapore and Malaysia. These industries offer high international market growth potential and can be expected to maintain production and employment levels over relatively long periods. However, the amount of value added that remains in the domestic economy is not necessarily large. For example, even if the focus of assembly industries shifts from home appliances to personal computers, there is little real change in the processes involved.

The second aspect of industrial advancement is the expansion of the amount of value added that is generated domestically. This can be broadly divided into the reduction of reliance on imported intermediate goods and the promotion of knowledge-intensive industries.

Malaysia is approaching the former task through "cluster development" (see Takeuchi 1997b), whereas Thailand's approach is to provide incentives for investment in designated supporting industries. Schemes are being implemented not only to attract foreign investment but also to form linkages between the domestic operations of companies and local enterprises. Singapore has been pursuing this approach since the mid-1980s.

Examples of the latter approach include Singapore's "Singapore One" and Malaysia's Multimedia Super-Corridor plans, which aim to foster the development of the information and telecommunications industries, especially with regard to software. Thailand has designated the development of industrial parks for software industries as one area eligible for investment incentives.

The industrial advancement policies of ASEAN governments are becoming increasingly similar. Moreover, because of the advanced skill and technology elements involved in the promotion of these industries, foreign investment is an essential requirement. Industrial advancement is a way of gaining an edge over competing countries and has become the focus of competition for investment.

Overseas Investment by the ASEAN Economies

The 1990s ushered in a rapid increase in foreign investment by Singapore, Thailand, and Malaysia (table 6). A comparison of direct investment inflows and outflows on an international balance-of-payments basis reveals that foreign investment *from* Singapore has been equivalent to 50 percent or more of investment inflows *into* Singapore since 1992. Thailand's ratio is also rising. South Korea and Taiwan both became capital exporters in the late 1980s, while at the same time actively accepting foreign investment. In the 1990s, the ASEAN economies also are emerging increasingly as sources of investment.

There are several reasons for this change. First, there is the growth of local enterprises. Rapid economic growth has enabled ASEAN's companies to grow and to accumulate management resources, including capital and business know-how. Many companies have achieved rapid expansion by discovering business opportunities in such areas as privatization schemes and infrastructure projects involving private-sector participation—two developments that have been used increasingly as part of the structural adjustment process. Another factor is the improvement of access to funds due to the growing presence on domestic and overseas stock exchanges.

Second, changes in domestic economic environments have helped foster foreign investment. Manufacturing industries oriented toward domestic markets have

Table 6. Investment Outflows of ASEAN Economies (US$ million)

	Singapore	Malaysia	Thailand
1980	754.7	146.0	NA
1981	794.1	198.5	2.3
1982	975.2	191.5	−0.4
1983	1,056.8	136.9	1.3
1984	1,124.8	156.8	0.4
1985	1,025.9	104.8	0.7
1986	1,193.0	123.5	1.1
1987	1,406.2	83.6	168.3
1988	1,487.7	65.1	2.4
1989	2,711.7	120.6	49.8
1990	4,294.8	204.9	139.9
1991	5,612.4	312.8	167.7
1992	6,913.5	514.3	136.2
1993	8,083.5	1,325.7	281.2
1994	12,728.1	2,102.1	405.6
1995	17,729.2	2,652.8	780.7

Sources: Singapore Department of Statistics, Bank Negara Malaysia, and the Bank of Thailand.

Note: Figures for Singapore are based on stock of direct equity investment at year-end; for Malaysia, on investment reported to the central bank; and for Thailand, on net outflows.

Table 7. Investment Outflows by Country and Region (%)

		ASEAN-5	Indochina and Myanmar	China and Hong Kong	United States	Others
Malaysia	1993	23.0	0.5	24.8	18.4	33.3
	1994	24.3	1.2	30.9	8.1	35.5
	1995	46.6	1.7	15.5	7.2	29.0
Singapore	1993	27.5	NA	21.0	8.3	43.2
	1994	31.4	0.4	21.8	6.3	40.1
	1995	33.8	0.8	20.0	5.7	39.7
Thailand	1993	24.0	6.5	25.7	14.6	29.1
	1994	21.3	6.5	32.6	16.6	23.0
	1995	23.2	8.2	17.4	17.8	33.5

Sources: Singapore Department of Statistics, Bank Negara Malaysia, and the Bank of Thailand.

achieved growth through the formation of joint ventures with foreign capital in response to import substitution policies. Manufacturers need to prepare not only for the maturity of domestic markets but also for the competition from imported goods as the region moves toward trade liberalization. It has become difficult to maintain the competitiveness of labor-intensive industries because high growth leads to a tight labor market and rising costs. And privatization, which has been a source of business opportunities for private-sector companies, has also had consequences for government enterprises such as former telecommunications authorities, including the introduction of competition and the need to develop new income sources.

Third, business opportunities have expanded into neighboring economies. Liberalization and economic growth have generated many kinds of opportunities in China (stemming from its reform and open-door policies), Vietnam (which is currently implementing its *doi moi* reform policies), and Myanmar (which has also shifted to an open-door policy). Investment environments are also improving in Indonesia and the Philippines, where low wages and other costs are attracting increasing investment from Malaysia and elsewhere. The contribution of regional investment to cumulative foreign investment in Indonesia and the Philippines increased sharply from 1991 to 1996 compared with 1986 to 1990. Outward foreign investment statistics for Singapore, Thailand, and Malaysia from 1993 to 1995 similarly reveal a strong emphasis on neighboring economies, with investment in ASEAN, Indochina and Myanmar, and China/Hong Kong accounting for more than 50 percent of total outward foreign investment (table 7).

Investment in these economies can be broadly divided into five categories: infrastructure-related investment (including investment by former state-owned enterprises), resource-related investment (forestry and oil-field development), service-related investment (hotels, tourism, and real estate), investment in areas such as fish farming and apparel (as part of efforts to reduce costs through industrial adjustments), and investment in areas relating to local markets (food, beverages, and cement) (see Takeuchi 1995b).

The government of Singapore responded to economic stagnation in the 1980s by highlighting the potential of overseas investment as an option that would enable companies to grow beyond the limitations imposed by the market size of the national economy. It began to provide active support, including tax exemptions and loans. Incentives for investment in neighboring countries that offer business opportunities have been enhanced under a regionalization policy introduced in 1992. Government-related companies are also stepping up their investment activities, including the development and management of industrial parks in China, India, Vietnam, and Myanmar, to accommodate investment from Singaporean companies and foreign companies with bases in Singapore. These activities form part of Singapore's support for foreign investment. They also provide new arenas in which to reproduce the advantage enjoyed by Singapore's government and government-related companies, which have considerable experience in attracting foreign investment. Overseas investment also is seen increasingly as a source of business growth in Malaysia and Thailand. Related measures include incentives for overseas investment and government-led investment missions.

Each country's foreign investment total includes investment in third countries by foreign-affiliated companies with domestic business operations. At the end of 1991, investment by foreign-affiliated companies in Singapore accounted for as much as 51 percent of Singapore's overseas investment,[11] whereas in Malaysia 36 percent of the companies that undertook overseas investment in 1988 were foreign-affiliated (Bank Negara Malaysia 1992, 64–69). According to a survey conducted by the Japan External Trade Organization (JETRO) in 1995, more than 40 percent of Japanese-affiliated companies in Singapore had invested in third countries from Singapore, and more than 80 percent of that investment was channeled into the ASEAN economies, including Vietnam. There are clear signs that investment in third countries from Malaysia and

Thailand will expand in the future. According to the survey, Japanese-affiliated companies in Singapore are expanding their investment in third countries "in response to local demand" (JETRO 1996, 36.18).

The Role of FDI in the Transitional Phase

FDI by the NIEs has been expanding since the late 1980s. This trend has also been conspicuous in the ASEAN region. In the NIEs, direct investment has served a dual purpose: It has fostered the transfer of industries in which the NIEs have a comparative disadvantage overseas while simultaneously attracting new growth industries. In the ASEAN economies, the introduction of direct investment is recognized as a vital factor for industrial advancement, but outward direct investment does not play such a major role in industrial adjustment. In most ASEAN economies, a strong need still exists for the absorption of labor by modern sectors, such as manufacturing industries. The rapid advancement of industrial structures could lead to adjustment costs resulting from mismatching between the supply and demand of labor. It is therefore vital to maintain competitiveness by improving the efficiency of industries that have lost their competitive advantage. There appears to be considerable scope for this.

The domino currency crisis that started in Thailand in 1997 has raised questions about the achievements of the past decade in terms of economic growth and industrialization. One consequence has been a re-examination of the role of export industries that rely heavily on imported intermediate goods. Governments sought to attract projects with high export ratios by offering a variety of incentives, including the relaxation of restrictions on foreign ownership and exemptions from import tariffs on capital and intermediate goods, to companies that exported a certain percentage of their output. The typical manifestation of this approach was the export-processing zone.

Although exports of manufactured goods expanded as a result of these efforts, structural reliance on imports of intermediate goods and other items caused trade balances to deteriorate. Among the ASEAN economies, falling exchange rates are expected to restore export competitiveness due to the consequent reduction in labor costs and other production costs. In industries that rely heavily on imported intermediate goods, however, those benefits will be canceled out by the increased cost of those imports.

Local content ratios vary considerably according to product and company. At the macro level, the electronics industry (Malaysia's biggest export sector) requires at least 0.4 units of imports for every one unit of production. Thus, the electronics industry, which is typical of industries that have achieved dramatic growth on the strength of foreign investment, has produced only limited spin-off benefits for the rest of the national economy. Direct investment brings direct technology transfers to workers employed by the companies concerned. Moreover, technology transfer benefits also happen through corporate transactions. Benefits to local companies include the acquisition of management skills about such matters as quality and delivery through the supply of intermediate goods to foreign-affiliated companies and the improvement of technology to meet the requirements of those companies. In addition, this accumulation of knowledge could encourage domestic capital to participate in related industries, thereby helping to expand and deepen the industrial structure. However, the realization of these benefits takes a certain amount of time and industrial infrastructure.

Direct investment has been expected to play a variety of roles in the industrialization of the ASEAN economies, and the validity of imposing a variety of objectives on direct investment, which is just one type of economic transaction, has been pointed out (Sekiguchi and Tran 1986, 82). Since the 1980s, however, the increasing priority placed on such goals as the expansion of manufactured exports has inevitably led to the postponement of other objectives and to the expansion of measures that have been counterproductive in terms of fostering domestic capital and improving trade balances. To overcome structural problems, it will be necessary to focus on other aspects of direct investment, such as skill formation and technology transfers.

Regional Economic Integration and FDI

The 1990s have brought changes to ASEAN's role as a regional community. One is the start of moves toward economic integration through the creation of a single free trade area in the region. Another is the emergence of the ASEAN-10, which became a reality in April 1999.

Moves toward Economic Integration

ASEAN has a long history of regional economic cooperation, though efforts in that direction have not always been successful. Moves toward cooperation first began to gather momentum at the first ASEAN summit meeting in 1976. Thereafter, ASEAN members reached agreement on a succession of special economic cooperation schemes, including the Preferential Tariff Agreement in 1976, the ASEAN Industrial Project in 1978, the ASEAN Industrial Cooperation scheme in 1981, and the ASEAN Industrial Joint Venture scheme in 1983. All focused primarily on the use of preferential tariffs to overcome the limitations imposed by markets.

It proved difficult to reconcile the product categories and sectors that would be acceptable to individual members. Moreover, these schemes did not produce significant benefits (Yamakage 1997, 65–74). One scheme that has been relatively effective is the Brand-to-Brand Complementation (BBC) scheme for automobiles, which was proposed by private-sector companies in 1987. This scheme provides a 50 percent tariff reduction for the trade in automobile parts among the regional plants of automobile assemblers. It was initiated in 1988 by four ASEAN members (Indonesia was not among them).

The situation changed dramatically after the fourth ASEAN summit meeting in 1992, which marked the start of concrete moves toward economic integration. At that meeting, Thailand, which had previously been reluctant to open up its markets, proposed the ASEAN Free Trade Area (AFTA) concept. After deliberations, it was decided to adopt the Common Effective Preferential Tariff (CEPT) scheme proposed by Indonesia. Agreement was reached on a concept calling for the establishment of AFTA through the phased reduction of tariffs, with regional tariffs on all items falling somewhere between 0 percent and 5 percent by 2008 (see Takeuchi 1993). Members agreed to submit commitments on items included in or exempted from the CEPT, and on schedules for the reduction of tariffs on affected items. They vowed to work toward their targets by implementing tariff reductions and gradually extending their coverage in line with the commitments. At the fifth ASEAN summit meeting in 1995, members agreed on an even more active approach to liberalization, including the addition of unprocessed agricultural products to the CEPT list. They also approved moving up the deadline for the establishment of AFTA to 2003. The CEPT system was supposed to take effect from early 1993, but its introduction varied from country to country. Thailand and Indonesia started to apply the system in 1995, followed by the Philippines in 1996 (Yamakage 1997, 199). Trade in CEPT items now accounts for more than 80 percent of total intraregional trade (Asian Secretariat 1998).

The scope of liberalization is expanding to include investment and intraregional trade in services. For example, in December 1995, the ASEAN members signed a framework agreement for the liberalization of intraregional trade in services, and established the ASEAN Industrial Cooperation (AICO) agreement. In July 1997, the ASEAN Investment Area (AIA) concept was put forward. Under the AICO concept, the BBC scheme would be implemented without any limitation to specific industrial sectors, and a schedule for reducing intraregional tariffs for intracompany trade would be created. It was, however, a transitional mechanism: It would eventually be integrated into the CEPT.

With regard to the liberalization of intraregional trade in services, the ASEAN members will cooperate toward two goals. First, they aim to achieve a higher standard of liberalization than is provided for in the WTO's General Agreement on Trade in Services (GATS). Second, they want to improve efficiency and strengthen competitiveness in the service industries through trade liberalization. Because those areas can be monitored through the statistics on international balance of payments, those most likely to be affected by the liberalization of the trade in services are cross-border transactions in such fields as transportation, telecommunications, and overseas travel. In GATS, however, the trade in services is broadly defined as services provided under four modes: cross-border transactions, overseas consumption, the establishment of companies in prospective markets, and labor movement. The aim is to eliminate barriers to the expansion of these transactions. ASEAN's service trade liberalization program is similar in content but sets higher targets than those set down in GATS. A characteristic of services is that production and consumption occur simultaneously. For this reason, a large percentage of services are provided through companies or people situated in prospective markets. The most important aspect of service trade liberalization, therefore, is the liberalization of investment relating to the service industries. In practical terms, a close correlation with investment liberalization is likely (see Takeuchi 1997a). In December 1997, an initial package on the liberalization of intraregional trade in services was signed, committing members to liberalization.

Among the aims of the AIA concept are the formation of a free and highly transparent common investment environment that will encourage investment, the development of an ASEAN investment promotion program, and the promotion of free flows of capital, skilled workers, and technology among the ASEAN economies. In 1998, a framework agreement was concluded at the 1998 meeting of economic ministers.

Yet, if a "free and highly transparent common investment environment" means an investment agreement, it is apparent from the scope of such an agreement that considerable adjustment and work will be involved. Leaders at the unofficial summit meeting in December 1997 adopted ASEAN Vision 2020, which clarifies goals relating to the liberalization of capital movements by the year 2020, including the establishment of AFTA, the promotion of trade liberalization in services, and the formation of the AIA.

The increased interest of the ASEAN economies in regional economic integration since 1992 was prompted by several factors. First, competition escalated to attract investment. China's shift to an open-door policy was reflected in increased investment in that country and its vast domestic market. In addition, the former Soviet Union and the countries of Eastern Europe were also starting to seek foreign investment to feed their voracious demand for funds since the end of the cold war. ASEAN needed something that would enable it to maintain a continuing inflow of foreign investment. It needed to be able to offer the potential future benefits of a single market with a population in excess of 400 million.

Second, there was the need to diversify export markets. Conspicuous moves toward regional economic integration, including the North American Free Trade Agreement (NAFTA) and the European Union, raised concerns that future exports to the markets of advanced economies might be affected. The ASEAN economies thus began to focus on regional as well as external markets.

Third, regional economic relationships were becoming increasingly close in real terms. There has been an increase in the involvement of countries within the region in the trade and investment activities of other ASEAN members. Particularly significant is the formation of regional divisions of labor by means of corporate networks created through direct investment. Awareness improved that this tendency was helping to drive economic growth and was reflected in an increasing emphasis on economic integration through the liberalization of regional activities as a way of supporting and promoting these investment flows.

Fourth, the establishment of the WTO and the introduction of regular APEC summit meetings was leading to the formulation of multinational trade and investment rules. Moreover, the possibility that such rules would become more and more binding in the future was growing. This trend raised two issues for ASEAN: Regional liberalization would be meaningless if it lagged behind liberalization through the WTO or APEC, and the impact of trade and investment liberalization involving countries outside of the region on ASEAN's industries would be incomparably greater than the effects of regional trade and investment liberalization. To avoid these two undesirable situations, it would be necessary to keep regional liberalization one step ahead of the WTO and APEC at all times and to treat this period as a warm-up during which competitiveness could be enhanced by implementing liberalization measures across a wider area. That is why ASEAN has expanded the scope of its regional cooperation from trade liberalization to service trade and investment liberalization.

The Emergence of the ASEAN-10

Another change that has affected ASEAN's role as a regional community is steady progress toward the formation of the ASEAN-10, which now includes all the Southeast Asian nations. Vietnam joined in December 1995, followed by Laos and Myanmar in June 1997. Had the political situation in Cambodia remained stable, the ASEAN-10 would have been achieved in June 1997.

The following analysis focuses on the significance of the economic development perspective of the ASEAN-10. What benefits and costs will the expansion of ASEAN bring to the new members and the ASEAN-6?

For the new members, membership in ASEAN signifies a higher profile in the international community, a change that will likely encourage foreign investment. Low wage levels give the new ASEAN members a comparative advantage in labor-intensive industries, and they are expected to attract investment in export-oriented labor-intensive industries.

The new members should also benefit from increased opportunities to obtain economic cooperation from countries in the region and from ASEAN. Singapore is already assisting Myanmar in the area of human resource development, and Malaysia, which has expressed strong interest in economic assistance for the least of the less developed countries (called "South-South cooperation" in Malaysia), could also expand its aid. ASEAN is currently attempting to unify the various systems of its members, including tariff procedures and codes, in preparation for 2020. Plans to assist the new members with the development of tariff systems and trade statistics are under way. Meetings among the heads of the ASEAN Investment Agencies have been held since 1996, and plans are being drawn up to integrate investment systems and to develop joint

Table 8. Approved Foreign Direct Investment by Country and Sector

	Vietnam		Myanmar		Laos		Cambodia	
	US$mn	%	US$mn	%	US$mn	%	US$mn	%
ASEAN-5	8,259	27.1	3,090	49.5	2,880	42.5	74	22.9
Indonesia	242	0.8	211	3.4	5	0.1	3	0.9
Malaysia	1,347	4.4	524	8.4	264	3.9	24	7.4
Philippines	291	1.0	7	0.1	0	0.0	0	0.0
Singapore	5,299	17.4	1,215	19.5	16	0.2	35	10.8
Thailand	1,080	3.5	1,133	18.1	2,595	38.3	12	3.7
NIEs-3	10,963	36.0	137	2.2	554	8.2	136	42.1
Hong Kong	3,720	12.2	64	1.0	28	0.4	11	3.4
South Korea	3,124	10.3	73	1.2	455	6.7	5	1.5
Taiwan	4,119	13.5	0	0.0	71	1.0	120	37.2
Oil and gas	1,005	3.3	2,193	35.1	4,500*	66.4	–	–
Agriculture and forestry	396	1.3	279	4.5	220	3.2	123	38.1
Industry	11,912	39.1	1,140	18.3	545	8.0	73	22.6
Hotels and real estate	6,459	21.2	1,638	26.2	605	8.9	103	31.8
Infrastructure	10,023	32.9	450	7.2	562	8.3	10	3.1
Total	30,465	100.0	6,243	100.0	6,779	100.0	323	100.0
Period	1988–Dec.1997		1988–Jul.1997		1988–Apr.1997		Jan.–Dec.1996	

Source: Investment agencies in each country.

Note: Hotels and real estate includes tourism.

*Entire energy sector.

efforts to attract investment. Participation in these meetings is expected to result in significant technology transfers to the new ASEAN members, including enhanced understanding of the systems used in other countries and the ways they are managed.

A third benefit for new members is likely to be increased private-sector interest in the region. The ASEAN-5 are already important sources of investment for the new members and Cambodia, and account for 20 percent–50 percent of foreign investment approvals (table 8).

The biggest cost will be participation in the liberalization plans that are being promoted within the region. With the exception of Vietnam, levels of industrialization among the new members are low: Agriculture accounts for more than 60 percent of GDP in both Myanmar and Laos. If they open up their markets in this early stage of industrialization, their industries could well become decimated by products from the ASEAN-6. Vietnam, Laos, and Myanmar announced that they would join the CEPT after becoming ASEAN members, and they produced lists of items that would be included or excluded from tariff reductions. Among the new members, the percentages of items covered by tariff reductions

Table 9. Inclusion and Exclusion Lists for the CEPT Scheme

	Inclusion List		Temporary Exclusion	General Exclusion	Sensitive List
	No.	%			
Brunei	6,060	92.8	220	236	14
Indonesia	6,597	90.9	593	45	23
Laos	533	15.0	2,820	102	96
Malaysia	8,690	93.5	406	60	137
Myanmar	2,356	43.1	2,987	108	21
Philippines	5,099	88.3	589	28	58
Singapore	5,738	97.9	–	120	–
Thailand	9,033	98.8	74	26	7
Vietnam	1,497	53.3	1,127	165	23

Source: ASEAN Secretariat.

are 53.3 percent for Vietnam, 15.0 percent for Laos, and 43.1 percent for Myanmar. These figures are extremely low compared with the 88 percent–99 percent ratios announced by the ASEAN-6 (table 9). Compared with the tariff reduction deadlines established for the ASEAN-6, the new members have been granted grace periods of three to five years. The deadline for Vietnam is 2006, whereas that for Laos and Myanmar is 2008.

The question is what happens after that. By 2010, all members are required to reduce tariffs to a maximum of 5 percent on all goods, including those currently excluded. The grace periods before the newest members are required to lower tariffs on excluded items are extremely short. They can seek further exemptions if tariff cuts cause problems such as deteriorating balance of payments or a serious impact on domestic industries. However, it is not certain that such exemptions would be accepted indefinitely. Faced with fierce competition in their export markets, the ASEAN-6 are constantly searching for new markets. They have high hopes for the markets of new members, which might be regarded as ASEAN's backyard. But extreme delays in reducing tariffs could become a source of confrontation among ASEAN members. Over the long term, however, even the new ASEAN members will inevitably join the global free trade system, as symbolized by the WTO.[12] Members will need to view regional liberalization positively as a preparatory stage for this.

From the viewpoint of the ASEAN-6, the new members are geographically close and offer potentially large markets. The participation of these economies in regional trade and investment liberalization will bring increased export and business opportunities for the ASEAN-6. Moreover, the addition of new members will increase the size of AFTA, which will eventually be a single regional market, thereby raising the level of interest in ASEAN among countries outside the region. However, the process of regional economic integration will become increasingly difficult as the new members begin to participate. The addition of new members at significantly different economic levels could easily bog down consensus formation and increase the possibility that plans will not be completed. The new members had per capita GDP figures in the US$200–US$300 range in 1995. This is significantly lower than Indonesia's US$980 in 1995, which was the lowest among the ASEAN-6.

Two factors have made economic integration in ASEAN a more realistic proposition in the 1990s: the reduction of economic gaps among members and increasing complementation through the networks of foreign companies with business operations in the region. The reduction of economic gaps among the region's economies through the economic development of new members is a vital prerequisite for economic integration. This is likely to require the cooperation of the ASEAN-6. Direct investment and economic cooperation play an especially important role.

The new members have clearly stated that they intend to make active use of foreign investment in their economic development. And, one after another, they have established investment laws since 1987. They have essentially copied the foreign investment strategies of the ASEAN-6, including the establishment of tax holidays and the provision of tariff exemptions for capital and intermediate goods used by export industries. Areas in which a strong need exists for foreign investment include infrastructure improvement and the development of export industries. Regional investment is already actively involved in infrastructure development.

The investment environments of the new ASEAN members have two distinct drawbacks: political risk and a lack of transparency in the way things work. Moreover, foreign investment in Vietnam and Myanmar has started to decline. To restore the confidence of investors, it will be necessary to demonstrate that earlier projects based on investment from the ASEAN-5 are proceeding satisfactorily.

Regional Economic Cooperation and FDI

The economic benefits of economic integration can be summed up as follows. First, the trade creation effect leads to the expansion of trade among economies within the region. Second, a trade replacement effect is created, whereby import sources outside of the region are replaced by regional sources. Third, the investment transition effect triggers inflows of investment into the region. Fourth, the competitiveness effect kicks in, whereby the competitiveness of regional companies is enhanced through economies of scale resulting from the expansion of markets and from efficiency improvements driven by competition with other companies in the region (Ōno 1994, 7). Moves toward the formation of a free trade area in ASEAN are clearly targeted toward the realization of these benefits and especially toward the investment transition effect. These effects are interlinked, and investment has especially important implications for trade and competitiveness.

In ASEAN, too, foreign-affiliated companies have undertaken many investments within the region, and intracompany trade generated by the resulting divisions of labor has become a driving force for the expansion of intraregional trade. This pattern is typified in the electronics industry, which is oriented heavily toward exports. Until the 1970s, the formation of international divisions of labor in the ASEAN region was hindered by trade barriers. However, the ASEAN governments have now adopted export-oriented industrialization policies, leading to the creation of export-processing zones and other types of enclaves. These policy changes have made it easier to form international divisions of labor, and the export sectors have shown strong performances.

Yet this growth strategy has reached a turning point in two senses. First, an increasing number of countries are adopting similar growth strategies, resulting in the acceleration of the pace of change in the competitiveness of manufactured goods in export markets. This can easily lead to a situation in which industries created by direct investment can shift to other countries where costs are lower before they have time to put down roots and commence self-sustained development in the economy.

Second, the strategy has become increasingly incompatible with national economic development. Divisions of labor within the region are based on links between enclaves; they can actually hinder the formation of links between national economies. Those enclaves are likely to disappear with the liberalization of trade and investment. However, the establishment and growth of industries require the improvement of a wide range of environmental factors, including human resources, infrastructure, and supporting industries. Host country governments and ASEAN will need to increase their contributions in these areas.

Conclusion

Since the late 1980s, the ASEAN economies have achieved high economic growth by using inflows of FDI to transform themselves into exporters of manufactured goods. However, the 1990s have created a turning point for the factors that made this growth possible. First, there has been an escalation of competition. More and more countries are using foreign investment inflows as a stepping stone to participation in export markets, just as the ASEAN economies have done. This is reflected in increasingly fierce competition in world markets and in changes in the competitiveness of manufactured goods over short periods.

Second, the production environment has deteriorated due to rising labor costs and other factors. Rapid growth has caused labor costs to rise in the ASEAN economies, and the limited accumulation of specialists in the labor market is reflected in increasingly serious shortages of workers in this category. The ASEAN economies are responding to the declining competitiveness of their key export industries by working to develop more advanced industrial structures, which they aim to build by attracting "quality" investment.

However, most ASEAN economies still face a strong need to absorb labor into modern sectors. The rapid development of more sophisticated industrial structures would inevitably involve adjustment costs, especially in the area of labor. The achievement of efficiency improvements to maintain competitiveness in sectors that have lost their comparative advantage is an important priority; considerable scope for such improvements is likely. In particular, the ASEAN economies need to raise the level of local processing technologies through such means as technology transfers based on transactions with foreign-owned companies, and to rationalize their material industries through the reduction of tariff rates. Since the 1980s, the ASEAN economies have increasingly insisted that direct investment should contribute to export expansion. To survive the present turning point, they will need to place greater emphasis on the improvement of industrial capabilities and on the transfer of technology.

Direct investment is an important requirement for the economic development of the ASEAN economies, but it is not sufficient in itself. Even with a base of direct investment, the ASEAN economies will not be able to overcome structural weakness unless they have the capacity for self-driven industrial development. During this transitional phase, they will need to increasingly focus on the role of direct investment in such areas as technology transfers and the improvement of efficiency. The ASEAN economies need to develop more advanced industrial structures and are seeking quality investment as a way of meeting that need. They should recognize that the quality of investment is also determined by the stance of the host country.

Notes

1. Unless otherwise stated, the "ASEAN economies" refer to the ASEAN-5: Indonesia, Malaysia, the Philippines, Singapore, and Thailand.

2. Thailand began to provide incentives for export-oriented industries with the introduction of the Promotion of Investment Act of 1972. However, real benefits appear to have been minimal: The tightening of restrictions on foreign investment and the maintenance of advantageous conditions for import-substitution industries have hampered Thailand. For a detailed discussion, see Takeuchi (1996, 54–55).

3. Indonesia previously required companies to localize at least 51 percent of their paid-up capital within 15 years of establishment. The deadline and regulation on the foreign capital ratio were abolished in the 1994 package.

4. In relation to investment statistics by sector, the scope of statistics and the industrial classifications used vary widely from country to country. In Singapore, there are no statistics relating solely to foreign investment, and investment approval figures include domestic as well as foreign investment. The figures for Thailand are based not on investment approvals but rather on net inflows, as published by the Bank of Thailand.

5. ibid.

6. In 1994, Thailand responded to these demand-side changes by liberalizing participation in the petrochemical industry.

7. Numbers on export-oriented projects approved in Malaysia have not been available since 1992.

8. Because investment statistics published by Malaysia do not support continuity with the period up to 1988, the figures are based on cumulative totals for 1989–1996.

9. This covers items with three-digit Standard International Trade Classification (SITC) codes. However, items that account for less than 3 percent of total exports according to U.N. trade statistics have been excluded, with the result

that the number of items covered differs from country to country. The 1995 totals were 58 for Singapore, 54 for Thailand, 47 for Malaysia, 43 for Indonesia, and 34 for the Philippines.

10. In industrial statistics, office machines and data processing machines are classified as machinery, but for the purposes of this chapter, office machines and data processing machines and parts thereof (SITC 751, 752, 759) are included in the electronics industry.

11. Until 1991, Singapore's overseas investment reports provided separate figures for overseas investment by foreign-affiliated companies and local companies.

12. A growing possibility exists that the scope of the WTO's activities will not be limited to trade and that the organization will also be involved in the establishment of multilateral rules in such areas as investment protection and liberalization.

Bibliography

ASEAN Secretariat. 1996. *AFTA Reader Vol. 3.* Jakarta: ASEAN Secretariat.
———. 1998. <http://www.asean.or.id/>.
Bank Negara Malaysia. 1992. *Annual Report 1991.* Kuala Lumpur, Malaysia: Bank Negara Malaysia.
Chia Siow Yue and Joseph L. H. Tan, eds. 1996. *ASEAN in the WTO.* Singapore: Institute of Southeast Asian Studies.
Department of Statistics, Singapore. 1993. *Direct Investment Abroad of Local Companies 1991.* Singapore: Department of Statistics.
———. 1994. *Singapore's Direct Investment Abroad 1993.* Singapore: Department of Statistics.
———. 1997. *Foreign Direct Investment Activities of Singapore Companies 1995.* Singapore: Department of Statistics.
Imada, Pearl, and Seiji Naya. 1992. *AFTA: The Way Ahead.* Singapore: Institute of Southeast Asian Studies.
Japan External Trade Organization. 1989. *Asia sangyō kakumei no jidai* (Era of Asian industrial revolution). Tokyo: Japan External Trade Organization.
———. 1996. *JETRO tōshi hakusho* (JETRO white paper on investment). Tokyo: Japan External Trade Organization.
Kojima Kiyoshi. 1985. *Nippon no kaigai chokusetsu tōshi* (Foreign direct investment of Japan). Tokyo: Bunshin-dō.
Maxwell, J. Fry. 1992. *Foreign Direct Investment in Southeast Asia.* Singapore: Institute of Southeast Asian Studies.
Ōno Kōichi, ed. 1994. *Keizai tōgō to hatten tojōkoku* (Economic integration and developing economies). Tokyo: Institute of Developing Economies.

Ramstetter, Eric D. 1991. *Direct Foreign Investment in Asia's Developing Economies and Structural Change in the Asia-Pacific Region.* Oxford, U.K.: Westview.

Sekiguchi Sueo and Noda Makito. 1994. *Economic Interactions and Interdependence in East Asia.* Tokyo: Ushiba Memorial Foundation Study.

Sekiguchi Sueo and Ono Akihiko, eds. 1991. *Asia keizai kenkyū* (Asian economic research: Policies in trade, investment, and technology transfer). Tokyo: Chuo Keizai-sha.

Sekiguchi Sueo and Tran Van Tho. 1986. *Chokusetsu tōshi to gijutsu iten* (Direct investment and technology transfer). Tokyo: Japan Center for Economic Research.

Takeuchi Junko. 1993. "Effect of AFTA on ASEAN Industrial Structure." *RIM* 19: 10–41. Published by the Sakura Institute of Research.

———. 1995a. "Trends and Prospects for Foreign Investment in ASEAN Countries in the 1990s." *RIM* 27: 22–41. Published by the Sakura Institute of Research.

———. 1995b. "Shinkō shijō e no kuikomi o hakaru ASEAN kigyō" (Overseas investment by ASEAN companies). *RIM* 29: 58–71. Published by the Sakura Institute of Research.

———. 1996. "Henyō suru Thai no kōgyōka" (Changes in industrialization in Thailand). *RIM* 32: 52–67. Published by the Sakura Institute of Research.

———. 1997a. "ASEAN Moves toward Service Trade Liberalization." *RIM* 35: 2–26. Published by the Sakura Institute of Research.

———. 1997b. "The New Industrialization Strategy of Malaysia as Envisioned in the Second Industrial Master Plan." *RIM* 37: 2–21. Published by the Sakura Institute of Research.

Tran Van Tho. 1992. *Takokuseki kigyō to sangyō hatten* (Multinational companies and industrial development). Tokyo: Tōyō Keizai Shinpō-sha.

Tsao Yuan, Lee. 1994. *Overseas Investment: Experience of Singapore Manufacturing Companies.* Singapore: McGraw-Hill.

United Nations Conference on Trade and Development (UNCTAD). 1996. *World Investment Report 1996.* New York: UNCTAD.

———. 1997. *World Investment Report 1997.* New York: UNCTAD.

Urata Shūjirō, ed. 1995. *Bōeki jiyūka to keizai hatten* (Trade liberalization and economic development). Tokyo: Institute of Developing Economies.

World Trade Organization. 1996. *Annual Report 1996.* Geneva: World Trade Organization.

Yamakage Susumu. 1997. *ASEAN Power.* Tokyo: Tokyo University Press.

– 7 –
Vietnam in ASEAN

Kashiwagi Takahiro

V IETNAM'S ECONOMY, which grew at an average annual rate of more than 8 percent from 1992 to 1995 (table 1), has attracted considerable foreign direct investment (FDI) owing to its explosive growth potential and inexpensive labor. In the early 1990s, Vietnam shifted from a "highly centrally planned economy" to a "market oriented economy regulated by government."[1] In 1986, at the 6th Congress of the Communist Party of Vietnam, the *doi moi* reforms were adopted to restructure the centrally planned economy. The present high economic growth has resulted from a series of reforms that followed in the 1990s, including the devaluation of the currency (dong), expanded autonomy for state-owned enterprises (SOEs), the abolition of government subsidies for SOEs, the legislation of new tax laws, and an amendment to the foreign investment law. Vietnam also deepened its political and economic relationships with other East Asian countries and joined the Association of Southeast Asian Nations in July 1995. Vietnam now enjoys high and continuing economic growth.

Following reunification in 1976, Vietnam experienced political upheaval and economic difficulties. A border war with China and the 1978 invasion of Cambodia curtailed economic development. Vietnam formally joined the Council for Mutual Economic Assistance (CMEA) in 1978 and strengthened its relationship with the Soviet Union. Economic assistance from the Soviet Union and trade with other CMEA members

I wish to thank Dr. Carolyn L. Gates and Dr. Manuel F. Montes of the Institute of Southeast Asian Studies for their helpful comments. This chapter greatly benefited from the constructive comments of Tran Van Tho of Obirin University. And I gratefully acknowledge the thoughtful discussion with project members on an earlier draft of this chapter.

Table 1. Vietnam's Basic Economic Indicators

	1986	1987	1988	1989	1990	1991	1992	1993	1994	1995
GDP real growth rate (%)										
Total	NA	3.7	5.9	8.0	5.1	6.0	8.6	8.1	8.8	9.5
Agriculture and forestry	NA	−0.6	3.9	6.9	4.6	2.2	7.1	3.8	3.9	4.7
Industry and construction	NA	8.8	5.3	−2.6	−2.4	9.0	14.0	13.1	14.0	13.9
Others	NA	5.5	9.2	18.3	10.8	8.3	7.0	9.2	10.2	10.9
State-owned sector	NA	5.9	7.3	4.6	2.5	8.6	12.4	11.6	12.8	14.4
Non-state-owned sector	NA	2.5	5.2	9.7	6.4	4.7	6.8	6.2	6.7	6.7
Sectoral share of GDP in constant 1989 prices (%)										
Agriculture and forestry	43.8	42.0	41.2	40.8	40.7	39.2	38.6	37.1	35.4	33.9
Industry and construction	25.7	27.0	26.8	24.2	22.5	23.1	24.2	25.4	26.6	27.7
Others	30.5	31.0	32.0	35.0	36.9	37.7	37.1	37.5	38.0	38.5
State-owned sector	33.1	33.8	34.2	33.2	32.4	33.2	34.3	35.4	36.7	38.3
Non-state-owned sector	66.9	66.2	65.8	66.8	67.6	66.8	65.7	64.6	63.3	61.7
Sectoral share of labor force (%)										
Agriculture and forestry	72.9	73.0	72.5	72.2	72.3	72.6	72.9	73.0	72.8	73.7
Industry and construction	13.9	13.8	14.1	13.9	13.9	13.6	13.4	13.4	13.6	13.8
Others	13.2	13.2	13.4	13.9	13.8	13.8	13.6	13.6	13.6	12.5
State-owned sector	14.7	14.6	14.2	13.1	11.3	10.2	9.3	9.0	8.7	8.8
Non-state-owned sector	85.3	85.4	85.8	86.9	88.7	89.8	90.7	91.0	91.3	91.2
Labor productivity by sector (000 dong in constant 1989 prices)										
Agriculture and forestry	520	506	519	549	548	545	566	571	578	588
Industry and construction	1,601	1,710	1,740	1,683	1,575	1,715	1,928	2,134	2,324	2,573
Others	1,993	2,071	2,180	2,452	2,601	2,758	2,909	3,096	3,316	3,934
(% of GDP)										
Overall budget deficit	−6.2	−4.7	−7.1	−7.5	−5.8	−1.5	−1.7	−4.6	−1.6	−0.5
Trade balance	−5.1	−13.0	−5.0	−6.7	−0.8	−0.9	−0.6	−4.3	−7.7	−11.5
Current balance	−5.3	−13.3	−5.4	−11.2	−5.0	−2.0	−0.1	−6.1	−7.6	−9.2
Change in consumer prices (%)	487.2	301.0	310.9	95.8	67.5	81.8	37.6	8.4	14.4	12.7
Exchange rate (dong/US$)	22.5	281.3	1,125.0	5,375.0	8,125.0	11,500.0	10,565.0	10,842.5	11,050.0	10,962.1

Source: World Bank (1995b; 1996a), General Statistical Office (1995), International Monetary Fund (1996), and Asian Development Bank (1997a; 1997b).

supported the Vietnamese economy. The collapse of the Soviet Union and the CMEA in 1991 temporarily worsened Vietnam's economic difficulties.

At the 8th Congress of the Communist Party of Vietnam in June 1996, Vietnam adopted a new economic development strategy for the year 2000 that aimed to further high economic growth and enhance development in the rural provinces (Takeuchi 1997). The congress targeted industrial sector growth of 14 percent–15 percent per annum and gross domestic product (GDP) growth of 9 percent–10 percent per annum. Such growth requires an investment rate in excess of 30 percent. The congress estimated total investment to support this growth at US$41 billion–US$42 billion, of which the country would depend on foreign capital for US$13 billion–US$15 billion. The strategy prioritized investment in the industrial sector, especially in heavy industries. Forty-three percent of total investment was to be allocated to the industrial sector and 20 percent to the agriculture, forestry, fisheries, and water supply sectors. Investment in heavy industries was to account for 70 percent of total investment in the industrial sector.[2]

The strategy attached importance to equitable development among the provinces through expanded employment opportunities. To address the widening income gap between urban and rural areas, the strategy stressed gradual industrialization and resource reallocation to rural and mountainous areas.[3]

Per capita GDP in Vietnam was US$240 in 1995, even lower than that of Cambodia. Vietnam is ASEAN's poorest member. According to the *World Development Report 1997* (World Bank 1997a), Vietnam was the 15th poorest country in the world, even poorer than Bangladesh and Uganda, in terms of per capita GDP.[4] Even so, Vietnam's income distribution is similar to that of the other ASEAN economies. The inequities of income distribution, as measured by the Gini coefficient, are less pronounced in Vietnam than in Malaysia, Thailand, or the Philippines.[5] If the Kuznets inverted-U shape hypothesis[6] is true, inequality expands jointly with economic growth. In a socialist economy such as Vietnam's, where an artificial distribution mechanism has supported income equality, the changes that occur during the transition to a market economy will likely lead to further income disparities.

Vietnam faces a number of concerns in its efforts to sustain high economic growth. First, economic development requires investment. In developing countries, the current account balance typically turns to deficit when domestic savings levels are insufficiently small to cover the investment that is needed to spur development. Vietnam had huge current account deficits in the late 1980s and again in the mid-1990s. Funding is a critical issue for Vietnam. If the country fails to secure investment, it will have difficulty industrializing and maintaining high growth, leading to a decline in the investment rate and/or an increase in cumulative external debt.

Second, economic efficiency must be improved and income disparities reduced. Large capital inputs typically drive economic growth in the early stages of industrialization, and growth subsequently slows as returns on capital diminish. The growth pattern in developing countries changes from a dependence on factor inputs to the improvement of productivity to sustain long-term growth. The restructuring of the SOEs and the promotion of the private sector are the keys to improving efficiency in Vietnam's transitional economy. In addition, the mobility of labor between the agricultural and nonagricultural sectors is important, because it can improve economic efficiency and reduce income disparities through optimal resource allocation.

Third, Vietnam has integrated itself into the international economy by joining the ASEAN Free Trade Area (AFTA). Under the CMEA trade system, members produced tradable goods irrelevant to their comparative advantages, and trade deficits were offset by borrowing from the Soviet Union. In a free trade system, trade is based on comparative advantages and fierce international competition, which forces productivity improvement in domestic industries. After the collapse of the CMEA, its members had difficulty participating in the open global economy, primarily because their export goods were not competitive. Vietnam responded by deepening its relationship with other Southeast Asian countries and by joining ASEAN in 1995 and AFTA in 1996. AFTA allows members to gradually move toward trade liberalization, but Vietnam still faces a challenge in reducing domestic protectionist tariff and nontariff barriers.

Securing Investment for Economic Development

In developing countries, the current account balance often runs at a deficit because investment cannot be entirely covered by domestic sources. Sustainable growth becomes possible only when investment for economic growth can be supplied by domestic savings or foreign capital—provided the latter does not lead to a debt crisis.

Structural Change in the Resource Balance

Vietnam's international balance of payments deteriorated rapidly from 1992 to 1995 following some improvement in the early 1990s. Vietnam's trade and current account deficits in 1995 reached 11.5 percent and 9.2 percent, respectively, of gross domestic product (table 1). The dong has been stable at around 11,000 per U.S. dollar since 1991,[7] but the currency has appreciated in terms of the real exchange rate given Vietnam's comparatively high inflation rate. Therefore, the price competitiveness of Vietnam's exports has weakened. This is one reason for the deterioration in the trade balance. However, the current account deficit is the result of the deterioration of the resource balance.[8] In fact, Vietnam's domestic investment rate has increased dramatically relative to the domestic savings rate.

In calculating the resource balance, we divided the economy into government and nongovernment sectors.[9] We then looked at the causes of the increase in the current account deficit and the structural changes in the resource balance.[10] Finally, we examined how Vietnam raised funds during its high-growth period.

Table 2 shows the resource balances of the government and nongovernment sectors as indicated by their ratio of GDP in 1990, 1992, and 1994. The resource balance of the whole economy reveals the general trend. Although the resource balance was at a deficit of 9.7 percent of GDP in 1990, it decreased to a deficit of 3.9 percent of GDP in 1992. However, it expanded again to a deficit of 8.4 percent of GDP in 1994.

The government's resource balance declined from a deficit of 5.8 percent of GDP in 1990 to a deficit of 1.7 percent in 1992; the deficit remained low, at 1.6 percent, in 1994. The nongovernment sector's resource balance decreased from a deficit of 3.9 percent of GDP in 1990 to a deficit of 2.2 percent in 1992; it expanded to a deficit of 6.8 percent in 1994. The improvement of the total resource balance in 1992 was caused by a reduction of the deficit in both sectors, and the deterioration of the total resource balance in 1994 was the result of a large amount of investment in excess of domestic savings into the nongovernment sector.

The savings and investment rates for each sector explain the changes

Table 2. Resource Balance by Economic Sector (% of GDP)

	GDP	Taxes	Transfers	Consumption	Savings	Investment	Resource Balance	Finance
1990								
Nongovernment sector								
State-owned sector	32.5	-8.6	3.1	-84.8	3.7	-7.5	-3.9	Foreign direct investment 2.3
Non-state-owned sector	67.5	-2.3						
External trade and others	—	-3.7						
Government sector	—	14.7	-3.1	-12.3	-0.7	-5.1	-5.8	Domestic loans 2.8
Total	100.0	0.0	0.0	-97.1	2.9	-12.6	-9.7	Foreign grants and loans 3.0
1992								
Nongovernment sector								
State-owned sector	36.2	-10.8	9.1	-80.5	9.6	-11.8	-2.2	Foreign direct investment 2.5
Non-state-owned sector	63.8	-3.0						
External trade and others	—	-5.3						
Government sector	—	19.0	-9.1	-5.8	4.1	-5.8	-1.7	Domestic loans -0.7
Total	100.0	0.0	0.0	-86.2	13.8	-17.6	-3.9	Foreign grants and loans 2.4
1994								
Nongovernment sector								
State-owned sector	40.2	-12.3	11.0	-74.6	12.1	-18.8	-6.8	Foreign direct investment 6.8
Non-state-owned sector	59.8	-3.1						
External trade and others	—	-8.9						
Government sector	—	24.3	-11.0	-8.3	5.0	-6.6	-1.6	Domestic loans 1.5
Total	100.0	0.0	0.0	-82.9	17.1	-25.5	-8.4	Foreign grants and loans 0.1

Source: World Bank (1996a) and Asian Development Bank (1997b).

Note: The resource balance of the government sector is equivalent to the budget balance.

in the resource balances. The savings rate of the government sector remarkably rose from a deficit of 0.7 percent of GDP in 1990 to positive 4.1 percent in 1992 and edged up to 5.0 percent in 1994. On the other hand, the government's investment rate from 1990 to 1994 advanced from 5.1 percent to 6.6 percent. The improvement in the government sector's resource balance resulted from a remarkable surge in savings and controlled investments. Table 2 shows that the increase in tax revenue caused the rise in government savings." Tax revenue from profitable SOEs expanded from 8.6 percent of GDP in 1990 to 12.3 percent in 1994, and tariff income from external trade rose from 3.7 percent to 8.9 percent during the same period. One reason the government was able to control investment was its decision to stop subsidizing the SOEs.

In the nongovernment sector, the savings rate soared from only 3.7 percent of GDP in 1990 to 12.1 percent in 1994. The increase in transfers from the government sector and the decrease in the average propensity to consume offset the expansion in tax payments to the government, thereby allowing the savings rate to improve. However, the resource deficit in the nongovernment sector expanded owing to significant investment in excess of savings.

The government financed its deficit with domestic loans and foreign grants and loans. Domestic loans were accompanied by an expanded money supply and mainly consisted of debt from the central bank in the late 1980s (table 7). Because the expansion of the money supply led to high inflation, domestic loans were curtailed in 1992 to reduce the money supply and slow inflation. In the nongovernment sector, the resource deficit was nearly equal to FDI inflows in 1992 and 1994. Thus, FDI inflows supported the rapid expansion of investment in the nongovernment sector.

A big change occurred from 1990 to 1994 in the structure of the resource balance. Although more than half of the total deficit was explained by the deficit of the government sector in 1990, the deficit of the nongovernment sector, which was financed by FDI, determined about 80 percent of the total deficit in 1994. The government succeeded in reducing its deficit to restrain inflation. The stability of the macroeconomy led to a rise in the nongovernment sector's savings rate and promoted FDI inflows. Vietnam has achieved its high economic growth in the 1990s by allocating foreign capital and domestic savings for investment in the nongovernment sector.

Table 3. Vietnam's Resource Balance (% of GDP)

	1990	1991	1992	1993	1994	1995	1996
Gross domestic savings	2.9	10.1	13.8	14.5	17.1	19.0	16.0
Gross domestic investment	12.6	15.1	17.6	24.9	25.5	27.1	27.9
Resource balance	−9.7	−5.0	−3.9	−10.4	−8.4	−8.2	−11.9

Source: Asian Development Bank (1997b).

Table 4. Comparison of Resource Balances (% of GDP)

	Gross Domestic Savings			Gross Domestic Investment			Resource Balance		
	1970	1980	1995	1970	1980	1995	1970	1980	1995
Singapore	18	38	51	39	46	33	−20	−8	18
Malaysia	27	33	37	22	30	41	4	3	−4
Thailand	21	23	36	26	29	43	−4	−6	−7
Indonesia	14	37	36	16	24	38	−2	13	−2
Philippines	22	24	15	21	29	23	1	−5	−8
Myanmar	NA	18	11	NA	21	12	NA	−3	−1
Cambodia	NA	NA	6	NA	NA	19	NA	NA	−13
South Korea	15	25	36	24	32	37	−10	−7	−1
Hong Kong	25	34	33	21	35	35	4	−1	−2
China	29	35	42	29	35	40	0	0	2

Source: World Bank (1995c; 1997b), and Asian Development Bank (1997a).

Resource Balances and the Role of FDI in East Asian Countries

Tables 3 and 4 compare Vietnam's domestic savings rates, domestic investment rates, and resource balances with those of other East Asian countries. Only Singapore and China had a resource surplus in 1995; South Korea's resource balance had improved remarkably since 1970 but was still in deficit. The deficits in Malaysia, Thailand, and the Philippines are expanding. The savings rates of the East Asian countries are generally high—exceeding 30 percent except in the Philippines and the Indochinese nations. However, the savings rates were not so high in the early stages of development. Indeed, the saving rates of Singapore, Indonesia, and South Korea were roughly 15 percent in 1970; afterward, they rose along with economic growth. Vietnam's savings rate of 16 percent in 1996 was still low compared with the past performance of East Asian countries.

FDI has played a significant role in the economic development of the East Asian countries and particularly so in Vietnam. Table 5 shows the ratio of net FDI to gross domestic capital formation. For Vietnam, this

Table 5. Role of Foreign Direct Investment (% of gross domestic capital formation)

	1980	1985	1990	1994	1995
Vietnam	NA	NA	18.5	26.7	32.3
Singapore	20.5	10.3	25.4	18.9	14.9
Malaysia	12.8	7.9	17.9	14.5	11.1
Thailand	2.0	1.4	6.7	1.6	1.6
Indonesia	1.2	1.3	3.2	3.6	5.1
Philippines	0.0	1.1	5.7	7.7	8.4
South Korea	0.5	0.9	−0.1	−0.9	−1.0
Taiwan	0.9	2.2	−10.7	−1.9	−1.9
China	0.1	1.0	2.2	14.4	11.8

Source: Asian Development Bank (1997b) and International Monetary Fund (1996).

figure was 32 percent in 1995—extremely high compared to other East Asian countries.

FDI inflows generally have a positive effect on developing countries. First, FDI introduces capital without debt accumulation. With foreign borrowing, the principal and interest must be paid regardless of the borrowing country's economic situation; default can occur when the economy falters. With FDI, enterprises are less likely to file for bankruptcy because dividends are paid based on profitability. Second, FDI ordinarily flows into the host country's industrial sector, thereby leading to expanded employment and exports in the host country and improved productivity through the introduction of efficient technology from more advanced countries. The funds raised by portfolio investment or foreign loans do not always flow into capital formation. Third, FDI makes it easy for the host country to enter into the international division of labor by using the procurement and sales channels established by more advanced countries (Sekiguchi 1988; Urata 1996; Tran 1996).[12]

FDI has driven Vietnam's rapid growth. However, FDI inflows, which account for one-third of domestic investment, will likely dissipate over time. Some analysts contend that the economic development of the East Asian countries was the result of FDI. In fact, the ratio of FDI to domestic investment was about 10 percent in Malaysia and China in 1995 and single digits in most of the other developing East Asian countries; the exception was Singapore, which had a rate of 15 percent in 1995 after reaching 25 percent in 1990 (table 5). The optimal ratio of FDI to domestic investment is theoretically unknown. However, the level of recent FDI

Table 6. Incremental Capital-Output Ratio

	1971–1980	1981–1990	1991–1996
Vietnam	NA	NA	2.8
Singapore	4.6	5.7	4.1
Malaysia	3.4	6.2	4.6
Thailand	3.9	3.9	5.2
Indonesia	3.1	5.2	4.4
Philippines	4.8	22.4	8.2
Myanmar	NA	−154.0	2.3
Cambodia	NA	NA	2.7
South Korea	3.0	3.5	5.0
Hong Kong	3.0	3.9	5.6
China	5.0	3.2	3.4

Source: Based on data from World Bank (1995c) and Asian Development Bank (1997a).

inflows into Vietnam cannot be sustained. In its new economic development strategy, Vietnam raised the minimum share for Vietnamese capital in joint ventures with foreign investors. In addition, Vietnam reduced preferential treatment for foreign investment so that domestic industries will receive equal treatment. These policy changes will have the effect of reducing FDI inflows.

At the same time, the funds required for further economic development will increase. In general, capital efficiency deteriorates along with capital accumulation owing to diminishing returns on capital. The incremental capital-output ratio shows this tendency (table 6). Vietnam's ratio of 2.8 from 1991 to 1996 indicates that its capital efficiency was better than that of other East Asian countries during this period. But maintaining this level over the long term will be difficult. The incremental capital-output ratios of the East Asian countries were roughly 3 at the beginning of their development. Afterward, these countries suffered a deterioration in capital efficiency and therefore an increase in the ratio. If Vietnam cannot counter this tendency, more investment will be necessary to maintain high economic growth.[13] Consequently, expanded domestic savings, continuing FDI inflows, and improved capital efficiency are indispensable to continued growth.

For Vietnam to sustain growth, the government must (a) facilitate FDI inflows by stabilizing the macroeconomy and softening artificial restrictions on FDI, (b) promote domestic savings, and (c) change the growth pattern from one driven by factor inputs to one driven by improvements in economic efficiency. The promotion of domestic savings and the change in the growth pattern will be difficult to attain in the short term. Responsible policy dictates that FDI inflows should not be constrained while the savings rate and economic efficiency remain low.

Stabilizing the Macroeconomy and Improving the Domestic Savings Rate

A stable macroeconomy is necessary both to increase the domestic savings rate and to sustain FDI inflows. The budget structure and especially budget deficits threaten economic stability. Many transitional economies experience high inflation, and Vietnam is no exception; it suffered triple-digit inflation in the late 1980s, primarily because the budget deficit was financed through expansion of the money supply. To deter inflation, Vietnam reduced its budget deficit by increasing tax revenue, abolishing subsidies for the SOEs, and directing the SOEs to banks for funding. The slowing of inflation helped stabilize the economy, which aided in the success of Vietnam's reforms.[14] However, weaknesses in the government's revenue structure will test its continuing capability to contain inflation.

Table 7 shows the government's revenue and expenditure structure from 1986 to 1995. This structure changed during the period from a dependence on nontax revenue to a dependence on tax revenue; hence, budget revenue increased dramatically. The ratio of budget revenue to GDP rose from 13.9 percent in 1986 to 23.9 percent in 1995. Tariff income and tax revenue from the non-state-owned sector contributed 5.6 percentage points and 1.6 percentage points, respectively, to this rise. The total revenue of tax and transfers from SOEs from 1986 to 1995 remained stable at roughly 10 percent of GDP.

SOE revenue decreased from 72.3 percent of total revenue in 1986 to 41.2 percent in 1995, although the government's dependency on SOE revenue remains high. Tariff income rose from 7.2 percent of total revenue in 1986 to 27.7 percent in 1995, which covered the decrease in the share of SOE revenue. Revenue from the non-state-owned sector was stable during the period at 14 percent–15 percent.

The government's revenue structure breaks down as follows: First, the SOEs represent the largest source of government revenue even though their share has decreased considerably. Second, the remarkable increase in tariff income accounts for more than half of the increase in government revenue as measured by GDP. Third, income from the

Table 7. Government Finance

	1986		1990		1992		1994		1995	
	% of GDP	Share	% of GDP	Share	% of GDP	Share	% of GDP	Share	% of GDP	Share
Revenue and grants	13.9	100.0	14.7	100.0	19.0	100.0	24.3	100.0	23.9	100.0
Tax	3.0	21.7	4.0	27.6	13.7	71.9	19.4	79.6	20.3	85.0
SOEs	0.0	0.0	0.0	0.0	8.7	45.8	10.4	42.6	9.1	38.2
Non-state-owned sector	2.0	14.5	2.3	15.7	3.0	15.6	3.1	12.7	3.6	15.0
Agricultural tax	0.7	4.8	0.7	4.8	1.2	6.2	0.7	2.7	0.7	2.7
Nonagricultural tax	1.3	9.6	1.6	10.8	1.8	9.5	2.4	10.0	2.9	12.3
External trade	1.0	7.2	1.7	11.9	2.0	10.4	5.3	21.8	6.6	27.7
Joint ventures	0.0	0.0	0.0	0.0	0.0	0.0	0.6	2.5	1.0	4.1
Other nontax revenue	10.9	78.3	10.6	72.4	4.6	24.1	4.2	17.2	3.0	12.5
Transfers from SOEs	10.0	72.3	8.6	58.8	2.1	10.8	2.0	8.0	0.7	3.0
Others	0.8	6.0	2.0	13.6	2.5	13.2	2.2	9.2	2.3	9.5
Grants	0.0	0.0	0.0	0.0	0.8	4.0	0.8	3.2	0.6	2.5
Current expenditure	13.7		14.7		14.0		17.6		17.3	
Capital expenditure	6.3	100.0	5.1	100.0	5.8	100.0	6.6	100.0	5.7	100.0
Agriculture, forestry, and irrigation	1.3	21.1	0.9	16.8	0.7	12.4	1.1	16.1	1.3	22.0
Industry and construction	2.0	31.6	1.8	35.1	2.1	35.4	1.7	25.9	0.6	11.3
Others	3.0	47.4	2.4	48.1	3.0	52.2	3.9	58.0	3.8	66.7
Overall primary balance	-6.2		-5.1		-0.8		0.1		0.8	
Interest (paid)	0.0		0.7		0.9		1.7		1.3	
Overall balance (cash basis)	-6.2		-5.8		-1.7		-1.6		-0.5	
Financing	6.2		5.8		1.7		1.6		0.5	
Foreign grants and loans	2.3		3.0		2.4		0.1		-0.7	
Domestic loans	3.8		2.8		-0.7		1.5		1.2	
State bank	3.8		2.0		-2.0		0.0		0.0	
Government securities	0.0		0.8		1.3		1.5		1.2	

Source: World Bank (1995b; 1996a).

non-state-owned sector is expanding, although its ratio to total revenue remains unchanged.

In the present structure, revenue depends too heavily on tariffs and the taxes on the SOEs because the non-state-owned sector has not grown quickly. The heavy dependence on the SOEs has led to their preferential treatment. When development of the non-state-owned sector is obstructed by this preferential treatment, competition among the various economic entities becomes constrained. With competition only among SOEs, their long-established market-poor behavior prevents technical and managerial innovation. Without competition among other sectors, the SOEs will not realize efficiency improvement and the government's tax revenue from the SOEs will gradually decline. Furthermore, tariff income will decrease in the future because of reductions to comply with AFTA's Common Effective Preferential Tariff (CEPT) scheme. By the year 2006, tariff rates must be 5 percent or less. However, government expenditures could easily expand as higher levels of investment enter the country for continued infrastructure and economic development.

Vietnam would benefit from a change in its government revenue structure away from a dependence on tariff and SOE revenue. The government should expand its tax base by promoting the non-state-owned sector. Reinforcement of the revenue structure would contribute to a balanced budget and a stable macroeconomy. If Vietnam fails to enact this structural change, it will suffer economic instability and deterioration of the resource balance. A revival of inflation would cause a decline in the domestic savings rate by making real interest rates negative and lowering the future value of assets. A stable macroeconomy is a prerequisite for improving the domestic savings rate.[15]

Improving Economic Efficiency and Reducing Income Disparities

Although economic growth is ordinarily driven by the quantitative augmentation of labor and capital inputs in the early stages of development, such growth eventually slows. To sustain growth, economic efficiency must be improved by restructuring the domestic economic system and gaining access to technological innovations. The collapse of countries that were part of the former Soviet Union resulted from a failure to improve economic efficiency. These countries failed to reform their centrally planned economic systems following high investment-driven growth.

Income disparities create another problem in the transition from a centrally planned to a market economy. Increased disparities often cause social problems in formerly socialist countries, where equality had been a high priority. Vietnam has attempted to simultaneously attain both sustained high growth and a reduction in income disparities.

Efficiency, Economic Growth, and Income Distribution

By using growth accounting, we can see the role of efficiency improvement in economic growth. Assuming an aggregate production function of a country as $Y = AF(L, K)$, we can represent the economic growth rate as $G(Y) = G(A) + \alpha G(L) + \beta G(K)$. Here, Y is GDP, A is the coefficient representing neutral technological progress, L is labor, K is capital stock, α is the production elasticity of labor, β is the production elasticity of capital, and G( ) is the growth rate of the respective variable.

Using this equation, the GDP growth rate can be divided into three parts: the contributions of growth in labor, capital, and total factor productivity (TFP). TPF includes all growth factors other than labor and capital inputs, including technological progress, improved efficiency through the restructuring of the economic system, and the optimal allocation of labor and capital among economic sectors (see Kashiwagi and Sekiguchi 1999).

In analyzing economic growth by means of growth accounting, we can estimate the parameters α and β, using time series data of Y, L, and K in empirical studies. But we cannot complete this analysis in Vietnam's case owing to a lack of data on capital stock; hence, our qualitative analysis is based on conjecture.[16]

First, we focus on labor. The labor population increased at an annual average growth rate of 2.7 percent from 1990 to 1995, whereas the total annual average population growth rate was 2.1 percent during the period.

A relationship exists between the growth rate of investment and that of capital stock. We have assumed constant growth of investment. When the capital stock is large enough at the beginning of the development process, the growth rate of capital stock is lower than that of investment initially but the former converges with the latter asymptotically. In contrast, when the capital stock is small in the early stages of development, the growth rate is higher than that of investment initially but the former converges with the latter asymptotically. Given that Vietnam's capital stock was relatively small in 1990, the capital stock probably grew more than 26 percent annually from 1990 to 1995, which is equivalent to the average annual growth rate of investment during the period.

Next, we examine the contribution of TFP to Vietnam's economic growth. Although we cannot know parameters α and β, we can project the extent to which TFP contributes to growth by providing some random α and β. If we suppose constant returns to scale pertaining to the production function, we can assume $\alpha + \beta = 1$. We can thereby calculate the growth rate of TFP from 1990 to 1995, where $\alpha = 0.2$, $\alpha = 0.5$, and $\alpha = 0.8$. Here, the actual average annual growth rate of real GDP is 8.3 percent and that of labor is 2.7 percent during the period. We assume that the growth rate of capital stock is equal to the annual average investment growth rate of 26 percent. Under these assumptions, we obtain growth rates for TFP of minus 13.0 percent, minus 6.1 percent, and plus 0.9 percent, respectively. As a result, we can conclude that the contribution of TFP to Vietnam's recent growth is negative or small, regardless of the α value.

Based on such growth accounting, we can forecast Vietnam's future economic growth. The growth rate of labor will probably be less than that of the total population over the long term; indeed, the labor ratio peaked at a relatively high 47 percent in 1995. The labor growth rate will likely converge with the population growth rate in the medium to long term. The United Nations estimates the average annual growth rate of Vietnam's population at 2.1 percent from 1995 to 2000, 1.8 percent from 2000 to 2005, and 1.5 percent from 2005 to 2010. The gradual decline in the growth rate of labor will restrain long-term economic growth.

The growth rate of capital stock also will likely decline in the medium to long term owing to the difficulty in securing investment. Sustained high growth in investment is indispensable for continuing rapid growth in the capital stock. If an economy's investment growth rate is equal to its economic growth rate, it can continue to invest without a rise in the domestic savings rate. However, if an economy, such as Vietnam's, has an investment rate higher than its economic growth rate, it cannot raise funds for sustained high growth of investment without a rise in the domestic savings rate.[17] Conversely, an upper limit exists on the increase in domestic savings because people cannot live without consumption. Therefore, high growth in the capital stock cannot be maintained unless the economy introduces foreign capital such as FDI and foreign loans. As for Vietnam, high growth in the capital stock might be possible if the country continues to attract FDI through further improvement of the investment climate such that FDI covers a substantial portion of domestic investment. However, this is an optimistic long-term scenario.

Vietnam's economic growth will also slow without a rise in the contribution of TFP. In fact, the decline of labor and capital growth is inevitable over the long term. To sustain growth, TFP must be raised through innovations in production technology, improvements in managerial efficiency, SOE and foreign trade system reforms, promotion of the private sector, and the reallocation of resources between the agricultural and nonagricultural sectors.

Income disparities seem to occur concurrently with economic growth. Hayami (1995) points out three causes of income disparities that developing countries experience in the early stages of development. First, changes occur in the labor and capital shares. With latecomers to developing status, the capital share increases because the newly developed countries entice capital via labor-saving technologies. The fall in the labor share in latecomers often exceeds the past records of developing countries. Second, in a dual economic structure, where large-scale capital-intensive enterprises coexist with cheap and abundant labor, the differentials of productivity and wages expand between large enterprises and small and medium-sized enterprises. Third, the differential between the agricultural and nonagricultural sectors creates further income disparities. Inequality expands if the productivity differential derived from the introduction of foreign technology into the nonagricultural sector is not reduced due to the immobility of labor among sectors.

Vietnam's investment policy, which gives priority to heavy industries and preferential treatment to SOEs, exacerbates income disparities. Furthermore, Vietnam's surplus labor in the agricultural sector has not sufficiently moved into the nonagricultural sector. If wages rise in the nonagricultural sector because of the failure to absorb cheaper labor from the agricultural sector, industrial investment will stagnate. Alternatively, the nonagricultural sector will specialize in capital-intensive industries that adopt labor-saving technologies to offset the rise in wages brought about by the labor shortage. If this occurs, the production of labor-intensive industries falls short of expectations. The immobility of labor among sectors causes not only the expansion of income differentials but also the stagnation of aggregate economic outputs. Assuming constant growth in factor inputs, the stagnation of economic growth owing to the immobility of labor could lead to a decline in the growth rate of TFP. Economic efficiency cannot improve without optimal resource allocation. Consequently, the top priority for improved efficiency and reduced income disparities is the development of labor-intensive industries that absorb surplus labor from the agricultural sector.

Enterprise Reforms and Economic Efficiency

Vietnam enacted reforms in 1981 that permitted the SOEs to sell that portion of products produced in excess of the amount mandated by government and granted them autonomy in the use of labor, capital, and land. More significant structural reforms were undertaken in the late 1980s. In 1987, the SOEs were granted extensive autonomy in production planning, financing, and labor management. Subsidies for the SOEs were abolished, and the SOEs were directed to raise funds via bank loans. In the 1990s, the performance of the SOEs has improved. According to Le (1996), the proportion of loss-making SOEs dropped from 30 percent–40 percent of all the SOEs in 1990 to about 10 percent in 1996. This improvement followed mass personnel cuts and the abolition and amalgamation of the SOEs in rural areas in the late 1980s and early 1990s. Employees in the state-owned sector declined from about 4 million in 1988 to under 3 million in 1992. Furthermore, the number of SOEs declined from 12,000 to about 6,000.

However, many analysts question whether efficiency at the SOEs has resulted in improvements in production and management methods despite the rise in labor productivity. Nguyen, Ngo, and Ho (1996) point out that 15 percent of the outputs from the SOEs in the early 1990s were too substandard to sell in both the domestic and international markets. More than 50 percent of the SOEs' assets depreciated more than 50 percent, and the organizational pattern of SOEs cannot respond to the needs of diversified business operations. To produce goods that are competitive in the international market, productivity must be enhanced through domestic competition. The 1992 Constitution of Vietnam confirmed the country's intent to develop a multisectoral market economy with state control and a socialist orientation. Legislation in 1990 promoted the private sector. However, the proportion of SOEs to private industrial enterprises is still high, and the SOEs continue to dominate the domestic market. Without exposure to domestic competition, the SOEs will find it difficult to improve efficiency.

The annual growth rate of the gross output of industrial production by the state-owned sector, at 13.2 percent, was far higher than that of the non-state-owned sector, at 7.0 percent, from 1989 to 1994. The share of the state-owned sector in industrial production increased from 66.4 percent in 1989 to 72.3 percent in 1994.[18] The SOEs enjoy monopolies in the electricity, fuel, and ferrous metallurgy industries, and they dominate the nonferrous metallurgy, electric and electronic technology, chemical, foodstuffs, weaving, and textile industries. The non-state-owned sector dominates only the other metallic products, wood and forestry product processing, and food industries. Thus, the non-state-owned sector has played a limited role in Vietnam's industrialization.

In what direction does Vietnam want to advance enterprise reforms in the future? In March 1994, Vietnam's prime minister advocated the formation of business groups (conglomerates) to pursue economies of scale. Policymakers regard small SOEs as ineffective because they do not enjoy economies of scale. A business group must have at least seven member enterprises and minimum legal capital of one trillion dong. In addition, heavy industries are prioritized.[19] Seventy percent of total investment will be allocated to heavy industries in the new economic development strategy for the year 2000. This policy is clearly designed to further develop the state-owned sector because the SOEs monopolize almost all of the heavy industries.

To improve productivity, a competitive market must exist between a developed non-state-owned sector and efficient SOEs. However, Vietnam's policy making to date has effectively strengthened the dominance of the SOEs.[20] Furthermore, the policy prioritizing heavy industries is not consistent with Vietnam's comparative advantage of abundant labor in rural areas. The policy obstructs not only the expansion of employment in the state-owned sector but also the development of labor-intensive industries in the non-state-owned sector. According to Dang (1995), 72 percent of Vietnam's laborers work in the non-state-owned agricultural sector, 10 percent in the non-state-owned industrial sector, and only 3 percent in the state-owned industrial sector.

Income Differentials and the Reallocation of Labor

Income differentials exist among the provinces in terms of labor allocation between the agricultural and nonagricultural sectors. Figure 1 shows the relationship between the agricultural value-added share of GDP and per capita GDP by province. The two variables have a negative correlation in those provinces where the agricultural ratio is at or below 40 percent. The lower the agricultural ratio, the higher the per capita

Figure 1. Attaining High per Capita GDP in Non-Agriculture-Intensive Provinces (1994)

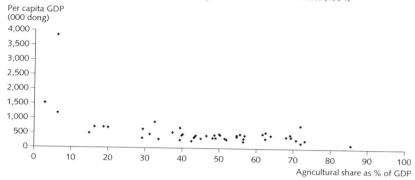

Source: World Bank (1995b).

Figure 2. Expanding Income Differentials in Agriculture-Intensive Provinces (1990–1994)

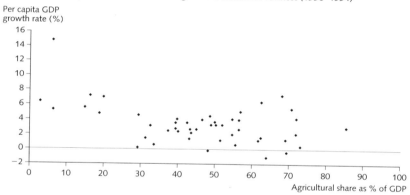

Source: World Bank (1995b).

GDP. If the agricultural ratio is more than 40 percent, per capita GDP is stable. This stability probably derives from social policies designed to support a minimum standard of living.

The relationship between the agricultural share of GDP and the growth rate of per capita GDP shows that income differentials are expanding in agriculture-intensive provinces (fig. 2). The two variables have negative correlations in provinces for which the agricultural ratio is at or less than 40 percent. But we see both positive and negative correlations when the ratio is more than 40 percent. The differentials of per capita GDP growth rate are extremely large in those provinces where agricultural ratios are about 70 percent. Because the income level and its growth rate in the provinces engaging in industry are higher than those in provinces engaging in agriculture, income differentials are expanding in both types of provinces.

Many agriculture-intensive provinces are low income and low growth because agricultural labor productivity continues to be sluggish. Agricultural productivity is lower than that of the other sectors, and the differential is expanding (table 1). Agricultural productivity cannot improve, even though the growth rate of the agricultural sector has been positive since 1988, because the agricultural labor force is continually increasing.

The agricultural share of GDP, including forestry, decreased from 43.8 percent in 1986 to 33.9 percent in 1995, whereas the agricultural share of labor was stable at roughly 73 percent for the same ten years. The agricultural labor force grew at 2.3 percent annually and increased by 4.53 million persons from 1986 to 1995, which accounted for 70 percent of the increase in the total labor force.

In general, labor reallocation from the agricultural sector, which has cheap and abundant labor, to the industrial sector makes it possible to accumulate capital rapidly in the industrial sector and to improve productivity in the agricultural sector. However, this mechanism does not currently work in Vietnam. The productivity and income levels of Vietnam's agricultural sector remain low because the sector has surplus labor. Although the industrial sector has grown rapidly in those urban provinces that have received foreign capital in the form of joint ventures with SOEs, this growth has not absorbed surplus agricultural labor. The policy that prioritizes heavy industries in the state-owned sector—and a concentration on labor-saving technologies in the SOEs—obstructs the development of labor-intensive industries in the non-state-owned sector.

Consequently, labor-intensive industries that are suitable for a labor-abundant country should be developed to reduce income disparities (see Tran 1996). If Vietnam intends to achieve sustainable growth, reduce income disparities, and improve economic efficiency, it must actively promote non-state-owned enterprises for industrialization in rural areas as advocated in its new economic development strategy.

Integrating into the International Economy

Vietnam has deepened its economic relationship with the East Asian countries and the developed countries since the collapse of the CMEA in 1991. Although Vietnam has struggled in its transition from a socialist trade system to a free trade system, participation in ASEAN and AFTA has played a key role in its reintegration into the international economy.

Trade and Investment

Vietnam's trade has been expanding since the early 1990s. Nominal exports and imports grew at average annual rates of 16.9 percent and 24.2 percent, respectively, from 1990 to 1995. Trade is crucial to Vietnam's economic activity. Vietnam's trade was strictly regulated in the 1980s, but the trading system reforms undertaken since the late 1980s have led to deregulation. For example, in 1990 the system that perpetrated the SOE trade monopolies was abolished and private enterprises were given the right to trade. In 1993, the government approved private trading companies. These reforms paved the way for trade expansion.[21]

Vietnam exports primary goods, such as foods and mineral fuels, and imports manufactured goods—mainly capital goods (table 8). Food and live animals (Standard International Trade Classification [SITC] 0) and mineral fuels (SITC 3) account for 60 percent–70 percent of total exports. Manufactured goods (SITC 5–8) represent just one-third of the total, although the share is rising owing to an increase in exports of miscellaneous manufactured goods such as garments and footwear. Vietnam's current comparative advantages lie in primary goods and labor-intensive goods. Imported manufactured goods, on the other hand, account for three-fourths of total imports. The share of machines and transport equipment (SITC 7) imports expanded rapidly in the early 1990s. This implies that Vietnam is entering into an international division of labor whereby it produces primary goods and labor-intensive goods for export using imported capital goods.

Table 9 shows the share of Vietnam's exports and imports, their annual growth rates, and trade balances by region and country. From 1990 to 1996, the biggest change was the shifting of main trading partners from former socialist countries, including the Soviet Union, to East Asian and/or industrial countries. Exports to the former Soviet Union accounted for 36.5 percent of Vietnam's total exports in 1990 but declined to just 0.4 percent in 1996. In contrast, exports to industrial countries, including Japan, surged from 20.9 percent of total exports in 1990 to 61.6 percent in 1996. Imports from East Asian countries, including the ASEAN economies and/or the newly industrializing economies (NIEs),

Table 8. Vietnam's Exports and Imports by SITC Section

		1990	1991	1992	1993	1994	1995
		Exports (% of total exports)					
SITC 0	Food and live animals	34.4	36.8	37.3	37.4	38.7	37.9
1	Beverage and tobacco	0.7	0.1	0.2	0.2	0.1	0.1
2	Crude materials excluding fuels	13.6	15.2	12.7	7.8	7.9	6.8
3	Mineral fuels, etc.	20.8	30.2	33.6	32.9	24.7	22.2
4	Animal, vegetable oil, and fats	0.4	0.1	0.2	0.2	0.3	0.3
5	Chemicals	0.7	0.4	0.4	0.5	0.3	0.6
6	Basic manufactures	4.5	3.9	3.6	5.4	5.6	6.4
7	Machines and transport equipment	0.0	0.3	0.3	0.7	2.4	1.6
8	Misc. manufactured goods	23.9	13.0	11.7	15.0	19.9	24.1
9	Unclassified goods	0.9	0.1	–	0.1	0.1	0.0
5 + 6 + 7 + 8	Manufactured goods total	29.2	17.5	16.0	21.5	28.2	32.8
	Total exports	100.0	100.0	100.0	100.0	100.0	100.0
		Imports (% of total imports)					
0	Food and live animals	4.1	5.8	5.8	3.0	3.3	4.7
1	Beverage and tobacco	0.4	1.8	2.2	0.9	1.2	1.0
2	Crude materials excluding fuels	3.3	3.3	0.8	1.4	2.6	5.6
3	Mineral fuels, etc.	23.3	23.2	25.3	18.1	13.0	11.1
4	Animal, vegetable oil, and fats	0.0	0.2	0.0	0.3	0.3	1.2
5	Chemicals	16.4	18.4	21.3	16.7	17.4	15.8
6	Basic manufactures	22.2	22.5	20.2	19.3	17.8	18.5
7	Machines and transport equipment	27.0	19.2	18.6	33.7	34.3	28.7
8	Misc. manufactured goods	2.4	4.7	4.7	6.5	10.2	13.5
9	Unclassified goods	0.8	0.9	1.1	0.0	0.0	0.0
5 + 6 + 7 + 8	Manufactured goods total	68.0	64.8	64.7	76.3	79.7	76.5
	Total imports	100.0	100.0	100.0	100.0	100.0	100.0

Source: Asian Development Bank (1997b).

surged from 29.6 percent of total imports in 1990 to 59.6 percent in 1996. Almost all of Vietnam's trade deficit can be explained by its deficit against East Asian countries—the ASEAN economies, the NIEs, and China. The deficits against Singapore, South Korea, and Taiwan are particularly striking.

Vietnam's trade with the ASEAN-4—Indonesia, Malaysia, the Philippines, and Thailand—has been relatively small. Vietnam's biggest trading partner is Singapore, although its share of trade with Singapore declined from 1990 to 1996. Exports and imports with the ASEAN-4 accounted for only 6.4 percent and 9.3 percent, respectively, of totals in 1996. However, imports from the ASEAN-4 grew at an average annual rate of 84.9 percent from 1990 to 1996. As a result, the share of Vietnam's

Table 9. Vietnam's Trade by Region

	Exports			Imports			Trade Balance (US$ mn)	
	% of Total		Growth* (%)	% of Total		Growth* (%)		
	1990	1996	1990–1996	1990	1996	1990–1996	1990	1996
Industrial countries	20.9	61.6	41.7	16.4	29.6	43.4	62	229
Japan	13.5	26.4	32.4	5.9	9.2	39.6	171	578
Developing countries	69.1	30.2	3.1	41.0	62.4	39.3	578	−6,435
Asia	26.7	25.5	17.4	29.6	59.6	46.0	−165	−6,377
ASEAN-4	5.1	6.4	22.7	1.1	9.3	84.9	97	−836
ASEAN-5	12.8	12.1	17.2	18.6	23.2	34.7	−205	−2,327
ASEAN-7	13.8	14.1	18.8	19.0	24.4	35.4	−192	−2,359
Singapore	7.7	5.7	12.6	17.5	13.8	24.9	−302	−1,491
Malaysia	0.2	2.0	73.6	0.0	2.6	166.1	4	−21
Thailand	2.1	0.9	2.4	0.6	3.8	77.2	35	−466
Indonesia	0.6	1.3	35.5	0.4	1.9	72.1	5	−167
Philippines	2.3	2.2	17.6	0.1	1.0	80.0	53	15
Laos	0.6	0.4	11.0	0.1	1.1	82.5	12	−118
Cambodia	0.4	1.6	52.2	0.3	0.2	21.7	1	86
NIEs	11.8	6.7	7.7	10.2	27.2	52.9	8	−3,252
Hong Kong	9.6	2.6	−5.0	6.9	4.8	22.4	46	−482
South Korea	1.1	0.0	−100.0	1.9	12.9	79.4	−26	−1,764
Taiwan	1.1	4.2	46.6	1.4	9.5	77.8	−12	−1,006
China	0.3	4.0	80.9	0.2	6.8	138.7	3	−646
Europe	41.2	2.0	−28.8	11.4	2.5	0.9	716	−206
USSR/Russia	36.5	0.4	−43.8	7.4	1.0	−7.4	709	−104
Others	10.0	8.3	14.6	42.6	8.1	−1.6	−957	−529
DOTS Total	100.0	100.0	–	100.0	100.0	–	–	–
Amount (US$ million)	2,524	6,933	18.3	2,841	13,668	29.9	−317	−6,735

Source: International Monetary Fund (1997).

Note: ASEAN-4 consists of Malaysia, Thailand, Indonesia, and Philippines; ASEAN-5 consists of the ASEAN-4 and Singapore; and ASEAN-7 consists of the ASEAN-5, Laos, and Cambodia.
*Average annual growth rate.
DOTS: *Direction of Trade Statistics.*

imports from the ASEAN-4 advanced from 1.1 percent in 1990 to 9.3 percent in 1996.

By source economy, Taiwan contributed the largest amount of aggregate FDI to Vietnam from 1988 to 1995 on an approved basis, followed by Japan, Hong Kong, Singapore, and South Korea (table 10). Following the lifting of the U.S. economic embargo on Vietnam in 1995, FDI sharply increased from Japan, the United States, and the United Kingdom. FDI from the NIEs, including Singapore, however, continued to

Table 10. Foreign Direct Investment in Vietnam by Source Country (approved basis) (US$million)

	1988	1989	1990	1991	1992	1993	1994	1995	1988–1995 Total	Share (%)
Industrial countries	12	252	141	179	635	412	760	2,779	5,170	30.5
France	3	49	4	13	125	168	110	124	596	3.5
United Kingdom		119		5	167	1	1	864	1,157	6.8
Netherlands	7		47	69	6	9	46	108	292	1.7
Japan		83	2	13	221	76	333	1,130	1,858	11.0
United States						0	220	531	751	4.4
Australia	2	1	88	79	116	158	50	22	516	23.0
ASEAN	1	0	36	174	181	698	888	907	2,885	17.0
Singapore	1		20	15	78	250	598	488	1,450	8.6
Malaysia				71	21	347	126	94	659	3.9
Thailand			5	20	20	68	162	190	465	2.7
Indonesia			10	31	62	15		8	126	0.7
Philippines			1	37		18	2	127	185	1.1
NIEs	10	45	162	706	856	1,177	1,177	1,818	5,951	35.1
Hong Kong	10	44	53	181	219	402	547	104	1,560	9.2
South Korea			0	41	107	371	265	565	1,349	8.0
Taiwan		1	109	484	530	404	365	1,149	3,042	17.9
Others	124	67	173	88	254	328	897	1,020	2,951	17.4
Total	147	364	512	1,147	1,926	2,615	3,722	6,524	16,957	100.0

Source: Iwami (1996).

be significant. In addition, FDI from the ASEAN-4 increased in the early 1990s. Although FDI from the ASEAN-4 has been weak so far, it is expected to strengthen through regional integration with AFTA. Despite a short-term decline in FDI from the ASEAN-4 owing to the regional economic crisis, the complementarity between Vietnam and the ASEAN members will facilitate FDI over the long term.

AFTA's Tariff-Reduction Scheme

The Framework Agreement on Enhancing Economic Cooperation and AFTA's CEPT scheme were concluded at the fourth summit of ASEAN in January 1992. AFTA members are obligated to reduce import tariff rates to less than 5 percent by 2008 according to the original CEPT plan; the ASEAN economic ministers in September 1994 decided to bring forward the target date to 2003. However, the CEPT scheme permits AFTA members to temporarily delay implementation of tariff reductions given members' respective developmental stages and internal affairs.

Vietnam participated in AFTA at the fifth summit of ASEAN in

December 1995. As conditions for joining AFTA, Vietnam agreed (a) to reduce its import tariff rates to less than 5 percent by January 2006, (b) to transfer temporarily excluded products other than unprocessed agricultural products onto its inclusion list for tariff reduction in five equal installments beginning in January 1999 and ending in January 2003, and (c) to transfer unprocessed agricultural products from the temporary exclusion list onto the inclusion list beginning in January 2000 and ending in January 2006. Vietnam was granted a three-year postponement relative to other AFTA members.

The impact of the CEPT scheme on trade liberalization for the respective countries depends on the kinds of items on the tariff reduction list. If a country decreases the number of products on the inclusion list and/or places only items with low import tariff rates on the list, the effect of tariff reduction through the CEPT will be limited. Countries can delay substantial trade liberalization by temporarily excluding products they want to protect.

Although some AFTA members have placed 80 percent–90 percent of their total products on inclusion lists for tariff reduction, Vietnam has included only 39 percent of its total products; the temporary exclusion list accounts for 54 percent of all products. The import tariff rates of the items on Vietnam's inclusion list are already less than 5 percent (table 11).

Vietnam's simple average and maximum import tariff rates are high relative to those of other AFTA members. Vietnam's temporary exclusion list probably contains all of the items currently protected by tariffs, considering that the average import tariff rates for product categories on the inclusion list are already less than 5 percent. Accordingly, the effects of trade liberalization will feed through only after the protected items are moved to the inclusion list. After Vietnam transfers products other than unprocessed agricultural products to the inclusion list, their tariff rates will be gradually reduced to less than 5 percent by January 2006. Vietnam can choose which products to transfer onto the inclusion list, thus it can continue to protect domestic industries in the short term.

Vietnam has two alternatives concerning trade liberalization. First, Vietnam can reduce import tariffs at a pace that allows the adequate development of domestic industries. Second, Vietnam can initiate trade liberalization earlier and force domestic industries to become competitive through fierce international competition.

Japan, for example, had time to develop competitive machinery and

Table 11. Vietnam's Import Tariff Rates (%)

HS Code		Simple Average	Maximum	Minimum	Average Rate for Products in the CEPT Inclusion List
1–5	Live animals	8.4	25	0	4.29
6–14	Vegetable products	15.1	50	0	2.87
15	Fats and oils	11.4	30	1	4.00
16–24	Prepared foodstuffs	40.9	150	2	5.00
25–27	Mineral products	4.5	70	0	1.20
28–38	Chemicals	4.9	70	0	1.12
39–40	Plastics	16.8	50	0	3.06
41–43	Hides and leathers	16.1	50	1	3.67
44–46	Wood and wood articles	15.7	40	1	4.50
47–49	Pulp and paper	17.6	40	0	1.71
50–63	Textiles and apparel	27.8	100	0	1.37
64–67	Footwear	33.4	50	1	1.00
68–70	Cement and ceramics	17.1	45	0	1.88
71	Gems	11.8	35	0.5	–
72–83	Metals and metal articles	9.4	30	0	0.45
84–85	Machinery and electrical appliances	12.2	60	0	0.09
86–89	Vehicles	20.2	200	0	0.31
90–92	Optical, precision, and musical instruments	8.3	30	0	0.71
93	Arms	11.5	40	0	–
94–96	Miscellaneous manufactured articles	19.5	50	0	0.00
97–98	Antiques and works of arts	4.7	20	0	–

Source: <http://www.batin.com.vn/vninfo/tariff/> (14 July 1997) and <http://www.asean.or.id/economic/tariff/> (3 July 1997).

HS: Harmonized Commodity Description and Coding System; CEPT: Common Effective Preferential Tariff.

automobile industries by postponing trade liberalization. However, Japan's success featured intense domestic competition among several enterprises in markets protected by tariff barriers against foreign enterprises (Komiya, Okuno, and Suzumura 1984). The Japan experience implies that a competitive domestic market is a necessary condition for postponing trade liberalization to protect domestic industries. Given the less competitive domestic market in Vietnam, Vietnam should begin trade liberalization as early as possible to improve the efficiency of its domestic industries.

Effects of AFTA Membership

Vietnam's trade deficit is expanding each year, and the largest proportion of the deficit is with AFTA members, primarily Singapore. Because Singapore is essentially a free port with tariff rates of almost zero, Vietnam's exports to Singapore are unlikely to expand through the price effect of tariff reductions in Singapore. Conversely, Vietnam's imports from Singapore will increase owing to import tariff reductions in Vietnam. Thus, Vietnam's trade balance against Singapore will likely deteriorate further.

Vietnam's imports from AFTA members other than Singapore are also expanding and its trade balances with these countries are rapidly deteriorating. Vietnam's tariff reductions will accelerate this tendency as it expands imports of intermediate goods from those countries. Furthermore, we cannot expect Vietnam's exports to experience any short-term benefit from AFTA membership. Agricultural products are Vietnam's main exportable goods. However, because AFTA members can protect products by postponing tariff reductions and the price elasticity of demand is low, Vietnam has little possibility of increasing exports of agricultural products. The extent of trade balance deterioration against AFTA members other than Singapore will remain small because the trade linkage with those countries is still weak.

Vietnam imports mainly capital goods from extraregional AFTA members, such as Japan and the NIEs. When Vietnam reduces import tariffs on capital goods only for AFTA members, the supply from intraregional countries will partly substitute for the supply from extraregional countries. This will lead to an improvement in Vietnam's trade balance against extraregional countries but a deterioration in the balance against AFTA members.

The increase in the trade deficit against AFTA members will govern Vietnam's overall trade balance trend. The inevitable short-term trade deficit might cause political pressure to extend the deadline for reducing tariff rates. Furthermore, rising protectionism could result from the effect of tariff reductions on the profitability of the SOEs, which produce over 70 percent of Vietnam's industrial products. The decline in tariff revenue, which accounts for one-fourth of budget revenue, could also result in political pressure to postpone trade liberalization.

Vietnam's long-term comparative advantage lies in labor-intensive industries. Here, *long term* refers to the period in which product mix changes through the reallocation of factors of production. Because the reduction in import tariff rates will mean lower prices for intermediate and capital goods in the domestic market, profitability in these industries will decline. In general, capital moves from low-return industries to high-return industries unless capital allocation is restricted. If the prices of capital-intensive goods drop, capital will move to labor-intensive industries. When laborers follow the flow of capital into these industries, the production of labor-intensive goods will expand. Surplus labor in the agricultural sector has caused severe income disparities in Vietnam. If laborers move into labor-intensive industries, Vietnam should improve economic efficiency and reduce its income disparities. FDI from AFTA members should have a positive effect on Vietnam's economy in this regard.

Middle-income countries such as Malaysia and Thailand have had to reshuffle priorities among domestic industries owing to wage increases. If these countries change their specialization to capital-intensive industries and transfer their labor-intensive industries to Vietnam through FDI, complementarity with Vietnam will strengthen and trade will expand. This would lead to an increase in Vietnam's exports and a decrease in the trade deficit relative to the other ASEAN economies, and facilitate the absorption of surplus labor into the industrial sector. Hence, Vietnam should deregulate FDI and abolish the policy that prioritizes heavy industries.

The process of trade liberalization through tariff reduction will likely be thorny for Vietnam because liberalization will extend the trade deficit and decrease tariff income in the short term. However, Vietnam should attain its longer-term targets of improving economic efficiency and reducing income disparities if it reallocates the factors of production into labor-intensive industries. The expected increase in FDI inflows from AFTA members should ease Vietnam's funding crunch and promote labor-intensive industries.

Conclusion

Vietnam has targeted two primary concerns as it enters the next stage of its economic development: sustaining high growth and reducing income disparities. This chapter has addressed the circumstances of Vietnam's initial stages of development and the requirements for continuing to fund investment for economic growth.

Although inflation was exacerbated in the mid-1980s by expanding the money supply to finance the budget deficit, it was restrained through cuts in the budget deficit. Vietnam's resource balance has deteriorated primarily because of a deficit increase in the nongovernment sector. This deficit is chiefly financed by FDI; hence, Vietnam has had some success in sustaining high economic growth while controlling inflation.

Vietnam's ratio of FDI to gross domestic capital formation is extremely high compared to that of other East Asian countries. Although FDI plays a key role in Vietnam's economic development, these inflows will not likely continue over the long term. Furthermore, capital efficiency has a tendency to deteriorate with economic development because of the diminishing returns on capital, and investment has a tendency to increase. The issues for continued growth are (a) to facilitate FDI inflows by deregulating FDI and (b) to promote domestic savings by stabilizing the economy. However, the weak government revenue structure could hamper economic stability. Government revenue depends heavily on tariffs and taxes on the SOEs because the non-state-owned sector is not yet a sizable tax base. Vietnam can expand its tax base by promoting the non-state-owned sector.

Improvements in economic efficiency are indispensable to sustaining growth in Vietnam. Vietnam's growth in the 1990s has been dependent on factor inputs rather than efficiency improvement. If the contribution of TFP growth does not rise, a slowing of economic growth is inevitable. Progress in production technology, the reform of the economic system, and optimal resource allocation will improve economic efficiency. On the other hand, Vietnam has targeted a reduction in income disparities as well as continued high economic growth. However, the income differential between the agricultural and nonagricultural sectors is expanding. Such disparities come from a policy that prioritizes heavy industries in the state-owned sector. The policy does not contribute to the reallocation of surplus labor from the agricultural sector to the industrial sector.

The non-state-owned sector has played a limited role in Vietnam's industrialization; industrial development has come mainly from growth in the state-owned sector. But the lack of exposure to market competition keeps the SOEs from improving their efficiency. Vietnam has tried to reform the SOEs by creating business groups (conglomerates) and promoting heavy industries. These reforms are not appropriate for Vietnam in that they strengthen the dominance of the state-owned sector in the marketplace and fail to address the problem of surplus labor in the agricultural sector. To improve economic efficiency and to reduce income disparities, labor-intensive industries must be developed in the non-state-owned sector.

Vietnam joined AFTA in an effort to integrate its economy into the world trading system. To participate, Vietnam agreed to reduce tariff rates to less than 5 percent by the year 2006. However, the import tariff rates of items in Vietnam's tariff-reduction inclusion list are already less than 5 percent. Hence, the immediate effect of AFTA for Vietnam is nil. Full-scale tariff reduction will occur gradually from 1999 to 2006. Accordingly, Vietnam has sufficient time to assess two alternatives for trade liberalization. First, trade liberalization can be realized only after domestic industries become competitive. Second, Vietnam can carry out earlier trade liberalization so that domestic industries become more competitive through intensified international competition. The latter option would most benefit Vietnam.

Vietnam's trade deficit against AFTA members will increase in the short term. Furthermore, tariff reduction will cause a decrease in profitability at the SOEs and in tariff income for the government. Such changes might incite protectionism and intensify political pressure to delay the deadline for reducing tariff rates. To realize trade liberalization in compliance with the CEPT scheme, the SOEs must be strengthened through competition and the government's revenue structure must be changed.

Longer term, trade liberalization via AFTA membership offers merit to Vietnam. If the prices of capital-intensive products drop owing to tariff reductions, resources will shift into labor-intensive industries. In addition, AFTA will likely facilitate FDI inflows into Vietnam from middle-income countries such as Malaysia and Thailand in conjunction with the reshuffling of their industrial structures. AFTA could contribute to a reduction in Vietnam's trade deficit through an increase in exports and the absorption of surplus labor in the agricultural sector. Consequently, Vietnam should abolish its artificial restrictions on FDI and promote industries suitable for FDI inflows from AFTA members. If Vietnam overcomes the pressure of protectionism and makes the most of its AFTA affiliation, the country can successfully enter the international economy.

Notes

1. This policy was instituted at the 7th Congress of the Communist Party of Vietnam in 1991.

2. Industries in socialist nations are usually divided into heavy and light, but the distinction is ambiguous. Heavy industries seem to include such sectors as petroleum, coal, steel, and chemical fertilizers.

3. Vietnam aims to complete its industrialization by 2020, with an increase

in GDP of 8 times–10 times compared with 1990 and balanced growth among the various economic entities, including the state-owned sector.

4. If we estimate per capita GDP using an exchange rate based on purchasing power parity, the ranking changes because the exchange rates of developing countries tend to be overvalued.

5. According to the World Bank (1997a), Vietnam's Gini coefficient (an indicator of the extent to which the distribution of income among individuals or households within an economy deviates from a perfect equal distribution) is 35.7, whereas those of Malaysia, Thailand, and the Philippines are 48.4, 46.2, and 40.7, respectively.

6. This hypothesis states that economic growth brings about the expansion of income disparity in an early stage of economic development, while the growth equalizes the income disparity in the process of further development.

7. Vietnam devalued the official exchange rate to 11,800 dong per U.S. dollar in February 1998.

8. According to a basic equation of macroeconomics, the relationship between the current account balance and the resource balance is as follows: current account balance = domestic saving − domestic investment = resource balance.

9. Here, the resource balance of the government sector is equivalent to the budget balance, which is calculated as follows: tax revenue − government expenditure of transfers − government consumption − government investment. The resource balance of the nongovernment sector is calculated as follows: GDP + transfers from government − tax payments − nongovernment consumption − nongovernment investment.

10. Sekiguchi Sueo (1992) discusses the resource balance of Vietnam in the 1980s and concludes that the resource deficit was caused by a budget deficit. However, the cause of the resource deficit has changed in the 1990s to the nongovernment sector.

11. Here, tax revenue includes transfers from the SOEs. However, these transfers decreased dramatically after 1991 when tax revenue largely replaced the transfers.

12. FDI can also produce negative effects in the host country. For example, Komiya, Okuno, and Suzumura (1984) point out that (a) FDI worsens the service balance owing to the remittance of the return on investment; (b) when FDI comes from international monopolistic enterprises, FDI causes the overseas outflow of monopolistic rent created by their price control in the host country; and (c) joint ventures with foreign enterprises have less incentive to develop new technologies and new products compared with domestic enterprises.

13. Infrastructure construction will also extend investment requirements. According to estimates by the Economic Planning Agency of Japan, Vietnam's infrastructure investment needs from 1995 to 2015 will reach US$34.9 billion.

14. Riedel and Comer (1997) view the stabilization of Vietnam's economy during this period as a successful example of shock therapy.

15. Vietnam's domestic savings rate fell to 16.0 percent in 1996, although it had increased from 2.9 percent in 1990 to 19.0 percent in 1995.

16. In growth accounting, factors such as work hours, quality of labor and capital, and the operating ratio of capital are ignored.

17. Assuming a neoclassical production function, GDP, labor, and capital grow at the same rate in a balanced growth path. According to neoclassical economic theory, in an economy in which the growth rate of capital is higher than that of labor and GDP, the capital growth rate falls to the level of the labor growth rate through the adjustment of the price mechanism in the factor market, so that the GDP growth rate declines to the same rate as well. In Vietnam, because such price mechanisms do not work, the determinant of capital growth is domestic savings.

18. The share is overestimated because the production of the state-owned sector statistically includes that of joint ventures with foreign companies regardless of industry. Tran (1998) estimates the 1995 share excluding joint ventures at 52.5 percent.

19. Vietnam also began equitization of the SOEs on a trial basis. However, this experiment has yet to bear fruit.

20. The government provides preferential treatment to the SOEs because it relies on them for tax revenue. Vietnam needs to expand its tax base and thereby its budget by promoting non-state-owned enterprises.

21. Governmental trade controls remain in place for such exportable goods as rice and crude oil, and for such importable goods as fertilizer, steel, and cement. Trade liberalization reforms are not yet complete.

Bibliography

ASEAN Secretariat. 1995. *AFTA Reader Vol. 3.* <http://www.asean.or.id/reader/vol3/> (6 August 1997).

———. 1996. *AFTA Reader Vol. 4.* <http://www.asean.or.id/reader/vol4/> (30 July 1997).

Asian Development Bank. 1997a. *Asian Development Outlook 1997 and 1998.* Oxford, U.K.: Oxford University Press.

———. 1997b. *Key Indicators of Developing Asian and Pacific Countries 1997.* Oxford, U.K.: Oxford University Press.

Dang Duc Dam. 1995. *Vietnam's Economy 1986–1995.* Hanoi: Gioi Publishers.

Dodsworth, John R. et al. 1996. *Vietnam: Transition to a Market Economy.* Washington, D.C.: International Monetary Fund.

General Statistical Office. 1995. *Statistical Yearbook 1995.* Hanoi: General Statistical Office.

Gotō Fumio and Takeuchi Ikuo, eds. 1994. *Shakaishugi Betonamu to doi-moi* (Socialist Vietnam and doi-moi). Tokyo: Institute of Developing Economies.

Hayami Yūjirō. 1995. *Kaihatsu keizaigaku* (Development economics). Tokyo: Sobun-sha.

International Monetary Fund. 1996. *International Financial Statistics Yearbook Vol. XLIX 1996*. Washington, D.C.: International Monetary Fund.

―――. 1997. *Direction of Trade Statistics 1997*. Washington, D.C.: International Monetary Fund.

Iwami Motoko. 1996. *Betonamu keizai nyūmon* (Economic development in Vietnam). Tokyo: Nihon Hyōron-sha.

Kashiwagi Takahiro and Sekiguchi Sueo. 1999. "Gaienteki seichō to naiteki seichō: Nicchū hikaku" (Extensive growth and intensive growth: A comparison—Japan and China). *Nihon Keizai Kenkyū* (JCER Economic Journal) 38: 62–92.

Komiya Ryūtarō, Okuno Masahiro, and Suzumura Kōtarō, eds. 1984. *Nihon no sangyō seisaku* (Industrial policy of Japan). Tokyo: Tokyo University Press.

Krugman, Paul. 1994. "The Myth of Asia's Miracle." *Foreign Affairs* 73(6): 62–78.

Le Dang Doanh. 1996. "Legal Consequences of State-Owned Enterprise Reform." In Ng Chee Yuen et al., eds. *State-Owned Enterprise Reform in Vietnam*. Singapore: Institute of Southeast Asian Studies.

Leung, Suiwah, ed. 1996. *Vietnam Assessment*. Singapore: Institute of Southeast Asian Studies.

Naya, Seiji Finch, and Joseph L. H. Tan, eds. 1995. *Asian Transitional Economies: Challenges and Prospects for Reform and Transformation*. Singapore: Institute of Southeast Asian Studies.

Nguyen Ngoc Tuan, Ngo Tri Long, and Ho Phuong. 1996. "Restructuring of State-Owned Enterprises towards Industrialization and Modernization in Vietnam." In Ng Chee Yuen et al., eds. *State-Owned Enterprise Reform in Vietnam*. Singapore: Institute of Southeast Asian Studies.

Riedel, James, and Bruce Comer. 1997. "Transition to Market Economy in Viet Nam." In Wing Thye Woo et al., eds. *Economies in Transition: Comparing Asia and Eastern Europe*. Cambridge, Mass.: MIT Press.

Sekiguchi Sueo. 1988. *Chokusetsu tōshi to gijyutsu-iten no keizaigaku* (Economics on direct investment and technology transfer). Tokyo: Chūō Keizai-sha.

―――. 1992. "Betonamu no chochiku-tōshi baransu to shihon chikuseki" (Saving-investment balance and capital accumulation in Vietnam). In Sekiguchi Sueo and Tran Van Tho, eds. *Gendai Betonamu keizai* (The economy of contemporary Vietnam). Tokyo: Keisō Shobō.

Takeuchi Ikuo. 1997. "Betonam Kyōsantō dai-8-kai-taikai to shin keizai kaihatsu senryaku" (The 8th Congress of the Communist Party of Vietnam and the New Economic Development Strategy). *Ajia keizai* (Monthly journal of the Institute of Developing Economies) 38(8): 2–20.

Takeuchi Ikuo and Murano Tsutomu, eds. 1996. *Betonamu no shijōkeizaika to keizai kaihatsu* (Transition to market economy and economic development in Vietnam). Tokyo: Institute of Developing Economies.

Tran Van Tho. 1996. *Betonamu keizai no shin-tenkai* (New development of the Vietnamese economy). Tokyo: Nihon Keizai Shimbun-sha.

———. 1998. "Keizai kaihatsu to shijō ikō—Betonamu no guradyuarizumu no ichi kōsatsu" (Economic reforms and development: The gradualism in the Vietnamese experience). *Kokumin-keizai zasshi* (Journal of economics and business adminstration) 177(1): 83–100.

Urata Shūjirō. 1996. "Chokusetsu tōshi no kettei yōin to ukeire-koku eno eikyō" (Determinants of direct investment and the effects on host countries). In Sekiguchi Sueo, Tanaka Hiroshi, and Nihon Yusyutsunyū Ginkō Kaigai Tōshi Kenkyūsho, eds. *Kaigai chokusetu tōshi to Nihon keizai* (Foreign direct investment and the Japanese economy). Tokyo: Tōyō Keizai Shinpō-sha.

Watanabe Shin'ichi. 1995. "Betonamu ni okeru kinyū shisutemu no kaikaku to kaigai yōin" (Vietnam: Financial reform and external factors). In Itō Kazuhisa, ed. *Hatten-tojōkoku no kinyū-kaikaku to kokusaika* (Financial reform and internationalization of developing countries). Tokyo: Institute of Developing Economies.

World Bank. 1995a (23 January). *Viet Nam: Poverty Assessment and Strategy.* Report No. 13442-VN. Washington, D.C.: World Bank.

———. 1995b (17 October). *Viet Nam: Economic Report on Industrialization and Industrial Policy.* Report No. 14645-VN. Washington, D.C.: World Bank.

———. 1995c. *World Tables 1995.* Washington, D.C.: World Bank.

———. 1996a (31 October). *Viet Nam: Fiscal Decentralization and the Delivery of Rural Services: An Economic Report.* Report No. 15745-VN. Washington, D.C.: World Bank.

———. 1996b. *World Development Report 1996.* New York: Oxford University Press.

———. 1997a. *World Development Report 1997.* New York: Oxford University Press.

———. 1997b. *World Development Indicators 1997.* Washington, D.C.: World Bank.

– 8 –
The Role of Nonstate Actors in Building an ASEAN Community

Noda Makito

I N AN ARTICLE on the goals and prospects of the Association of South-east Asian Nations over the next 25 years, Noordin Sopiee, one of the most internationally renowned strategists in Southeast Asia, states that ASEAN should aspire to be "what can be called the ASEAN Community" to achieve "sub-regional and regional resilience" (Sopiee 1992, 18). *Resilience* is a term often used by Southeast Asian leaders, particularly in reference to nations' ability to withstand communist threats. The concept of regional resilience, a natural and logical extension of the national version, requires ASEAN members to "cooperate with each other in every possible way in order to promote their strength as a region based on the principles of self-confidence, self-help, mutual respect, mutual cooperation, and solidarity, which are the foundations for a solidified and viable community of Southeast Asian nations, in their pursuit of regional prosperity and security" (Tamaki 1995, 217). Whatever its specific objectives may be, a regional group of countries, such as ASEAN, is certain to be most effective in attaining its goals and strongest against aggression when it reaches the level of a transnational community. As his first proposal for a full-fledged ASEAN community, Sopiee suggests that members should "generate a higher level of sense of community, cohesion and commitment to ASEAN" (1992, 17).

What then are the requirements for a transnational community? It should be underpinned by a formal political framework, such as a treaty and a treaty organization. If, however, this is the sole foundation of the group's solidarity, it is liable to disintegrate should the treaty be abrogated. Most of today's regional and subregional groupings are economically motivated, based on the prospects of mutual benefits resulting from a high degree of economic interdependence. Excessive interdependence, however, can be anticommunal, as frequently exemplified by the economic frictions between the United States and Japan. "It can be argued that mere economic interaction and linkages are not sufficient as a basis for a regional community. In fact, these could turn out to be a source of acrimonious economic tensions and conflicts among the nations of the region" (Yamamoto 1995, 3).

It obviously takes something more to upgrade a group of nations to a regional community. Yamamoto Tadashi notes, "It is hard to establish a community without some viable shared visions or interests and greater stability in the human and institutional interactions among the nations within the region" (1995, 3). Numerous other writings on the process of building an Asia Pacific community testify to the same needs. Robert Manning and Paula Stern, for example, agree that "even now, as the Asia-Pacific's regional institutions are embryonic, a host of economic, political, military, and psychological trends suggest that the cherished aspiration—a common psychology of belonging, reflecting shared interests, responsibilities, values, and mutual respect—may prove to be a chimera" (1994, 80). They go on to declare that "trade, investment, and a Pacific coastline do not necessarily make for a broader sense of community" (80).

Yasui Sankichi offers additional insight into this matter. Although he admits that moves to create an Asia Pacific regional community are motivated by the desire "to strengthen and further intensify the region's economic dynamism and mutual interdependence," he also observes that "many have pointed out the indispensability of the establishment and intensification of some sorts of interactions in the cultural sphere in order for the Asia Pacific to realize genuine regional integration" (1994, 67). He goes on to quote several experts, including Watanabe Akio, of Aoyama Gakuin University, who emphasizes the importance of cultural exchange, including student exchange programs, to nurture the "shared human sympathy" that is essential for sustained economic cooperation among nations; Aoki Tamotsu, of Osaka University, who stresses the importance of building a "common Asian home" or Asian community; Funabashi Yōichi, of the *Asahi Shimbun*, who claims that, to stabilize and institutionalize the Asia Pacific community, it will have to nurture a spiritual community for coprosperity; and former U.S. Secretary of State

James Baker, who underscores the need for "a strong sense of community based on prosperity and common values" (Yasui 1994, 71). All of these comments point to a common understanding that a transnational regional grouping requires some shared sense of community.

Jeanne Kirkpatrick, a former U.S. ambassador to the United Nations, has said that although ASEAN is one of the smallest blocs in the United Nations, on many issues it has been the second most effective bloc (Sopiee 1992). If governmental agreements and business transactions are not enough, what has been the source of this third, and perhaps most crucial, requirement for the formation of a regional community capable of winning Kirkpatrick's admiration? My hypothesis is that this critical requirement has been supplied by so-called nonstate actors—that is, "civil society" organizations, particularly policy research institutions and nongovernmental organizations (NGOs)—and that this will continue to be the case for the ASEAN-10.

It has been some time since the role of nonstate actors in international relations first attracted intellectual attention. In a famous *Foreign Affairs* article, Jessica Mathews stated:

> The end of the Cold War has brought no mere adjustment among states but a novel redistribution of power among states, markets, and civil society. National governments are not simply losing autonomy in a globalizing economy. They are sharing powers—including political, social, and security roles at the core of sovereignty—with businesses, with international organizations, and with a multitude of citizens groups, known as nongovernmental organizations (NGOs). The steady concentration of power in the hands of states that began in 1648 with the Peace of Westphalia is over, at least for a while." (1997, 50)

A few years earlier, Jusuf Wanandi, the dean of Southeast Asia's international relations experts and a staunch advocate of the Asia Pacific community, asserted that "international relations, which have been based on relations among sovereign states as laid down by the Treaty of Westphalia in 1648, are now undergoing a fundamental change because relations among groups of people and even among individuals have also become an essential part of international relations" (1992, 7). These "relations among groups of people and even among individuals" seem to be a perfect vehicle for building a sense of community across national boundaries.

Indeed, the contribution of nonstate actors to the consolidation of an international community has a precedent in one of the most successful and effective regional communities, namely, that linking the United States and Europe across the Atlantic.

The Role of Nonstate Actors
in Postwar Transatlantic Relations[1]
Pre–World War II

U.S.-European relations in the post–World War II era are commonly referred to as "special" or "unique." They have been tested by a number of grave challenges but have survived and persisted, serving as the basis for the world's most successful regional community, particularly during the height of the cold war. Transatlantic relations are regarded as unique not only because of the degree of integration among the parties involved but also because of the active participation of informal, nongovernmental institutions in dialogues on managing the relationship and keeping it healthy. The contributions of these nonstate actors to the close relationship among policy leaders and thinkers across the ocean have been remarkable, and they are something any other aspiring international community would like to emulate.

The involvement of nongovernmental institutions actually predates World War II. Two of the most influential research institutions in international relations, the Council on Foreign Relations in New York (established in 1919) and the Royal Institute of International Affairs in London (1920), were founded on the basis of a nongovernmental agreement between people in the United Kingdom and the United States that independent institutions for public enlightenment should be established to facilitate discussions and dialogues on issues facing the two countries and the entire world among leaders of the private sector as well as political leaders, a precursor of today's track two diplomacy. At the base of this agreement was a keen common awareness across the Atlantic that international relations were too important to be left solely to governments, which had, after all, failed to contain World War I. The same awareness led to the establishment of a series of like-minded institutions, including the Foreign Policy Association (1918), the Hoover Institution on War, Revolution and Peace (1919), the Century Foundation (1919; formerly the Twentieth Century Foundation), the National Bureau of Economic Research (1920), the Chicago Council on Foreign

Relations (1922), the Brookings Institution (1927), the National Planning Association (1934), and the American Enterprise Institute for Public Policy Research (1943) in the United States, and the Graduate Institute of International Affairs (1927) and the Institute of Policy (1932) in the United Kingdom.

These and other independent U.S. institutions actively opposed the isolationist policy of the U.S. government and contributed to the expansion of the U.S. role in prewar international affairs. U.S. interest in the League of Nations was encouraged by the activities of these groups, leading to the U.S. commitment to the foundation of the United Nations after the war. The Council on Foreign Relations, in particular, promoted the public movement to demand that the U.S. government assist the British and French governments in response to the rise of Nazi power. Its Research Project on War and Peace, which aimed to explore America's political, economic, and strategic goals after the war, is considered to have made a great contribution to the establishment of the United Nations, the World Bank, and the International Monetary Fund.

Most of the large-scale philanthropic foundations in the United States, which have assisted these nongovernmental activities financially, were also established in this period, including the Carnegie Corporation in 1911; the Rockefeller Foundation in 1913; the Ford, Lilly, Kettering, Sloan, and Kellogg foundations in the 1920s and 1930s; and the Rockefeller Brothers Fund in 1940.

Post–World War II to the Mid-1960s

The period immediately following World War II through the mid-1960s is regarded as that of reconstruction of the transatlantic relationship after the devastation during the war. In light of the simultaneous challenges of defense against the Soviet Union and the reconstruction of war-devastated Europe, political leaders and policy planners on both sides decided that transatlantic relations were the cornerstones of security and economic development. From this conviction, a layer of Atlanticists emerged among policy elites in Europe and the United States. As governments faced mountains of tasks that they obviously could not handle alone, nongovernmental institutions played an important role in sponsoring a variety of forums for policy consultations among political and intellectual leaders, immensely contributing to mutual confidence among leaders. This eventually led to the evolution of new economic and political institutions within Europe and across the Atlantic, thus supporting both the transatlantic alliance and European integration.

The most outstanding example of these activities was indisputably the Bilderberg Conference inaugurated in May 1954 at the Bilderberg Hotel in the Dutch city of Rotterdam. This annual, nongovernmental conference on important transatlantic issues is still attended by presidents, prime ministers, and key cabinet members from participating countries as well as leading private citizens. In the 1950s and 1960s, the regular participants in this conference were referred to as the Atlanticists, and their major concerns were how to resolve issues and problems that could damage U.S.-European relations. Aside from the policy impact of these discussions, the true contribution of the Bilderberg Conference is said to lie in the personal relationships conference participants cultivate with their counterparts. A founding U.S. participant testifies that by the time he became a key member of the U.S. State Department, he had come to know almost all of Europe's political leaders on a personal level (Yamamoto 1988). With these kinds of personal relationships, potential problems, bilateral or regional, can be dealt with, even by a few phone calls, before they become politicized, a situation that does not exist in the case of the U.S.-Japan relationship despite an equal, if not higher, degree of economic interdependence.

U.S. nongovernmental initiatives led to the establishment of a few institutions for research and policy dialogue, including the American Council on German Affairs (1946) to promote bilateral relations and mutual understanding, the Salzburg Seminar (1947) to promote mutual understanding between Europe and the United States, and the Atlantic Council of the United States (1961) to promote the Atlantic community, as well as more general international relations institutions such as the Rand Corporation, the Hudson Institute, and the Georgetown University Center for Strategic and International Studies. Most of these institutions initially focused on transatlantic relations. U.S. philanthropic foundations also helped establish a number of research institutions and organizations for policy consultation in Europe in the absence of assistance from European governments, which were preoccupied with the more urgent reconstruction requirements.

On the other side of the Atlantic, too, partly supported by U.S. foundations, a few important nongovernmental institutions were established, including the Koenigswinter Konferenz (Anglo-German Conference), established in 1950 to democratize Germany and strengthen Anglo-German relations; the Wilton Park Conference, started in 1946 to discuss political, economic, and social issues common to the Atlantic countries; Atlantik Brucke (Bridge over the Atlantic), established in 1951; the Ditchley Foundation, established in 1958 to promote understanding on issues of common concern between the United Kingdom and the United States; and the Atlantic Institute, which promoted dialogue and cooperation among members of the Atlantic alliance.

Though embryonic, U.S.-European relations in those days, before the great schism caused by U.S. involvement in the war in Vietnam, are often referred to as the golden age of transatlantic diplomacy. Nongovernmental initiatives were the driving force behind that golden age.

The Mid-1960s to the Late 1970s

The ten-odd years from the mid-1960s through the late 1970s were the low tide of the postwar U.S.-European relationship. Disagreements over the Vietnam War and policies toward the Soviet Union as well as increased economic competition forced leaders on both sides to review the viability of the relationship and its underlying foundations. The emergence of new actors on the international stage, particularly Japan and China, also complicated the picture. Although a number of leading nongovernmental institutions and forums tried to respond by adopting Asia Pacific–related and/or Japan-related agendas or inviting participants from Asia, efforts were also made to rejuvenate transatlantic relations by reestablishing the channels of dialogue between future leaders of the two continents, including the Anglo-American Conference for the Successor Generation, which was cosponsored by the Royal Institute of International Relations and the Johns Hopkins University School of Advanced International Studies in 1985, as well as similar programs by the Ditchley Foundation, the Atlantic Council, the Anglo-German Association, and Atlantik Brucke.

Since the Late 1970s

From the late 1970s, stress has accumulated between the United States and Europe. Discord across the Atlantic became all too obvious, particularly with the heightening of East-West tensions resulting, for example, from the Soviet invasion of Afghanistan and the crisis in Poland. Disagreements between the two sides became significant on a range of issues from arms control to Middle East policy, and some scholars started referring to structural problems and fundamental perception gaps in transatlantic relations. During this period, the United States became heavily preoccupied with its own problems, whereas Europe, too, was more concerned with common problems on the continent and the prospects for a European community. Europeans were also concerned about what appeared to be an Asian shift by the United States. The Atlantic was described as having widened, and some observers spoke of a crisis in U.S.-European relations.

But again, with the help of layers of dialogue networks across the Atlantic, U.S.-European relations restrengthened by the mid-1980s. Michael Armacost, a veteran diplomat, once described Atlantic relations as underpinned by informal connections among leaders on every level and the ability to appeal directly to the public opinion of the other side. Particularly noteworthy contributions in this context were provided by the so-called Four Directors Report of 1981 by heads of the leading international relations institutions in the United States, Germany, France, and the United Kingdom on Western security, which aimed to revitalize policy consultation and coordination across the Atlantic on all security-related issues; a multiyear Europe-America Project of the Council on Foreign Relations, launched in 1983 to clarify the differences in interests in and perceptions of several key issues between the two regions and to promote mutual understanding across the Atlantic; a joint research project, "A New Approach to Nonproliferation" (1982–1985), by the European Policy Research Centre and the Council on Foreign Relations; a series of nongovernmental conferences with the participation of scholars as well as high-ranking foreign and defense officials on issues too delicate to be addressed via official channels; and the Center for Strategic and International Studies' efforts to focus on the dialogue between the successor generations across the Atlantic, including the European Policy Group, which provided a forum for exchange of views on short- and long-term problems in U.S.-European relations.

An applicant to the British foreign service, asked in a finalist interview what was most important to him, responded, "love and the relations with the U.S." (quoted in Rosenthal 1998). Throughout a half-century of ups and downs, transatlantic relations have remained intact and are still regarded as the most important thing in a British youth's life. One can witness here the resilience of a regional community. This special relationship across national borders and an ocean has survived, persisted, and even advanced further because there was something more than political and economic interdependence. The relationship has found its expression in the form of a sense of community among intellectuals and policy elites based on mutual confidence.

This brief review of postwar transatlantic relations shows that nongovernmental actors and initiatives, in the form of independent research institutions and private policy dialogues, have played an indispensable role in consolidating the Atlantic community. Their most outstanding achievement has been the creation of a sense of community among policy elites and intellectual leaders across the ocean.

For ASEAN to be as successful a regional community as the transatlantic community, it must possess similar nongovernmental initiatives to promote a sense of community among the policy elites and intellectual leaders of the member countries. The verification of a similar trend in ASEAN, however, alone does not prove that ASEAN is endowed with sufficient infrastructure for regional community building. After all, the ASEAN members are at different stages of national integration. The impact of nongovernmental initiatives will not be the same for the people of Southeast Asia as is the case in the more mature and more highly integrated societies of Europe and the United States. In developing societies, activities that involve a grass-roots approach should also be examined.

NGOs in Developing Countries
An Associational Revolution

With the overall progress of globalization, through which problems and issues are interrelated across national boundaries, the sovereign power of national governments has become increasingly limited. Furthermore, it has become obvious that they now have to share power with various nonstate actors, most notably with NGOs.

William van Dusen Wishard thus writes, "As a consequence of this globalization, every nation's control over its economic future is diminishing. Well over 50 percent of the variables affecting the United States economy are outside the control of policy makers in Washington. The Chinese government recently estimated that Beijing can control only about half of the factors affecting China's economy" (1994, 65). Wishard goes on to quote U.N. Secretary-General Boutros Boutros-Ghali: "It is undeniable that the centuries-old doctrine of absolute and exclusive sovereignty no longer stands" (65–66).

Mathews recalls that the prevalence of nonstate actors is not un-precedented, citing the example of the East India Company and some other centuries-old intergovernmental institutions, but she admits that "both in numbers and in impact, nonstate actors have never before approached their current strength" (1997, 52). Timothy M. Shaw notes the same phenomenon: "The international community has had to come to accept the legitimacy and activity of several types of influential non-state actors. These have historically included multinational corporations (MNCs) and major religions, but they now extend to international and local non-governmental organizations (INGOS and NGOs) such as ethnic, environmental, indigenous peoples', women's and youth groups" (1994, 140).

The prevalence of NGOs in the developing world makes it virtually impossible to provide a reliable quantitative measurement of their impact. Mathews (1997, 52–53) estimates that 35,000 NGOs are active in developing countries, although she also reports that in South Asia alone there are more than 12,000 NGOs active specifically in the field of ir-rigation. Julie Fisher of Yale University endorses an estimate of 30,000 to 35,000 "active grassroots support organizations in the Third World" (1996, 7). In another work, she mentions that as early as 1985, "the Club of Rome estimated that 'Southern' NGOs may involve as many as 60 million people in Asia, 25 million in Latin America, and 12 million in Africa" (1993, 8). These trends and the similar spread of NGOs in the industrialized world are collectively referred to as an "associational revolution" by Lester Salamon in a 1994 *Foreign Affairs* article in which he declares that, based on comparative studies among 14 countries, "this associational revolution may well give a tremendous impact on the world of the late 20th century similar to the impact of the rise of the nation-state on the late 19th century world" (109).

NGOs and Community Building

NGOs, typically composed of dedicated individuals with professional knowledge and expertise in their various fields, can be versatile and ca-pable of delivering almost anything governments normally deliver. In fact, Mathews suggests, "Internationally, in both the poorest and richest countries, NGOs, when adequately funded, can outperform government in the delivery of many public services" (1997, 63). In the context of this chapter, however, the focus is on NGOs' ability to help nurture a sense of community across national boundaries.

NGOs are not confined by national boundaries. In line with their characteristics, activities, modes of conduct, and missions, they are capable of nurturing a sense of community across national boundaries in a variety of ways.

ISSUE ORIENTATION   NGOs are naturally issue-oriented or even issue-specific. The international implications of this inclination should be obvious, given the cross-border and regional expansion of issues. These organizations can easily promote a sense of shared destiny and common interests among countries within a region that together confront the same issues. Environmental problems seem to be the best example of such issues, but Mathews (1997) introduces an example of solidarity among NGOs in the United States, Canada, and Mexico that took clear shape when they collaborated in demanding that the U.S. and Mexican governments disclose the draft of a bilateral trade agreement, particularly the articles on health-care and safety, cross-border environmental pollution, consumer protection, migration, fluidity of labor, child labor, sustainable agriculture, social contracts, and debt relief.

COMMUNITY AMONG PROFESSIONALS   Participants in NGO activities with professional skills and knowledge may well develop a sense of community with professionals from other countries in the same region who deal with the same issues. What Mathews writes about intellectual and technical elites can be applied to some NGO participants (who may, of course, themselves be members of such elites), namely, that "those elites…are also citizens groups with transnational interests and identities that frequently have more in common with counterparts in other countries, whether industrialized or developing, than with countrymen" (1997, 52). Wishard backs up this point, observing, "We see the proliferation of countless non-governmental organizations (NGOs) operating on a transborder basis, technological alliances crossing national boundaries" (1994, 67).

SENSE OF COMMUNITY AT THE GRASS-ROOTS LEVEL   Fisher reports, "In Asia, Latin America, and, more recently, in Africa, this organizational explosion is creating a partnership between some of the best- and least-educated people in each society as intellectuals and technically trained professionals seek out and work with grassroots village and neighborhood groups" (1993, 5). This partnership should help promote a sense of community with neighboring countries on a grass-roots level. And Isagani Serrano states, "Democratization from below has crossed local and national frontiers and spread throughout Asia-Pacific. Peoples' movements and other voluntary organizations are now linked regionally by structures and processes they have created over the years" (1994, 301).

CROSS-NATIONAL NETWORKING BASED ON ELECTRONIC COM-MUNICATIONS NGOs, not having access to traditional means of cross-border transmission, such as the diplomatic pouch, rely on communication through networks. The very nonnational nature of computer-based communication is bound also to help promote a sense of community among members of these organizations, who are geographically scattered but likely to be living in neighboring countries.

As Fisher explains, "South-South networks of NGOs [networks of NGOs among developing countries] have proliferated rapidly since the early 1960s within each region of the Third World" (1996, 15). She attributes this phenomenon to (a) the proliferation of indigenous NGOs in the Third World; (b) international or Northern support, both official and voluntary; (c) the rise of computer and communications technology; and (d) the process of NGO networking surrounding major U.N. conferences. Yamamoto (1995), who conducted a 15-country survey on the emergence of civil society in Asia Pacific, analyzes the general pattern of international NGO networking as beginning with groups of like-minded NGOs within a country, which in turn collaborate with similar groups in neighboring countries, eventually forming an issue-oriented regional network of NGOs. He goes on to underscore the positive effects of such networking on the sense of community within the region.

NGO activities, particularly their networking across national boundaries, have a great potential in cultivating and nurturing the kind of sense of community that seems to be required for a regional group of countries, such as ASEAN, to become a community.

Forces for Community Building

In the previous sections, an attempt was made to anatomize the two paths through which a regional grouping of countries might become an effective regional community: a sense of community through activities that will enhance mutual confidence among policy elites and intellectual leaders and, in light of the shallowness of national integration and political coherence in developing countries, a sense of shared destiny, interests, and goals that are promoted by numerous NGO activities that are, in actuality, changing the basic structure of international relations. Are these two paths present and effectively functioning in ASEAN?

Track Two Activities

The term *track two* (or track two diplomacy) is commonly used by international experts in reference to relations in ASEAN and East Asia. The term usually refers to international conferences, symposia, workshops, and seminars on policy-oriented topics on East Asian international relations and economic relations. Paul Evans has monitored these track two activities, particularly in the field of regional security in Asia, since 1993. He refers to a "dialogue enterprise" and says that "by 1993 the dialogue business had become a growth industry. It is now difficult to even list the various track two channels. The number of meetings listed in a recent compilation for 1993 averaged about four per month" (1993, 23) (tables 1 and 2).

Desmond Ball notes that "there has been a burgeoning of nongovernmental activities and institutional linkages, now generally referred to as the 'second track' process" (1993, 42). Carolina Hernandez defines track two diplomacy as "the generation and conduct of foreign policy by nonstate actors, including government officials in their private capacity" (1994, 6). Hernandez says that such diplomacy "includes the participation of scholars, analysts, media, business, people's sector representatives, and other opinion makers who shape and influence foreign policy and/or actually facilitate the conduct of foreign policy by government officials through various consultations and cooperative activities, networking and policy advocacy" (6). The South China Sea Informal Working Group contends that "track-two diplomacy . . . has no official standing, and participants, even though they may be government officials, do not represent the state

Table 1. Track One and Track Two Dialogues in East Asia

	Track One	Track Two
1993	3	34
1994	19	93
1995 (Jan.–June)	4	34
1995 (July–Dec.)	13	49
1996 (Jan.–June)	12	36
1996 (July)–1997 (June)	10	49
1997 (July–Dec.)	10	23
1998 (Jan.–Mar.)	2	14

Source: Joint Centre for Asia Pacific Studies (1995–1998).

Table 2. Track Two Dialogues Related to ASEAN (July 1996–December 1997)

The New Geopolitical Order in Southeast Asia and Europe-Asia Relations	4th ASEAN Colloquium on Human Rights
Working Group on Maritime Security in East Asia	1st Meeting of the CSCAP Study Group on Transnational Crime
South-East Asian Security: Coping With Rising Tensions (Wilton Park Conference 473)	6th Southeast Asia Roundtable on Economic Development: Building the Ground Work for a Strong Southeast Asian Economy
Peace and Cooperation: Different Approaches to the Maintenance of Peace in Southeast Asia, Asia and Europe	2nd ASEAN Congress
International Conference on Navigational Safety and Control of Pollution in the Straits of Malacca and Singapore: Modalities of International Cooperation	ASEAN Regional Forum Track II Conference on Preventive Diplomacy
	39th Annual Conference of the International Institute for Strategic Studies
ASEAN-Taiwan Dialogue	CSCAP Comprehensive and Cooperative Security Working Group Meeting
One Southeast Asia in a New Regional and International Setting (CSIS 25th Anniversary International Seminar)	2nd Meeting of the CSCAP Study Group on Transnational Crime
Workshop on ASEAN Maritime Security	International Conference on Promoting Trust and Confidence in Southeast Asia: Cooperation and Conflict Avoidance
ASEAN Young Leaders Forum: External Influences on Foreign Policy	ASEAN Young Leaders Forum
5th Meeting of the CSCAP Working Group on Confidence and Security Building Measures	7th CSCAP CSMB Working Group Meeting
	Asia-Pacific Security for the 21st Century
Asia-Europe: Strengthening the Informal Dialogue: First Plenary Meeting of the Council for Asia-Europe Cooperation (CAEC)	Asia Pacific Security Outlook 1998
ASEAN Regional Forum Inter-sessional Support Group Meeting on Preventive Diplomacy	Informal Meeting of the ASEAN Law of the Sea Experts on the Implementation of Certain Provisions of the 1982 UN Convention on the Law of the Sea
2nd Workshop on Security and Stability in Southeast Asia	
3rd Meeting of the CSCAP Working Group on Maritime Cooperation	SEAPOL's System Compliance Project Workshop
	3rd CSCAP North Pacific Working Group Meeting
3rd Meeting of the CSCAP Working Group on Comprehensive and Cooperative Security	Asia Pacific Agenda Project Yokohama Forum
Seminar on Nuclear Non-Proliferation	8th CSCAP Steering Committee Meeting
ASEAN in Transition: Implications for Australia	CSCAP-Japan Open Symposium
Data Sharing and Maritime Security	5th ASEAN-ISIS Colloquium on Human Rights
2nd Asia-Pacific Agenda Forum	Cambodia's Future in ASEAN: Dynamo or Dynamite?
Defense Asia Forum 1997	8th Southeast Asia Forum
ASEAN-India Dialogue	8th CSCAP CSMB Working Group
2nd Meeting of the CSCAP North Pacific Working Group	12th Asia Pacific Roundtable
	2nd Asia-Pacific Regional Security Workshop

Source: Joint Centre for Asia Pacific Studies (1997; 1998).

or government, and therefore the conclusions of the meeting, if any, are not in any way binding upon governments, and nor are the proceedings of the meeting declamatory of the position of any state. . . . This gives participants an unusual degree of freedom to speak and express their views, and to debate topics which, in ordinary circumstances, would be either taboo, or of such sensitivity that the approach to discussions is necessarily cautious" (Townsend-Gault 1998, 1). These track two measures mirror the nongovernmental policy-oriented initiatives of the postwar transatlantic community.

Hernandez further states that "track two diplomacy became possible because of growing interdependencies such that relevant actors in the multiple channels of integration are no longer confined to states. The function of diplomacy has been increasingly shared by nonstate and nongovernmental actors" (1994, 15). Such diplomacy reflects the structural changes in overall international relations—the power shift, or associational revolution.

ASEAN-ISIS AND ARF/CSCAP   Why is there such a heavy concentration of track two activities in East Asia, particularly in and around the ASEAN countries? One contributing factor is the ASEAN Institutes of Strategic and International Studies (ASEAN-ISIS) and its member institutions. Many of the regional track two activities have been related to the Council for Security Cooperation in the Asia Pacific (CSCAP). And a single institution—ASEAN-ISIS—is at the core of most CSCAP-related programs. ASEAN-ISIS is involved in many other regional dialogue programs as well. Ball asserts that "the ASEAN-ISIS association is central to much of the networking and discourse with respect to security cooperation in the region" (1993, 42). In recent years, topics of ASEAN-ISIS–initiated regional dialogues have expanded beyond security-related issues to include economic and so-called new security issues.

ASEAN-ISIS was "formalized as a regional non-governmental organization with the signing of its charter on June 28, 1988," but it was preceded by "a number of informal regional meetings . . . beginning in the early to mid-1980s amongst heads and experts from these groups upon the initiative of Mr. Jusuf Wanandi of the CSIS (Centre for Strategic and International Studies, Jakarta)" (Institute of Strategic and International Studies [ISIS] 1993, 1). Its genesis was a group of regular Southeast Asian participants at international conferences who had built up professional and personal relationships through these encounters in the international arena. The group was formed because "the need for more regional meetings of experts and scholars in the region was established in the face of politico-security and economic issues and problems affecting ASEAN" (Hernandez 1993, 1). Originally, the group consisted of five institutions from the ASEAN-5: the CSIS in Indonesia, the Institute of Strategic and International Studies in Malaysia, the Institute of Strategic and Development Studies in the Philippines, the Singapore Institute of International Affairs, and the Institute of Security and International Studies at Chulalongkorn University in Thailand. Subsequent participants included the Institute for International Relations of the Vietnamese Ministry of Foreign Affairs from 1996, and the Laotian and Myanmar Institutes of Strategic and International Studies from 1997. Brunei has not established an independent counterpart institution. All ASEAN-ISIS functions are attended by the region's foreign ministry officials in a private capacity. The group acknowledges that "initiating policy dialogues with each other, with ASEAN partners and other states in the region through non-official channels was an important step towards reducing tension and building confidence in the region" (Hernandez 1993, 1).

As an institution with the purpose of enhancing confidence in the ASEAN region, ASEAN-ISIS has coordinated numerous conferences and research projects to promote policy-oriented intellectual dialogue. Hernandez describes the role of ASEAN-ISIS in its support of ASEAN as follows:

- a major source of policy inputs for consideration of the respective governments and decision-makers in ASEAN countries;
- a significant venue for experts and scholars in strategic studies to exchange information and analysis of issues and concerns common to ASEAN and its major partners;
- a laboratory and nursery of tentative, perhaps even volatile, ideas [on the conviction that] the cutting edge of regionalism is the ability to go through a process of discussion of various issues, rather than simply the act of agreeing on specific ideas;
- the "comfort zone" in ASEAN which enables governments to adopt ideas safely and with legitimacy;
- something like an ozone layer (which) help[s] filter, screen, and modulate potentially "harmful rays" or ideas;
- a pathfinder, carving out options and approaches for the main party; [and]

- the task for ASEAN-ISIS is to think ahead to prevent disunity and crisis. (ISIS 1994, 9).

Through the personal prestige of participating members, and the relevance and timeliness of its activities, ASEAN-ISIS was quickly recognized by ASEAN governments as an important actor in the region. ASEAN-ISIS attained international recognition in 1992 when ASEAN officially announced the launching of the ASEAN Regional Forum (ARF), the first official institution for consultation on security affairs in the Asia Pacific region.

The establishment of ARF was truly a historical event. Nishihara Masashi, writing on the participation of 17 countries and one international organization (the European Union) at ARF's first conference, said, "It is a historic event that all the countries in the region which were divided into two blocs during the Cold War get together" (1994, 60). The ARF's historical significance lies primarily in its ability to generate a sense of mutual confidence between former opposing blocs through "mutual reassurance measures," as then Japanese Foreign Minister Kōno Yōhei characterized it (68).

ASEAN-ISIS perceived, articulated, tested, and formally proposed ARF. An ASEAN-ISIS report, "A Time for Initiative: Proposals for the Consideration of the Fourth ASEAN Summit," introduced the concept, which later became the basis for ARF. Hernandez notes "that the specifics of the ASEAN Regional Forum (ARF) reflect the main arguments of the ASEAN-ISIS proposal for this initiative" (1994, 18).

ASEAN-ISIS also contributed to the further institutionalization of ASEAN when it proposed what later was adopted as the senior officials' meeting. According to Ball, "It has been recognized that the PMC [Post Ministerial Conference] process must be supported by the development of some institutionalized infrastructure at both the official and nongovernmental level. In June 1991, the ASEAN Institutes of Strategic and International Studies proposed that a 'senior officials meeting' (SOM) made up of senior officials of the ASEANs and the dialogue partners be instituted to support the ASEAN PMC process" (1993, 41). The establishment of ARF was announced at an ASEAN-SOM in May 1993. Referring to the deliberations at ASEAN-ISIS, Evans reports that "[this SOM] meeting borrowed concepts and took advantage of a climate of opinion that have been generated through track two activities over the past two years" (1993, 33).

In an effort to strengthen ASEAN horizontally, ASEAN-ISIS officially proposed inviting Vietnam as ASEAN's seventh member. ASEAN-ISIS submitted a memorandum to ASEAN on this subject in late 1993, and this proposal "found its way into the July 1994 decision to invite Vietnam as a full member after certain formalities are met" (Hernandez 1993, 24). Meanwhile, a number of study missions composed of ASEAN-ISIS members and associates visited Vietnam to prepare the necessary groundwork.

ASEAN-ISIS has demonstrated that a nonstate actor can make a difference in regional relations. Its initiative to establish ARF, the first security community in the region, cannot be overemphasized. But, perhaps more important, ASEAN-ISIS has contributed to a sense of community and shared interests among foreign policy planners and other intellectuals across the region through its open and active agenda.

One of ASEAN-ISIS's most significant contributions in community building was CSCAP, which was formally launched in June 1993. ASEAN-ISIS developed CSCAP together with the Seoul Forum for International Affairs, the Japan Institute of International Affairs, and the Pacific Forum/CSIS in Honolulu, Hawaii. Participants later included the Strategic and Defence Studies Centre, Australia National University, and the University of Toronto–York University Joint Centre for Asia Pacific Studies in Canada. CSCAP has stretched its track two diplomacy more extensively than ASEAN-ISIS, and is underpinned by a Pacific Economic Cooperation Council–style national committee in each member country that is tripartite in composition, with scholars/academics, businesspeople, and government officials.

Ball views "the establishment of CSCAP [as] one of the most important milestones in the development of institutionalized dialogue, consultation and cooperation concerning security matters in the Asia Pacific region since the end of the Cold War. It is designed not only to link and focus the research activities of non-governmental organizations devoted to work on security matters across the whole of the Asia Pacific region, but also to provide a mechanism for linkage and mutual support between the second track and official regional security cooperation process" (1993, 50). Hernandez adds that "the usefulness of CSCAP's track two diplomacy" is cherished "as a source of intellectual strength and expertise whose findings can be made available to the ARF and other official regional security fora" (1994, 31).

The impact of these track two institutions on mutual confidence among countries in the Asia Pacific region is remarkable after decades of mutual suspicion and acrimony. One security flashpoint in the post–cold war Asia Pacific region remains the South China Sea. Managing Potential Conflicts in the South China Sea, a project supported by the Canadian International Development Agency, concluded "that confidence building measures are a non-negotiable requirement for any form of cooperation in the South China Sea" (Townsend-Gault 1998). The architects of CSCAP and ASEAN-ISIS clearly had these insights in mind when they perceived this framework.

ASEAN-ISIS AND THE ASEAN-10 COMMUNITY   From the viewpoint of enlarging the ASEAN community, ASEAN-ISIS plays an important role in the informal socialization, or indoctrination, of new members in ASEAN.

Sopiee, writing on the future of ASEAN in 1992, was somewhat ambivalent about the expansion of ASEAN. Although he admits that "our basic instinct in favour of a cohesive Southeast Asian organization of more than six and preferably 10 is sound," he also introduces a school of thought, which was popular in Southeast Asia at the time, that argued "that increased membership will excessively slow down, or even break down, the present process and momentum of ASEAN. . . . An expanded ASEAN would result in the excessive heterogenization of ASEAN in terms of strategic and policy concerns and perspectives, procedures and activities and grossly complicate the already laborious process of consensus formation, which is the basis of ASEAN decision-making" (1992, 20). One can sense the hesitation of a founding member of ASEAN, albeit on the private side. ASEAN has obtained international respect but expansion brings about the entry of newer, unsophisticated members. The ASEAN-5 are, at least on the institutional level, democratic in that they have general elections and their results are more or less respected. But the prospective new members all have been, from a Western perspective, shameless violators of democratic rules and human rights principles. Entry of these countries will surely lead to friction within the international community.

Also looking ahead to ASEAN's future, Jusuf Wanandi, the de facto dean of ASEAN-ISIS, reached a more proactive conclusion. Admitting that "among the many new issues in international relations, two stand out, namely human rights and the environment" (1992, 7), he contends that the positions of the new members should not hamper the new members within the ASEAN community. Wanandi believes that "self-righteous means and 'preachings' by the Western countries (many of which were colonialists during the period of imperialism) towards the developing countries will not be effective and are often counter-productive," and asserts that "the best approach is when the one party could give advice as a friend to another country" (1992, 10). The ASEAN-5 also went through a period of staunch criticism from the West not that long ago. Track two institutions are well positioned to ease this transition. Wanandi, therefore, concludes that "such cooperation should not be confined to governments but should also be developed among NGOs" (1992, 7). ASEAN-ISIS can offer friendly advice on these matters to the policy elites and intellectual leaders of Laos, Myanmar, and Vietnam. This socialization function by ASEAN-ISIS is crucial not only from the viewpoint of preparing the Indochinese countries for full-fledged membership in the ASEAN community but also for these countries to be accepted as legitimate members of the international community.

However, ASEAN-ISIS does not monopolize this role. Organizations with similar activities include a Thai educational institution that provides midcareer Vietnamese officials with training in planning in English; another Thai research institution, with the financial help of a U.S. foundation, that helped the Vietnamese government draft its first commercial and business laws; and a Singaporean educational institution that trains midcareer Vietnamese economic bureaucrats in planning and improving their English-language skills, which has long been the weak link of Vietnam's otherwise promising capability. Such activities contribute to a sense of community among participants and their host institutions.

The Myanmar Institute of Strategic and International Studies (MISIS) admits looking forward to participating in the various track two functions of ASEAN-ISIS, which it has just joined, because it will provide Myanmar's intellectuals with opportunities to explain their positions and exchange views with their U.S. and European counterparts—not otherwise an outlet available to them. In fact, the existence of a counter-part research institution to ASEAN-ISIS seems to be a prerequisite for membership in ASEAN. MISIS, however, exists in name only, and its leadership is seeking guidance from more experienced institutions on how to establish a full-fledged institution.

Thus, phenomena similar to postwar transatlantic relations exist in ASEAN. Nongovernmental activities contribute to the formation of a sense of community among policy elites and intellectual leaders throughout the region which, in turn, contributes to the overall confidence building in the region. In this important endeavor, ASEAN-ISIS, in particular, has played a role comparable to that of the Council on Foreign Relations in New York, the Brookings Institution in Washington, D.C., and the Royal Institute of International Affairs in London combined. T. G. McGee must have had ASEAN-ISIS in mind when he wrote, "While the degree of commitment to facilitate economic interaction between these new subglobal regions (including ASEAN) varies widely, they are all characterized by networks of collaborative institutions that act as the foundation for their regional cooperation" (1997, 12).

NGO Networks

The activities of ASEAN-ISIS have contributed significantly to the formation of a sense of community among the policy elites and intellectual leaders in the region by establishing reliable channels of communication and, thus, enhancing mutual confidence. The organization has worked to socialize new members toward eventual participation in the ASEAN-10. At least one condition for an effective regional community seems to be fulfilled.

For countries in the South, including the ASEAN members, however, a sense of community among the elites in the different countries does not guarantee cohesion of the group. In developing countries, where the gaps between the elites and the masses are wide, a regional community also requires grass-roots interactions. The networking capability of NGOs has been extremely effective in promoting a more grass-roots sense of community, especially among the developing countries. Therefore, it is relevant to examine whether NGOs actually help to underpin a regional community on the grass-roots level in ASEAN.

Because of a focus on issues that is more East Asian or Asian as opposed to Southeast Asian, the scope of NGO networks and collaborations among NGOs has been more Asia-wide or, sometimes, Asia Pacific–wide. Yamamoto, in his integrative 15-country study *Emerging Civil Society in the Asia Pacific Community*, writes that "there clearly has been an emergence of a number of associations, networks, and other forms of interactions among NGOs in Asia Pacific in recent years" (1995, 19). NGOs in various ASEAN members report a similar trend. The Singaporean report, for example, observes that "the increasing trends towards economic regionalization in Asia Pacific . . . have led to the necessity of NGOs working at the regional level in order to effectively address these [environmental and social problems that are transnational in nature] problems" (219). Likewise, the Philippines report states that "global issues such as human rights, the environment, women, migration and refugees, the spread of AIDS, and population growth all pose major challenges to the Asia Pacific region. Widespread concern has induced the formation of linkages of like-minded NGOs across national boundaries in Asia Pacific" (202). And the Thai report concludes that "nongovernmental organizations in Asia . . . have joined hands to work together" and that "the role of NGOs in countries in Asia and the Pacific cannot be denied. Networks of NGOs have been established across national borders" (261, 268).

Some of the more outstanding NGOs involved in regional networking include the following:[2]

- People's Plan for the 21st Century was established in 1988 to "counterpose a people-based, people-centered vision of an alternative Asian future to regional economic, political, and cultural integration" by linking the largely autonomous activities of grassroots and citizens' movements throughout the Asia Pacific region.
- CODE-NGO is the largest coalition of major-development NGO networks in the Philippines, forging linkages with development NGOs in other developing countries in Asia and in sub-Saharan Africa.
- The Centre for the Development of Human Resources and Rural Asia (CENDHRRA) was established in 1974 to develop linkages and networks among NGOs in Asia. The organization gave birth to the South East Asia Development of Human Resources and Rural Areas Forum (SEADHRRA), a solid regional network among national chapters of CENDHRRA in East Asian countries (Indonesia, Japan, Malaysia, the Philippines, South Korea, and Thailand).
- The Asian NGO Coalition for Agrarian Reform and Rural Development (ANGOC) was founded in 1979 as a regional association of 23 development NGOs and NGO networks from eight countries: Bangladesh, India, Indonesia, Malaysia, Pakistan, the Philippines, Sri Lanka, and Thailand. The coalition facilitates people-centered development in the region by promoting South-South and North-South dialogue through training and research programs.
- The Asian Alliance of Appropriate Technology Practitioners, Inc. (APPROTECH ASIA), is a network committed to the development of appropriate technology and its promotion for grass-roots communities. Member organizations come from Bangladesh, India,

Indonesia, Malaysia, Pakistan, the Philippines, Thailand, Singapore, and Sri Lanka.

- The Southeast Asian NGO Consortium for Sustainable Development (SEACON) was founded in 1989 to promote regionwide people's participation and social reform in ensuring sustainable development approaches. The consortium includes regional networks and representatives of NGOs from Indonesia, Malaysia, the Philippines, and Thailand.
- The Asia Pacific People's Environment Network, founded in 1983, holds regional seminars on the environment and development for NGOs throughout Asia.
- The Asian-South Pacific Bureau of Adult Education (ASPBAE) was founded in 1964 in Sydney to promote people empowerment through education with the membership of more than 15 national associations and institutions and individuals representing more than 35 countries.
- The South-North Project for Sustainable Development in Asia was founded in 1990 by six Asian organizations—AWARE of India, Project for Ecological Recovery of Thailand, PRRM of the Philippines, PROSHIKA of Bangladesh, SAM of Malaysia, WALHI of Indonesia, and NOVIB of the Netherlands—to research and lobby around the themes of agriculture, forestry, and micro-ecosystems.
- The Asian Cultural Forum on Development (ACFOD) was founded by an international group of Asian intellectuals in 1976 with the purpose of "bringing the grass roots to the international level." "Fishermen from Thailand, for example, were sent to Malaysia to learn about cockle cultivation from Malaysian fishermen. ACFOD has helped fishermen from seven countries organize an international network" (Fisher 1996, 36). Member countries include Bangladesh, India, Japan, Malaysia, Nepal, the Philippines, Sri Lanka, and Thailand.
- The Asian Council for People's Culture sponsors regional meetings, workshops, cultural festivals, slides, posters, and training in building networks.
- Action for Rational Drugs in Asia (ARDA) promotes essential drugs and education about harmful ones.
- The Asia Pacific Desertification and Deforestation Control Network enables forestry organizations to communicate with each other using a computer-based information system.

These groups cover all aspects of people's lives and social engagement in Asia. Judging from the networks' focal points, it is not difficult to imagine a villager in, say, the Philippines feeling a shared destiny with villagers in Indonesia on the basis of common agricultural and/or environmental problems that are brought to their attention by a regional NGO network. Meanwhile, leaders of the member NGOs in the same network cultivated a community of professional concerns and interests with each other. In this sense, Asian countries, including the ASEAN members, are well endowed with the mechanisms through which to generate a grass-roots sense of community.

Conclusion

This chapter has examined whether ASEAN has the conditions that seem to be essential for regional community building, on the assumption that whatever goal ASEAN may have is most easily attained if and when it becomes a regional community. The history of postwar transatlantic relations has illustrated the importance of a sense of community among intellectuals and policy elites. The unusual role of NGOs in linking people across national borders, particularly in developing areas, was also analyzed. An attempt was made to verify if these crucial elements are present and functioning in ASEAN.

Despite geographical proximity, the ASEAN members show a great diversity in historical legacy, religion, ethnicity, political system, and stage of economic development, all of which can adversely affect community building. In the past, there were cases of hostility and acrimony between and among members, including historical antagonism on the Indochinese peninsula; territorial disputes among Indonesia, Malaysia, the Philippines, and, more recently, Vietnam; and a near state of war between Indonesia and Malaysia during the *konfrontasi* policy days of the former. Economically, there are more elements of competition among members than factors for interdependence or mutual complementarity. In short, ASEAN does not present an easy, natural case for a regional community.

Against these hazards, ASEAN's track record in terms of its resilience and internal cohesion has been outstanding. The myriad of webs of personal relationships among intellectuals, professionals, and grass-roots-level citizens throughout Southeast Asia could not have emerged without the role of nongovernmental initiatives. NGOs are also destined to play an equally crucial role in ASEAN's quest for its next challenge: the completion of the ASEAN-10 community.

For these nongovernmental initiatives to be more effective and constructive toward future community building, a few steps must be taken. The genesis of ASEAN-ISIS was the personal friendship among the heads of leading international institutes in the ASEAN members. Although this origin provided an additional, personal factor to the group's cohesion, it also had the potential to convert this catalytic group into an exclusive and inflexible club. Some argue that the prevalence of ASEAN-ISIS is at least partially attributable to the underdevelopment of formal foreign service bureaucracies among the ASEAN members and that it will therefore lose its current status and utility, from the viewpoint of the political leaders in each country, once national bureaucracies are fully developed. To avoid total annihilation by the national bureaucracy, ASEAN-ISIS should welcome newer institutions with similar orientations and a sense of mission as they emerge in the region. As issues facing each country multiply and the values of citizens diversify within the ASEAN region, there should be more than one institute in each member country that is concerned with regional community development. In this sense, the launching of the ASEAN Economic Forum in November 1997 among some ASEAN-ISIS member institutes and nonmember institutes (University of Asia and Pacific, the Philippines; Institute of Southeast Asian Studies, Singapore; Institute of Policy Studies, Singapore; and National Institute of Development Administration, Thailand) is a welcome development.

Of course, for more independent institutions to emerge, funding sources must be secured. As in the case of earlier transatlantic relations, U.S. foundations have again played a crucial role not only in the establishment of ASEAN-ISIS but also in the funding of member institutions. Although contributions by these U.S. foundations are admired and appreciated, there must emerge more indigenous funding sources that can offer alternatives with less baggage (e.g., U.S. financial contributions to an Asian institution can label this particular institution as pro-American or pro-Western). As the region's major economy, Japan shares a large responsibility in this regard.

NGOs share the problem of diversification and vernacularization of funding sources. Serrano laments that "some grassroots movements and development support organizations are totally dependent on foreign funding. Their dependency gives rise to a number of problems, the most important of which is the loss of autonomy of the recipient organizations" (1994, 308). Recent years have seen the emergence of a number of private foundations in Asia. But Fisher notes that "the proliferation of Asian grant making foundations in recent years offers Asian networks a potential source of funding not available to networks in other regions. Yet despite well established NGO networks and rising foundation interest in NGOs, connections between Asian philanthropists and NGOs appear to be weak" (1996, 23). A Singaporean researcher on NGOs agrees that "first and foremost, grant-making institutions should be sensitive to the needs of NGOs" (Yamamoto 1995, 221).

Although there should be more foundations and other institutions to help finance NGO activities, NGOs must make themselves more eligible for foundation grants. The main method of networking by NGOs has been conferencing and personal relationships. Although the importance of these activities cannot be overemphasized, more substantive activities will be necessary for deeper relations. Aurola Tolentino observes that "there must be efforts to start joint projects and deeper involvements beyond conferencing and exchange of reports and points of view" (Yamamoto 1995, 210), and this requires professionalization on the part of grass-roots NGOs. Particularly in light of the need for more international communication for networking, English-language skills are important. Speaking of Indonesian NGOs, Andra Corrothers stated that "the lack of English language skills put a damper on efforts made by some Indonesian NGOs to communicate broadly among potential partners in the region and beyond," and concluded that "encouraging donors to include English language training for NGO activists in their programs is one method to increase the efficacy of networking communication" (Yamamoto 1995, 134). Of course, the need for professionalism is not confined to language skills. Overall, the upgrading of NGOs' capability is required, including organization, project coordination, and general communication skills. Again, Japanese foundations and NGOs can play a constructive role here. Finally, the availability of information is a crucial factor for effective coordination.

Notes

1. The author relies heavily for historical facts and quotations in this section on *Firansuropī no yakuwari* (The role of philanthropy), a research report

commissioned by the Japan Center for International Exchange for the National
Institute for Research Advancement in 1988 (see Yamamoto 1988).

2. This list is primarily extracted from three documents: *Emerging Civil Society in the Asia Pacific Community* (Yamamoto 1995), *International Networking* (Fisher 1996), and *Civil Society in the Asia-Pacific Region* (Serrano 1994).

Bibliography

Ball, Desmond. 1993. "CSCAP: The Evolution of 'Second Track' Process in Regional Security Cooperation." In Desmond Ball, Richard L. Grant, and Jusuf Wanandi. *Security Cooperation in the Asia-Pacific Region*. Washington, D.C.: Center for Strategic and International Studies.

Evans, Paul. 1993. "The Origins, Context and Prospects of CSCAP." In Desmond Ball, Richard L. Grant, and Jusuf Wanandi. *Security Cooperation in the Asia-Pacific Region*. Washington, D.C.: Center for Strategic and International Studies.

Fisher, Julie. 1993. *The Road from Rio: Sustainable Development and the Non-Governmental Movement in the Third World*. London: Praeger.

———. 1996. "International Networking: The Role of Southern NGOs." PONPO Working Paper No. 228 and ISPS Working Paper No. 2228. New Haven: Program on Non-Profit Organizations, Institution for Social and Policy Studies, Yale University.

Hernandez, Carolina. 1993. "The Role of the ASEAN-ISIS." *ASEAN-ISIS Monitor*, no. 6 (April): 1–3.

———. 1994. *Track Two Diplomacy, Philippine Foreign Policy, and Regional Politics*. Quezon City: The University of the Philippines Press and University of the Philippines.

Institute of Strategic and International Studies, Kuala Lumpur. 1993. *ASEAN-ISIS Monitor*, no. 6 (April).

———. 1994. *ASEAN-ISIS Monitor*, no. 9 (April).

Joint Centre for Asia Pacific Studies, ed. 1995–1998. *Dialogue Monitor*, nos. 1–5. Toronto: University of Toronto–York University, Joint Centre for Asia Pacific Studies.

Manning, Robert A., and Paula Stern. 1994. "The Myth of the Pacific Community." *Foreign Affairs* 73(6): 79–93.

Mathews, Jessica T. 1997. "Power Shift." *Foreign Affairs* 76(1): 50–66.

McGee, T. G. 1997. "Building Research Networks in the Asia-Pacific Region as a Basis for Academic Cooperation." *Asian Perspective* 21(2): 9–36.

Nishihara Masashi. 1994. "Ajia taiheiyō to takokukan anzen hoshō kyōryoku no wakugumi" (The Asia Pacific region and the framework for multilateral security cooperation). *Kokusai Mondai* (International Affairs), no. 415: 60–74.

Rosenthal, A. M. 1998. "On My Mind: Love, America and Britain." *New York Times* (24 March).

Salamon, Lester. 1994. "The Rise of the Nonprofit Sector." *Foreign Affairs* 73(4): 109–122.

Serrano, Isagani R. 1994. "Civil Society in the Asia-Pacific Region." In CIVICUS, ed. *Citizens Strengthening Global Civil Society.* Washington, D.C.: Civicus, World Alliance for Citizen Participation.

Shaw, Timothy M. 1994. "Beyond Any New World Order: The South in the 21st Century." *Third World Quarterly* 15(1): 139–146.

Sopiee, Noordin. 1992. "ASEAN into the Second Generation: Potentials and Proposals in the Political and Security Dimension." *ASEAN-ISIS Monitor,* no. 5 (Oct./Dec.): 18–22.

Tamaki Kazunori. 1995. "Tōnan ajia no kaiiki mondai to asean" (Sea territorial issues in Southeast Asia and ASEAN). In Okabe Tatsumi, ed. *Posuto reisen no ajia taiheiyō* (The Asia Pacific in the post–cold war era). Tokyo: Japan Institute of International Affairs.

Townsend-Gault, Ian. 1998. "The Role of 'Track-Two' Diplomacy in Ocean Affairs." <http://www.law.ubc.ca/centres/scsweb/track2.htm> (2 November).

Wanandi, Jusuf. 1992. "Human Rights and Democracy in the ASEAN Nations: The Next 25 Years." *ASEAN-ISIS Monitor,* no. 5 (Oct./Dec.): 7–12.

Wishard, William van Dusen. 1994. "Global Trends Reshaping Civil Society." In Don E. Eberly, ed. *Building a Community of Citizens—Civil Society in the 21st Century.* New York: University Press of America.

Yamamoto Tadashi et al. 1988. *Firansoropī no yakuwari* (The role of philanthropy). *Nira Output.* Tokyo: National Institute for Research Advancement.

———, ed. 1995. *Emerging Civil Society in the Asia Pacific Community.* Singapore and Tokyo: Institute for Southeast Asian Studies and Japan Center for International Exchange.

Yasui Sankichi. 1994. "'Ajia taiheiyō' no chiiki teki wakugumi ni kansuru ichi kōsatsu" (A study on the regional framework of 'Asia Pacific'). *Kokusai Bunka Gaku Kenkyū* 1: 55–78.

– 9 –
Prospects for Intra-
and Extraregional Relations

Sekiguchi Sueo

CHAPTERS 2–8 focused on specific aspects of the ASEAN-10, and rather than sum up previous arguments, this chapter fills in the gaps. Some earlier chapters were descriptive, whereas others were primarily quantitative. All looked at specific topics, in other words, the trees. This chapter, by standing a little farther back, looks at the forest of broader issues.

After discussing the interaction among members of the Association of Southeast Asian Nations and changes in their relations with non-members through regional integration, this chapter examines some significant economic mechanisms with direct implications for regional cooperation. It then looks at ASEAN's relations with important non-member partners, such as Japan, China, the United States, and the European Union. Although we are interested in the ASEAN-10's future relations with major nonmembers, the preceding chapters focused on ASEAN itself with only general remarks about ASEAN-Japan relations. This chapter too considers Japan in the context of ASEAN only generally. A more comprehensive study is needed to outline the future of ASEAN's relations with major nonmember economies, including Japan.

Interdependence among the ASEAN-10 Members

Until the late 1970s, most of the ASEAN-5—Indonesia, Malaysia, the Philippines, Singapore, and Thailand—traded mainly with countries outside this group. Only Singapore had relatively large intraregional trade as it served as a free port for the region. Most of the members competed among themselves as exporters of raw materials and labor-intensive manufactured goods. And these same members imported machinery and parts and consumer goods from industrialized countries. Foreign investment was substantially higher than intraregional investment.[1]

During the 1960s, most ASEAN economies adopted import substitution strategies for their industrialization. Hasty efforts to protect new industries so that domestic products could replace imports failed because protected companies did not improve their production efficiency. At the time, many international conferences, such as the Pacific Trade and Development Conference (PAFTAD), pointed out the defects of import substitution versus export promotion. In the mid-1970s, Fukuda Takeo, prime minister of Japan, declared that Japan would extend financial assistance to promote industrial cooperation among the ASEAN economies. Specifically, cooperation meant that ASEAN would agree on a division of labor that avoided duplication in industrial investment.[2]

The 1970s were a turbulent period, with two oil crises and heated conflicts between the northern and southern hemispheres as exemplified by "natural resource nationalism." Disputes also arose concerning direct investment by multinational enterprises in developing countries. At the same time, the ASEAN economies began to industrialize through export promotion.

Export promotion reduced the risk of government failure to industrialize because the ASEAN governments targeted industries that rapidly became internationally competitive. Increased investment in labor-intensive sectors and natural-resource-based industries expanded the ASEAN economies' exports and increased domestic employment. Although industrialization gained new momentum, intraregional trade remained small relative to extraregional trade because most of the ASEAN economies had similar industrial structures (fig. 1).

In the 1980s, the ASEAN economies' per capita income grew steadily and industrialization accelerated. Consequently, trade opportunities expanded among members and the ratio of intraregional trade as a percentage of ASEAN's total trade started to rise. Although the ASEAN Free Trade Area (AFTA) is incomplete in that members will not eliminate import tariffs within the region, tariff reductions will boost intraregional trade. In Figure 1, intra-ASEAN trade is small compared with the

Figure 1. ASEAN Trade, by Region, as Percent of Total ASEAN Exports

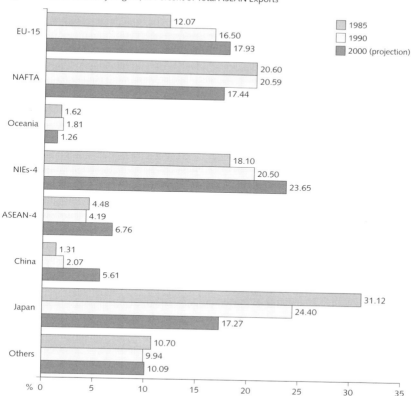

Source: Japan Center for Economic Research (1996).

Note: Singapore is included in NIEs-4: the newly industrializing economies of South Korea, Taiwan, Hong Kong, and Singapore. ASEAN-4 consists of Indonesia, Malaysia, the Philippines, and Thailand.

ASEAN-4's (the original members excluding Singapore) trade with Japan, the North American Free Trade Agreement (NAFTA) area, and the European Union (EU-15). Figure 2 shows that the ASEAN-4's share of Japan's total trade is small but rising.

Intra- and Extraregional Trade

The development of intraregional trade is limited by barriers in place for a decade or so that make members less complementary compared with other regions' integration. Under these circumstances, multinational

Figure 2. Japanese Trade, by Region, as Percent of Total Japanese Exports

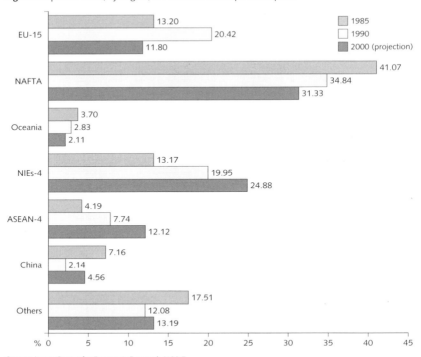

Source: Japan Center for Economic Research (1996).

Note: Singapore is included in NIEs-4: the newly industrializing economies of South Korea, Taiwan, Hong Kong, and Singapore. ASEAN-4 consists of Indonesia, Malaysia, the Philippines, and Thailand.

enterprises will continue to perform a key role in trade and investment within ASEAN.

Through the 1960s and 1970s, substantial direct and portfolio investment in ASEAN came from industrialized countries. Multinational enterprises and other companies established factories in the ASEAN economies that fit their global strategies. The ASEAN economies' domestic markets remained separated, however, as each member maintained high import barriers. If these barriers had been lower, multinationals might have invested in all members and thereby reduced transport costs because only a few geographical obstacles separate members. Because the ASEAN governments strictly controlled trade and investment, the multinationals had to export products to their home and/or third countries. From these destinations, the multinationals imported machinery and parts and other goods into ASEAN, which increased extraregional trade.

Intra- and Extraregional Investment

Throughout the 1960s and 1970s, the United States, Western Europe, and Japan contributed most of the foreign direct investment (FDI) in ASEAN. From the 1980s, however, the newly industrializing economies (NIEs), notably Singapore, joined as new investors. Later, Thailand began investing in its neighbors while continuing to receive substantial direct investment from industrialized countries. Although the scale is limited, there are signs of growth in intraregional investment. Most of the ASEAN economies are still net recipients of FDI and technology imports, but some have started transplanting traditional industries to ASEAN's less developed newcomers—Vietnam, Myanmar, and Laos. The majority of international investment still comes from non-ASEAN members, and the amount far exceeds trade in goods.

If AFTA is realized, multinational enterprises from non-ASEAN economies will be more motivated to invest in the ASEAN region. As a market of 480 million people, ASEAN is attractive to these multinationals. Obstacles limiting direct investment in ASEAN are inadequate infrastructures and a shortage of skilled labor in some member countries. Moreover, political instability and bureaucratic red tape have also constrained direct investment. Over the next few years, members suffering a currency crisis at present will have to reestablish the credibility of their financial systems. In Indonesia, a more critical issue is repairing the relationship between business and political leaders to avoid further chaos triggered by violent antigovernment protests.

Considering that institutional integration takes time (for example, AFTA), and taking into account the time lag between institution building and the actual effects thereof, the intensity of ASEAN's intraregional trade will not likely exceed its extraregional trade until 2010. As trade within ASEAN increases steadily, trade promoted by multinationals between ASEAN members and nonmembers will grow rapidly.

International Financial Links

Mahathir bin Mohamad, prime minister of Malaysia, has proposed that the ASEAN members substitute local currencies for other currencies in settling intraregional trade balances. His purpose was to save U.S. dollar reserves following the drastic depreciation of ASEAN currencies against the U.S. dollar in 1997. International and regional financial cooperation is badly needed to overcome the recent currency crises because the simultaneous depreciation of ASEAN currencies does not stimulate intra-ASEAN trade within East Asia.[3] If the devaluation is significant, ASEAN's exports to other regions would expand and rebalance trade at the expense of countries in other regions, which would suffer from lower exports. Steep devaluation would negatively affect these trade partners.

Ironically, despite Mahathir's plea, traders cannot rely on ASEAN currencies. In light of the current currency crises, the creation of a common ASEAN currency is unrealistic, considering how long it took Europe's euro participants to coordinate fiscal and monetary policies. At present, ASEAN still needs financial assistance from the International Monetary Fund (IMF) and industrialized countries. Although ASEAN governments face varied tasks, they share a common need to restructure their financial sectors and reestablish the credibility of their domestic financing. For some member countries, the elimination or drastic reduction of budget deficits is an urgent task.[4]

Because the ASEAN economies are linked financially, any member's default could start a chain reaction. In Singapore, for instance, neighboring countries' difficulties threatened Singapore's creditor status and caused the depreciation of the Singapore dollar. Similarly, but on a larger scale, Japanese banks could be damaged by defaults in the ASEAN region. On a smaller scale, ASEAN defaults could disrupt U.S. and European banks and corporate investment.

International financial cooperation is essential to resolve the currency crises. The recovery of domestic production and per capita income and less depreciation of currencies will stimulate intra- and extraregional trade. This scenario is more beneficial than ongoing currency depreciation. Mahathir's proposal to switch from extraregional trade to intraregional trade is neither feasible nor desirable. The proposal is not feasible because, under their current industrial structures, some ASEAN economies might depend more on trade with nonmembers. In addition, preferential arrangements, if established, would disrupt overall trade.

International financial cooperation might conflict with self-reliance and the reconstruction of industries through competition. Cooperation includes emergency assistance by governments to private financial institutions as well. To halt the spread of corporate defaults and avoid domestic chaos, taxes must be used. The issue is how to make corporate management responsible for its failures and assist employees and investors. When political leaders and other government officials are heavily involved in financial transactions, as is often true in many East Asian countries, they must be singled out and severely penalized for any illegal activities.

Having accomplished these tasks, the ASEAN economies as well as other East Asian economies should pursue financial cooperation to avoid diminishing domestic demand by the drastic and simultaneous depreciation of their currencies. Although monetary and fiscal discipline is important, austerity alone by all East Asian economies cannot save them.

Medium- and Long-Term Growth Potential

Most East Asians believe that the medium- and long-term growth potential of the ASEAN economies remains high in contrast to Paul Krugman's (1994) pessimism. True, almost all of the ASEAN economies, except Singapore, have grown through increased factor input, including the absorption of hidden unemployment and the importation of foreign capital. Reallocating resources among sectors has also played an important role. Typically, resources have been mainly allocated to manufacturing sectors rather than to traditional agricultural sectors. Technological progress has been promoted by importing technology. This situation is common in developing nations. It does not really matter whether technological progress comes from imported technology when catching up is the aim of high-growth developing countries.

The NIEs display a different feature in their growth accounting: The contribution of factor inputs is declining as that of technological progress is increasing. More precisely, technological progress, as measured by total factor productivity (TFP), is a mixture of resource reallocation and system reform as well as progress in production technology.[5] The NIEs differ from middle-income countries in that the NIEs face labor shortages, their resource reallocation plays a more important role, and their technological progress is promoted not only by importation but also by local investment in research and development. South Korea's recent economic difficulties, mostly attributable to excessive investment during the bubble period and the subsequent breakdown of the financial system, are failures to adjust as the former government-led economy makes the transition to a free market economy.[6]

Japan, a mature industrial economy, faces a decrease in labor input that must be offset by capital inflow and technological progress (table 1).

Table 1. Simple Growth Accounting of East Asian Economies

		1970–1980	1980–1990	1990–1995
		Contribution to growth by factor (%)		
Japan	Labor	4.1	18.3	−51.7
	Capital	39.6	43.0	52.1
	TFP	56.3	38.8	99.6
NIEs-4	Labor	21.9	16.6	11.4
	Capital	65.0	58.9	62.7
	TFP	13.1	24.5	25.9
ASEAN-4	Labor	16.8	21.8	14.9
	Capital	70.7	84.4	72.9
	TFP	12.6	−6.2	12.3
China	Labor	26.5	18.2	6.7
	Capital	48.8	34.0	32.1
	TFP	24.7	47.8	61.2
		Contribution to growth rate by factor (component of total)		
Japan	Labor	0.18	0.73	−0.63
	Capital	1.75	1.72	0.64
	TFP	2.49	1.55	1.22
	Growth rate	4.42	4.00	1.23
NIEs-4	Labor	1.94	1.37	0.75
	Capital	5.78	4.88	4.16
	TFP	1.17	2.03	1.72
	Growth rate	8.88	8.29	6.63
ASEAN-4	Labor	1.15	1.20	1.00
	Capital	4.85	4.65	4.90
	TFP	0.86	−0.34	0.82
	Growth rate	6.86	5.51	6.72
China	Labor	1.60	1.60	0.80
	Capital	2.95	3.00	3.84
	TFP	1.49	4.21	7.33
	Growth rate	6.04	8.81	11.97

Source: Japan Center for Economic Research (1996).

Note: Singapore is included in NIEs-4: South Korea, Taiwan, Hong Kong, and Singapore. ASEAN-4 consists of Indonesia, Malaysia, the Philippines, and Thailand. For the time period 1990–1995, estimated growth rates are used.

Because it has less room to reallocate resources, Japan must make technological progress through competition and innovation. Much as the U.S. economy recovered in the early 1990s from its long stagnation, Japan will eventually revitalize its economy.

Considering the long-term economic growth of nations, we believe that the ASEAN economies and the NIEs will maintain high growth rates in the coming decade, despite their recent economic turbulence.

Malaysia and Thailand, the fastest-growing economies in ASEAN after Singapore, will have to reallocate resources from traditional and labor-intensive industries to more sophisticated sectors. Cambodia, Laos, Myanmar, and Vietnam will take over the sectors in which the more advanced ASEAN economies previously enjoyed comparative advantages. Unless such a reallocation occurs, these newcomers will have few opportunities to sustain their economic growth.

During their own development, the core members of the ASEAN-10 came to recognize the importance of research and development and technology transfer. A decade ago, most ASEAN economies depended totally on foreign technology. This began to change, as symbolized by the December 1995 ASEAN Framework Agreement on Intellectual Property Cooperation (Institute of Developing Economies 1998). Although this agreement only declares the signatories' willingness to cooperate in protecting and promoting the development of intellectual property, the ASEAN members are expected to engage in specific activities in the near future that produce actual results.

In the past, the so-called overseas Chinese, who own companies and are partners in joint ventures in Southeast Asia, tended to be interested only in quick, high returns on their investments. They had no interest in technological progress as a means to expand their companies, which were not independent entities but instruments used to increase family wealth. In other words, the owners were not entrepreneurs. Thus, overseas Chinese have been good at commerce and services but not at manufacturing. This situation, however, is changing gradually.

In the ASEAN region, engineers' compensation has risen drastically during the recent boom initiated by FDI. Increasing demand for engineering has, in turn, increased the supply of engineers. This influx of engineers will lead to enhanced technological capability. Whereas industrialized countries have invested in higher education and R&D for the past century, the ASEAN economies started increasing their investment in these areas only a decade or so ago. Naturally, it will take time for ASEAN to see the fruits of its recent labors. It is a mistake to conclude that the ASEAN economies have low economic growth potential simply because their capability to develop technology is low at present.

A Greater Single Market?

Although the ASEAN-10 constitute a market with a population of 480 million, this market is far from unified. Most ASEAN economies maintain high import tariffs on sophisticated manufactured goods, though tariff rates on industrial raw materials are low (tables 2, 3, 4, and 5). Tariff escalation is sharp among most countries in the Asia-Pacific Economic Cooperation (APEC) forum region, especially among the ASEAN members. At present, tariff data is unavailable for Myanmar and the countries on the Indochina peninsula. Although the core members of the ASEAN-10 argue for freer trade within the association and for maintaining import barriers against nonmembers, the newcomers to ASEAN will resist because they want to invest more in the sectors in which the core members now have advantages. Politics is also a factor because many of the newcomers' political systems differ from those of the core members, and it will take time for the newcomers to adjust their trading systems to those of the core members.[7]

Mahathir proposed that ASEAN members promote intraregional trade instead of extraregional trade to save hard currency, particularly U.S. dollars. He also encouraged the use of local currencies to settle trade debts. He made these proposals as a means to cope with the recent currency crises in ASEAN. Although he did not suggest specific policies, any regulations or incentives that replace extraregional trade with intraregional trade are likely to harm the development of all ASEAN economies by distorting market mechanisms.

Creating a regional currency would facilitate intraregional investment and trade by saving hard currency, but a currency union is not feasible when most members face a currency crisis. The timing of Mahathir's proposals ironically coincides with the most difficult time for ASEAN to substitute currencies. No exporters would accept the currently unreliable local currencies. So there is no point in discussing the creation of a common ASEAN currency at this time. Even the EU spent many years preparing for its common currency, the euro. The EU took nearly a decade to determine the common monetary and fiscal policies that it launched in 1999. A similar option does not exist for ASEAN.

As the trade matrix in figure 1 indicates, ASEAN's intraregional trade remains small relative to its extraregional trade, despite the growth during the past decade. Therefore, the promotion of intraregional trade has had little effect on saving hard currency. The forced switch to intraregional trade might increase production costs in ASEAN. Thus, the danger of a switch seems greater than the hope of resolution by other means. The reality of ASEAN's trade situation is that its intraregional trade is low, but the short-term currency crises should be overcome without

Table 2. Import Tariffs and NTMs in APEC Countries on Men's or Boys' Shirts of Knitted or Crocheted Cotton (HS: 610510)

	Imports (000US$)	Exports (000US$)	MFN Range (%)		MFN Average (%)	Total Charge (%)	Specific Tariff	NTM (%)	QR (%)
			Minimum	Maximum					
Australia	29,375	2,432	37	37	37	37	No	0	0
Canada	58,555	8,738	24	24	23.6	23.6	No	0	0
Japan	709,884	8,580	10	16	12.9	12.9	No	0	0
New Zealand	5,587	3,122	30	NA	30	30	No	0	0
United States	1,362,932	116,019	21	21	20.7	20.7	No	0	0
Subtotal	2,166,333	138,891							
Taiwan	25,940	61,590	13	13	12.5	13	No	0	0
China	643	534,299	40	40	40	40	No	0	0
Hong Kong	225,804	236,470	0	0	0	0	No	0	0
South Korea	25,385	169,743	8	8	8	8	No	0	0
Subtotal	277,772	1,002,102							
Brunei	NA	12,123	10	10	10	10	No	0	0
Indonesia	207	120,995	40	40	40	42.5	No	0	0
Malaysia	2,467	104,342	20	20	20	30	No	0	0
Philippines	100	122,064	30	30	30	39	No	0	0
Singapore	74,044	48,742	0	0	0	0	No	0	0
Thailand	554	203,627	45	45	45	45	No	0	0
Subtotal	77,371	611,893							
Chile	3,593	88	11	11	11	11	No	0	0
Mexico	30,148	9,332	20	20	20	22	No	0	0
Subtotal	33,741	9,420							

Source: U.N. Conference on Trade and Development (1996).

NTMs: Non-tariff measures; HS: Harmonized Commodity Description and Coding System; MFN: Most-favored nation; QR: Quantitative restriction.

Table 3. Import Tariffs and NTMs in APEC Countries on Ethylene (HS: 290121)

	Imports (000US$)	Exports (000US$)	MFN Range (%) Minimum	MFN Range (%) Maximum	MFN Average (%)	Total Charge (%)	Specific Tariff	NTM (%)	QR (%)
Australia	2	33,511	0	0	0	0	No	0	0
Canada	97	3,230	0	0	0	0	No	0	0
Japan	166,349	96,856	3	3	2.8	2.8	No	0	0
New Zealand	2	0	0	0	0	0	No	0	0
United States	50,612	4,564	0	0	0	0	No	0	0
Subtotal	217,062	138,161							
Taiwan	30,075	466	0	0	0	0.5	No	0	0
China	4,572	31	5	5	5	5	No	0	0
Hong Kong	98	35	0	0	0	0	No	0	0
South Korea	24,575	141,856	5	5	5	5	No	0	0
Subtotal	59,320	142,388							
Brunei	NA	0	0	0	0	0	No	0	0
Indonesia	175,563	12,400	0	0	0	2.5	No	0	0
Malaysia	16,032	30,637	2	2	2	2	No	0	0
Philippines	210	0	10	10	10	19	No	0	0
Singapore	2,113	12,006	0	0	0	0	No	0	0
Thailand	67,650	0	12	12	12	12	No	0	0
Subtotal	261,567	55,043							
Chile	14	0	11	11	11	11	No	0	0
Mexico	557	52,333	10	10	10	11.7	No	0	0
Subtotal	571	52,333							

Source: U.N. Conference on Trade and Development (1996).

NTMs: Non-tariff measures; HS: Harmonized Commodity Description and Coding System; MFN: Most-favored nation; QR: Quantitative restriction.

Table 4. Import Tariffs and NTMs in APEC Countries on Automobiles with Reciprocating Piston Engines of 1,500–3,000 cc (HS: 870323)

	Imports (000US$)	Exports (000US$)	MFN Range (%)		MFN Average (%)	Total Charge (%)	Specific Tariff	NTM (%)	QR (%)
			Minimum	Maximum					
Australia	1,699,381	222,029	5	25	11.7	11.7	Yes	0	0
Canada	4,943,295	3,245,559	8	8	8	8	No	0	0
Japan	12,476,917	27,679,964	0	0	0	0	No	0	0
New Zealand	676,387	1,335	0	25	16.7	16.7	Yes	0	0
United States	32,803,232	8,425,763	3	3	2.5	2.5	No	0	0
Subtotal	52,599,212	39,574,650							
Taiwan	2,013,252	25,121	30	30	30	30.5	No	0	0
China	647,837	29,024	100	100	100	100	No	0	0
Hong Kong	1,987,322	12,128	0	0	0	0	No	0	0
South Korea	160,684	2,016,223	10	10	10	10	No	0	0
Subtotal	4,809,095	2,082,496							
Brunei	NA	7	20	20	20	20	No	50	50
Indonesia	121,875	1,795	75	125	100	172.5	No	0	0
Malaysia	795,077	51,940	5	50	35.5	44.1	Yes	82	82
Philippines	20,828	4,654	30	30	30	39	No	0	0
Singapore	483,946	6,255	45	45	45	45	No	0	0
Thailand	960,652	2,180	10	69	46.2	46.2	No	0	0
Subtotal	2,382,377	66,831							
Chile	389,571	3,336	11	11	11	11	No	0	0
Mexico	131,194	6,450,428	20	20	20	22	No	0	0
Subtotal	520,765	6,453,764							

Source: U.N. Conference on Trade and Development (1996).

NTMs: Non-tariff measures; HS: Harmonized Commodity Description and Coding System; MFN: Most-favored nation; QR: Quantitative restriction.

Table 5. Import Tariffs and NTMs in APEC Countries on Television Receivers* (HS: 852810)

	Imports (000US$)	Exports (000US$)	MFN Range (%) Minimum	MFN Range (%) Maximum	MFN Average (%)	Total Charge (%)	Specific Tariff	NTM (%)	QR (%)
Australia	48,826	9,640	5	5	5	5	No	0	0
Canada	381,729	82,713	7	18	8	8	No	0	0
Japan	1,824,534	1,932,907	0	0	0	0	No	0	0
New Zealand	96,596	364	0	13	2.6	2.6	No	0	0
United States	3,710,974	759,968	2	9	4	4	No	0	0
Subtotal	6,062,659	2,785,592							
Taiwan	269,809	309,802	5	15	12.5	13	No	0	0
China	319,892	1,111,705	20	50	43.3	43.3	No	0	0
Hong Kong	2,553,028	84,141	0	0	0	0	No	0	0
South Korea	53,053	1,106,314	8	8	8	8	No	0	0
Subtotal	3,195,782	2,611,962							
Brunei	NA	296	0	0	0	0	No	0	0
Indonesia	4,157	58,592	30	30	30	32.5	No	0	0
Malaysia	24,801	2,057,127	25	50	33.6	43.6	No	14	14
Philippines	3,193	107,863	30	30	30	39	No	0	0
Singapore	849,224	794,422	0	0	0	0	No	0	0
Thailand	92,075	870,406	30	30	30	30	No	0	0
Subtotal	973,449	3,888,706							
Chile	153,841	659	11	11	11	11	No	0	0
Mexico	168,634	2,687,952	15	20	19.7	21.7	No	0	0
Subtotal	322,475	2,688,611							

Source: U.N. Conference on Trade and Development (1996).

NTMs: Non-tariff measures; HS: Harmonized Commodity Description and Coding System; MFN: Most-favored nation; QR: Quantitative restriction.

*Including video monitors and video projectors.

disrupting the long-term strategies for integrating regional economies.

In the medium and long term, establishing a common settlement mechanism within ASEAN, including a common currency, and developing intraregional trade are closely related. An efficient and effective settlement mechanism will encourage intraregional trade, which, in turn, will promote a division of labor among the ASEAN economies that leads to higher trade intensity within the region. However, this cycle takes many years. It is therefore important that ASEAN leaders do not mix long-term strategies and short-term crisis management.

In conclusion, we would argue that establishing a greater ASEAN market is feasible within no less than 25 years. This common market might still be in an early phase by 2025 but should be firmly established by 2050.

Important Nonmember Partners

Most of the preceding chapters concentrated on ASEAN, except chapters 2 and 3, which discussed political relations and APEC, respectively. The following section focuses on three major regions closely related to ASEAN—the East Asian economies, including Japan; North America, particularly the United States; and the EU.

Relations with Other East Asian Economies

Naturally, the ASEAN-10's most intensive economic relations are with other East Asian countries, including Japan, China, and the NIEs. Japan was the dominant direct investor until the mid-1970s, and the NIEs became significant investors in the 1980s.[8] Because trade usually accompanies direct investment, trade relations have also grown significantly.

Foreign direct investors often export raw materials from ASEAN host countries and import machinery and other equipment as well as semiprocessed goods into the hosts. Sometimes, the investors export locally produced goods that replace similar exports from the investors' home countries. In aggregate, the dominant trend has been trade creation rather than trade replacement funded by FDI. Until the end of the 1970s, Japan and North American and Western European countries were ASEAN's dominant investors and major trading partners. The new trend is that trade between the ASEAN economies and the NIEs is growing rapidly as investment from the NIEs expands. Faster economic growth in the ASEAN economies and the NIEs in the recent decade is supporting increasing trade intensity.

Those NIEs with labor shortages must promote industrial restructuring because countries with lower wages are taking away many of their domestic industries. Some ASEAN economies are competing with the NIEs in standard manufacturing industries. More specifically, advanced industrial sectors in Malaysia and Thailand are competing against their counterparts in South Korea and Taiwan. In this respect, ASEAN and the NIEs compete, but the relationship is predominantly complementary as the NIEs rapidly shift to more sophisticated industries.

In contrast, relations between China and the ASEAN-10 may be characterized as more competitive than complementary. First, China has emerged as a large competitor for FDI. Because of its market of 1.2 billion consumers, multinational enterprises have increased their direct investment, despite complicated government intervention. Other things being equal, an increase in FDI in China reduces similar investment in ASEAN.

Second, China and India compete with ASEAN in exports of manufactured goods. In the early 1990s, exports from China and India replaced many ASEAN exports in world markets as most ASEAN currencies appreciated against the U.S. dollar. As China's and India's currencies remained stable, their export competitiveness strengthened against ASEAN exports. If the renminbi remains stable following most ASEAN currencies' significant depreciation in 1996–1997, Chinese exports will lose competitiveness vis-à-vis ASEAN. All of these factors point to competitive rather than complementary economies.[9]

In East Asia, Japan seems to complement the ASEAN-10 the most in trade, services, and investment. Nonetheless, Japan's share of foreign trade and investment in ASEAN has gradually declined, partly because of the NIEs' emergence and China's growing participation. More rapid economic growth in China, the NIEs, and the ASEAN economies relative to Japan has contributed to the diversification of ASEAN's foreign trade and investment.

The recent financial crises in ASEAN and some NIEs highlighted Japan's role in regional financial cooperation. South Korea, despite its brilliant debut as a trade partner and investor in ASEAN, eventually needed more financial aid than Thailand or Indonesia from international financial institutions and industrialized countries. Within the region, only Japan and Taiwan can extend substantial financial aid. Because of the China-Taiwan disputes, however, many ASEAN economies hesitate to request financial aid from Taiwan. But Malaysia and some other ASEAN economies faced with the urgency of their economic crises reportedly approached Taiwan for financial aid. As it was in the United States' best interest to assist Mexico during its crisis in 1994, it is in Japan's interest to support the ASEAN economies during their financial crises.

In view of broader regional cooperation in East Asia, which is important to ASEAN, disputes along the Taiwan Strait overshadow the otherwise cooperative climate. The disputes could disrupt cooperation when all East Asian economies are prospering. Indeed, the disputes hinder cooperation even as many regional economies face difficulties. Improved and stable relations between China and Taiwan will be the region's most important political task, given their influence over neighboring countries.

For ASEAN, Japan is an easy-to-manage partner because its political influence is minimal and its economic aid is substantial. Japan's declining economic power might create friction, but that will be managed easier than China's growing but less predictable influence in politics and economics. Change in China, considering its huge population, has a tremendous effect on ASEAN as well as on other neighbors.

The United States and North America

North America, especially the United States, maintains an important position in ASEAN's foreign economic and political affairs. The United States is a major market for ASEAN's manufacturing products as well as an important investor in local economies. It still influences ASEAN on security issues, though its role has diminished since the end of the cold war. Apart from its security role, the United States has exerted strong pressure on local political regimes and shaped the drafting and implementation of international rules for trade and investment.

Concern about U.S. dominance has deep roots among the ASEAN members and other East Asian countries. At the Pacific Economic Cooperation Council (PECC) in 1980, the ASEAN-5 expressed concern about their domination by industrialized countries, particularly the United States and Japan. This concern and other aspects of the PECC were echoed by APEC, a forum in which ASEAN members often expressed their misgivings about U.S. dominance over policy making. Whereas the Americans prefer clear rules and rigorous application, ASEAN's leaders favor consensus and harmony.

Mahathir's proposals to create the East Asian Economic Caucus

(EAEC) and to switch ASEAN from extra- to intraregional trade to save U.S. dollars, as well as his absence from the 1993 APEC summit in Seattle, Washington, are examples of the deep concern throughout ASEAN about U.S. dominance over policy making. Nonetheless, not all ASEAN leaders agree with Mahathir. At the 1994 APEC summit in Bogor, Indonesia, the majority of the leaders favored promoting relations with the United States. As realists, these leaders considered cooperation with the United States as indispensable. At best, ASEAN leaders and their people appear ambivalent toward the United States.

When the United States, a member of APEC, signed NAFTA with Canada and Mexico, negative reactions emerged across East Asia. Mahathir's proposed EAEC reflected this sentiment. The ASEAN members were less concerned about bilateral relations between Canada and the United States, perceiving any related trade diversion from ASEAN as minimal. However, ASEAN members feared that Mexican exports to North America would replace some ASEAN exports. These fears did not materialize after Mexico experienced a balance-of-payments crisis in 1994.[10]

The United States has been the second largest market for most of the ASEAN-5's exports. In terms of FDI, the United States has been one of ASEAN's three most important investors, together with the EU and Japan. The U.S. position declined until the end of the 1980s because of the NIEs and China. This trend reversed in the mid-1990s when most East Asian economies slumped while the United States enjoyed prosperity and a strong currency. U.S. enterprises have reportedly taken over many financially troubled ASEAN companies. To Mahathir's disappointment, the presence of and ASEAN's dependence on U.S. enterprises have been rising. These enterprises have benefited from financial crises in some ASEAN economies, which have significantly lowered acquisition costs, and the financial difficulties of individual companies.

As a member of APEC, the United States is expected to actively aid troubled Asia Pacific economies. But some members of the U.S. Congress argue that public funds should not be sent to the ASEAN economies. However, the East Asian market is so important to the United States that assisting ASEAN and East Asia in overcoming recent difficulties is within U.S. national interests. The IMF and the U.S. government insist that troubled economies must comply with the IMF's conditions prior to receiving financial assistance. This may provoke anti-American sentiments. In many respects, however, countries that receive foreign assistance should restructure their domestic systems, despite East Asian standards. In Indonesia, for example, situations in which the former president's family controls major industries should be changed as soon as possible. Avoiding arbitrary regulations on foreign trade is another example.

If the ASEAN-10's aim is to benefit from trade and investment and to receive substantial assistance within the framework of APEC, it is more reasonable to strengthen APEC than to create the EAEC, which would be a narrower regional institution. The United States has symbolic influence over ASEAN's will to develop the APEC framework.[11]

The European Union

Since its establishment as the ASEAN-5, ASEAN has promoted dialogue with its major trading partners—Japan, Western Europe, and the United States. Through the 1970s, the ASEAN-5 traded mainly with, and received its FDI almost equally from, Japan, the United States, and Western Europe (shares varied by country) (see Sekiguchi 1983). The EU's share of investment in some countries was small relative to the shares of Japan and the United States, but the EU's total regional share was comparable to those of the other two major partners. Therefore, the EU certainly has an interest in ASEAN. Short-term capital and FDI flowed from the EU into the ASEAN economies, so defaults in the ASEAN economies are of grave concern to the EU.

In the EU, investment risks related to ASEAN are dispersed across the EU's member countries. In this context, the EU might be less interested in the ASEAN economies' financial difficulties than Japan or the United States. Nonetheless, because the development of ASEAN benefits the EU through increased trade and investment, the EU has actively participated in financial cooperation with Thailand and Indonesia.

Greater Europe, as symbolized by the EU, and the expansion of the union into Eastern Europe might divert some of the EU's trade with nonmembers back to members. A broadening market and increasing investment opportunities within the EU might also divert the EU's ASEAN-bound investment back to the EU (Sekiguchi 1998). Because the EU is larger than AFTA or ASEAN, the effect of diverted trade is expected to be much larger, and the overall influence of the EU on terms of trade will also be greater. Some EU enterprises might acquire ASEAN companies that are facing financial difficulties, as U.S. companies have done.

Domestic instability in some ASEAN economies decreases their

attractiveness as a market for FDI by European companies. In antici-
pation of a rapid recovery, however, it is time to purchase ASEAN enterprises. As the ASEAN economies restructure their financial systems
and disciplined supply-demand management regains stability, the
ASEAN-10 will again become attractive to the EU. Given that ASEAN is
expected to grow rapidly, the EU's interest will intensify. Thus, the EU
will remain one of ASEAN's most important partners in trade and investment.

Conclusion

The ASEAN-10 have the potential to form a unified market with a population of 480 million. Unity takes time, however, because not only the
leading members but also the followers face a variety of tasks in con-
structing sound economies. As of early 1999, Cambodia had managed
to establish the Hun Sen government after prolonged political confrontation between two prime ministers and to dissolve the military power
of the Pol Pot group. Construction of the economy is just starting. Myanmar needs to democratize its political system and develop its economy.
Vietnam, though it has successfully introduced free market mechanisms
to revitalize its economy, still has to solve a number of problems. Laos'
economy has been stagnant for many years. For these newcomers, the
ASEAN-10 will have to slow its economic integration.

Human rights and democracy issues remain serious political con-
troversies among the ASEAN members and Western nations. East Asians
and Westerners view these issues differently. South Korea and Taiwan
have gradually shifted toward Western-style democracy after decades of
military dictatorship. Political factors have sometimes forced leaders to
keep military-led governments, particularly when confronting rivals.
Economic development was the top priority among these leaders. Despite the military shadow, South Korea and Taiwan have achieved rapid
progress in democratization.

Even ASEAN's leading members have not achieved full democracy
by Western standards. Although these countries could encourage more
active public participation in policy making in accordance with democratic processes, foreign pressure to do so might spark regionalism. It is
important for the ASEAN members to move steadily toward democracy
based on human rights.

The core members of the ASEAN-10 are in financial difficulty, and the causes differ by country: failure in supply-demand management, hasty and partial deregulation, and nepotism between political leaders and business circles. Enthusiasm for regional integration has shifted to regional protectionism. Such a trend is evident in Mahathir's statements. However, regionalism is unlikely to solve the current problems.

The East Asian economies are in trouble. Japan has been stagnant for a few years. South Korea suffered a currency crisis. Taiwan has been relatively stable, but its prospects are dimming. China has thus far avoided any balance-of-payments difficulties, partly owing to strict regulations and direct government control over foreign trade and exchange transactions. Thus, in general, the East Asian economies have lost their luster.

In contrast, economies in North America, and to a lesser extent in Europe, have revived or have continued to grow in the mid-1990s. Currency crises in many East Asian countries, including some ASEAN economies, have provided good opportunities for Western enterprises to acquire assets in the region. Financial firms throughout the region have become favorite takeover targets.

Although self-reliance is important for the ASEAN economies in overcoming recent hardships, a combination of currency devaluation and strict supply-demand management is not enough to strengthen their industrial bases. Regional currency depreciation does not change relative prices among East Asian nations, though it does make East Asian products less expensive than products from other regions. Thus, depreciation does not necessarily promote intraregional trade. Tight supply-demand management will reduce imports as well as demand for domestic products. This, in turn, will decrease intraregional trade as well as imports from outside the region.

There are good reasons for East Asian economies to promote regional financial cooperation to facilitate external balance of payments. Stable currency values and credible financial systems are needed. Because Japan and Taiwan have the means to extend financial assistance, they can provide emergency loans to countries trying to overcome short-term difficulties. Japan has already joined an international consortium to provide emergency assistance. In accordance with some ASEAN economies' requests, Taiwan is participating in such assistance, but China is not. Regional financial cooperation is a test case for solidarity and friendship among East Asian economies.

Financial cooperation should not be limited to East Asia. Broader cooperation through APEC is desirable and feasible. As a matter of fact, financial assistance to Thailand, Indonesia, and South Korea has been promoted through broad cooperation with other industrialized countries. Nonetheless, East Asian countries must take the initiative and explore ways to put their economies on the right track. This is in contrast to an inward-looking approach that protects insiders against outsiders. By analogy, trying to switch international trade to intraregional trade contradicts the idea of broader financial cooperation.

In all aspects of regional cooperation, Japan is in a position to play active roles in trade, investment, and finance. The Japanese government has, in fact, been promoting financial assistance. A more important task for the government, however, is the revitalization of Japan's economy. A stagnant Japan with shrinking imports cannot stimulate production in ASEAN. A long-term recession would prevent Japan from investing in ASEAN and from extending financial assistance.

Notes

1. One of the studies I made for the Asia-Pacific Economic Cooperation forum in the mid-1980s revealed that Singapore's investment in the region increased in the 1980s along with that from the other NIEs.

2. The concept of a division of labor did not make significant progress because most ASEAN economies wanted similar industries.

3. Most East Asian currencies depreciated for various reasons in 1997, but China's renminbi maintained its value. The Chinese currency might depreciate in the near future in response to changes in the economic environment.

4. These tasks are not limited to the ASEAN economies but are necessary in many other East Asian countries. Resource allocation under strong government intervention and guidance might cause excess investment as investors mistakenly assume that they are protected by government regulations.

5. This estimate is based on simple one-sector growth accounting. Total factor productivity, which we refer to as technological progress, includes the reallocation of resources, overall innovation, and technical progress.

6. Because of its huge foreign reserves, Japan did not face a currency crisis as South Korea did. As for the malfunctioning of financial institutions during the transition to a freer market economy, the causes of difficulties are the same: Past systems have failed to adjust to deregulation.

7. Table 2 covers tariffs of the earliest participants in ASEAN. TRAINS CD-ROM, published by the UN Conference on Trade and Development, does not provide a comparable database for newcomers. This symbolizes the lack of transparency in the trading systems of the newcomers.

8. Singapore also became an important investor in ASEAN at this time.

9. In general, given its size, China inevitably competes against other countries, though usually in a complementary manner because of its broad spectrum of industries.

10. Because the long-term changes do not directly relate to this financial crisis, trade diversion will continue, especially if NAFTA expands to include South America. It is unclear whether the crisis was related to hasty deregulation for regional integration. In the case of the ASEAN financial crises, factors relating to the formation of AFTA might be minor. They are worth investigating though.

11. Adapting domestic systems in China to those of market-oriented economies remains difficult. Therefore, it is uncertain in what respects the EAEC can cooperate in developing regional trade and investment.

Bibliography

Institute of Developing Economies. 1998. *Industrial Property Rights.* <http://www.ide.go.jp/economic/ASEAN/Industrial Property Rights>. (30 January).

Japan Center for Economic Research. 1996. *Globalization of Economic Activities and Regionalism.* Tokyo: Japan Center for Economic Research.

Krugman, Paul. 1994. "The Myth of Asia's Miracle." *Foreign Affairs* 73(6): 62–78.

Sekiguchi Sueo, ed. 1983. *ASEAN-Japan Relations: Investment.* Singapore: Institute of Southeast Asian Studies.

———. 1998. "Chiikitōgō to kokusaitōshi" (Regional integration and international investment). *Kaigaitōshi kenkyūshohō* (Journal of overseas investment) 24(3): 4–25. Published by the Export-Import Bank of Japan.

U.N. Conference on Trade and Development. 1996. *Trade Analysis and Information System.* TRAINS CD-ROM. Geneva: UN Conference on Trade and Development.

About the Contributors

SEKIGUCHI SUEO is Professor of Economics at Seikei University. After graduating from Yokohama National University in 1957, he joined the staff of the Japan Center for Economic Research and spent a year at the National Planning Association in Washington, D.C. He became Staff Economist at the Japan Center for Economic Research in 1968, then Senior Economist in 1974–1978. Professor Sekiguchi transferred to Osaka University as Professor of Economics in 1981 and assumed his current position in 1986. He was Director of the Center for Asian and Pacific Studies at Seikei University from April 1993 to March 1996. His recent publications include *Contemporary Vietnamese Economy* (co-edited, 1992), *Foreign Direct Investment and the Japanese Economy* (1996), *Will East Asian Economies Continue High Growth?* (1996), and *Industries and Employment in a Globalized Economy* (1999).

NODA MAKITO is Chief Program Officer and Director for Research Coordination at the Japan Center for International Exchange (JCIE). He joined JCIE as a Research Associate in 1974, while still attending Sophia University's Graduate School of International Relations. He received an M.A. in international relations from Sophia University in 1979 and an M.A. in international relations/economics from the Johns Hopkins University's School of Advanced International Studies (SAIS) in 1984; he then proceeded to the SAIS Ph.D. program. He co-edited with Sekiguchi Sueo *Economic Interactions and Interdependence in East Asia* (1994), and co-authored with Sekiguchi "China-Japan Economic Relations: Implications on ASEAN-Japan Relations," in *The Changing International Environment and ASEAN-Japan Relations* (1988), and *Recycling Japan's Current Overseas Account Surplus for Development Finance: With Special Reference to Direct Investment* (1992).

KASHIWAGI TAKAHIRO is Assistant Manager of the Legal and General Affairs Department at the Furukawa Electric Co., Ltd. Mr. Kashiwagi graduated from Hitotsubashi University with a B.A. in economics in 1983, after which he joined the Furukawa Electric Co., Ltd. From April 1994 to March 1996, he was seconded to the Japan Center for Economic Research. His scope of research is Asian transitional economies, particularly the economic development of China and Vietnam. His recent publications include "Flow of Resources between Agricultural and Non-Agricultural Sectors in China," in *Review of Asian and Pacific Studies* (1998), and "Extensive Growth and Intensive Growth: A Comparison—Japan and China," in *JCER Economic Journal* (co-authored, 1999).

OKUDA HIDENOBU is Associate Professor of International Economics in the Graduate School of Economics and APEC Study Center at Hitotsubashi University. Professor Okuda started his career as an economist in charge of country risk analysis at the Export-Import Bank of Japan in 1989. After earning his Ph.D. in economics from the Graduate School of Economics at the University of Minnesota in 1990, he became a Lecturer of International Economics at Hitotsubashi University in April 1991. He has been in his current position since April 1994. Professor Okuda specializes in monetary economics and development economics. His recent publications include "Financial Factors in Economic Development: A Case Study of the Financial Liberalization Policy in the Philippines," in *The Developing Economies* (1990), and *Introduction to Development Finance* (co-authored, 1998).

TAKANO TAKESHI is Associate Professor of International Relations, Faculty of Administration, at the Prefectural University of Kumamoto. Professor Takano graduated from the International College of Commerce and Economics (now Tokyo International University) in 1984 with a B.A. in international studies and from the Graduate School of Law and Political Science at Keio University in 1986 with an M.A. in political science. In 1988, he was awarded the Scholarship in Security Studies by the Research Institute of Peace and Security. He worked with the Faculty of Policy Management of Keio University from April 1990 to March 1992, and served as Research Associate at the Japan Center for International Exchange from 1992 to 1993. His recent publications include "The End of the Vietnam War and ASEAN," in *International Relations* (1994); "The Conceptual Change in 'Regional Security' in Southeast

Asia," in the *Journal of Law, Politics, and Sociology* (1995); *Politics of Southeast Asia: Multi-layered Dynamism of Region, State, Society and People* (1979, 1999); and *The Prospects of Southeast Asia* (forthcoming).

TAKEUCHI JUNKO is Senior Researcher at the Sakura Institute of Research. Ms. Takeuchi earned her B.A. in politics from Waseda University in 1984 and the same year joined the Japan External Trade Organization, where she conducted overseas research. She has been with Sakura Institute since 1990. Her research fields are ASEAN, foreign direct investment, and trade and industries. Her recent publications include "ASEAN Moves Toward Service Trade Liberalization," in *RIM* (1997); *The World Trade Organization and Economic Development in Asia* (co-authored, 1998); "Employment and Human Resource Development in Japanese-affiliated Manufacturers in Southeast Asia," in *RIM* (1998); and *Asian Economic Development and Small and Medium Enterprises* (co-authored, 1999).

YOSHINO FUMIO is Associate Professor of Economics at Takushoku University. Professor Yoshino graduated from Waseda University's School of Political Science and Economics in 1981. He earned his M.A. from the university's Graduate School of Economics in 1985. From September 1983 to June 1984, he studied at the Graduate School of the University of Chicago. His fields of interest are Asian economy and international economics. Currently he also serves as a Lecturer at Tokyo Women's Christian University, Tsuda Women's College, and St. Paul University. He is the author of "Korean Textile Industry," in *Industrial Policy in East Asia* (1991); *Economic Growth and Environment in APEC Countries* (working paper, 1996); and *Trade Impediments of Agricultural Products and Food* (working paper, 1996).

Index

Japan Center for International Exchange

FOUNDED IN 1970, the Japan Center for International Exchange (JCIE) is an independent, nonprofit, and nonpartisan organization dedicated to strengthening Japan's role in international affairs. JCIE believes that Japan faces a major challenge in augmenting its positive contributions to the international community, in keeping with its position as one of the world's largest industrial democracies. Operating in a country where policy making has traditionally been dominated by the government bureaucracy, JCIE has played an important role in broadening debate on Japan's international responsibilities by conducting international and cross-sectional programs of exchange, research, and discussion.

JCIE creates opportunities for informed policy discussions; it does not take policy positions. JCIE programs are carried out with the collaboration and cosponsorship of many organizations. The contacts developed through these working relationships are crucial to JCIE's efforts to increase the number of Japanese from the private sector engaged in meaningful policy research and dialogue with overseas counterparts. JCIE receives no government subsidies; rather, funding comes from private foundation grants, corporate contributions, and contracts.